Lecture Notes in Computer Science 4006

Commenced Publication in 1973
Founding and Former Series Editors:
Gerhard Goos, Juris Hartmanis, and Jan van Leeuwen

Luís Miguel Pinho
Michael González Harbour (Eds.)

Reliable Software Technologies – Ada-Europe 2006

11th Ada-Europe International Conference
on Reliable Software Technologies
Porto, Portugal, June 5-9, 2006
Proceedings

 Springer

Volume Editors

Luís Miguel Pinho
Polytechnic Institute of Porto
School of Engineering (ISEP)
Rua Dr. António Bernardino de Almeida, 431, 4200-072 Porto, Portugal
E-mail: lpinho@dei.isep.ipp.pt

Michael González Harbour
Universidad de Cantabria
Departamento de Electrónica y Computadores
Avda. de los Castros s/n, 39005-Santander, Spain
E-mail: mgh@unican.es

Library of Congress Control Number: 2006926424

CR Subject Classification (1998): D.2, D.1.2-5, D.3, C.2.4, C.3, K.6

LNCS Sublibrary: SL 2 – Programming and Software Engineering

ISSN   0302-9743
ISBN-10   3-540-34663-5 Springer Berlin Heidelberg New York
ISBN-13   978-3-540-34663-0 Springer Berlin Heidelberg New York

Springer is a part of Springer Science+Business Media

springer.com

© Springer-Verlag Berlin Heidelberg 2006

Typesetting: Camera-ready by author, data conversion by Scientific Publishing Services, Chennai, India
Printed on acid-free paper   SPIN: 11767077   06/3142   5 4 3 2 1 0

Preface

The 11th International Conference on Reliable Software Technologies, Ada-Europe 2006, took place in Porto, Portugal, June 5-9, 2006. It was as usual sponsored by Ada-Europe, the European federation of national Ada societies, in cooperation with ACM SIGAda. It was organized by members of the School of Engineering of the Polytechnic Institute of Porto, in collaboration with several colleagues from different institutions in Europe.

Following the usual style, the conference included a three-day technical program, during which the papers contained in these proceedings were presented, bracketed by two tutorial days where attendants had the opportunity to catch up on a variety of topics related to the field, at both introductory and advanced levels. Continuing the success achieved in the previous year, the technical program also included an industrial track, with contributions illustrating challenges faced and solutions encountered by industrialists from both sides of the Atlantic. Furthermore, the conference was accompanied by an exhibition where vendors presented their products for supporting reliable-software development.

The conference presented four distinguished speakers, who delivered state-of-the-art information on topics of great importance, both for the present and the future of software engineering:

- Correctness by Construction: Putting Engineering into Software
  by Rod Chapman (Praxis HIS, UK)
- Empirical Software Risk Assessment Using Fault Injection
  by Henrique Madeira (University of Coimbra, Portugal)
- Model-Driven Technologies in Safe-Aware Software Applications
  by Miguel Angel de Miguel (Technical University of Madrid, Spain)
- I Have a Dream: ICT Problems We All Face
  by John L. Hill (Sun Microsystems, USA)

We would like to express our sincere gratitude to these distinguished speakers, well known to the community, for sharing their insights with the conference participants.

A large number of regular papers were submitted, from as many as 23 different countries. The Program Committee worked hard to review them, and the selection process proved to be difficult, since many papers had received excellent reviews. Finally, the Program Committee selected 19 papers for the conference. The industrial track of the conference also received valuable contributions from industrialists, and the Industrial Committee finally selected 9 of them for the conference. The final result was a truly international program with contributions from Australia, Austria, Canada, China, France, Germany, Iran, Italy, Japan, Portugal, Spain, the UK, and the USA, covering a broad range of topics: real-time systems, static analysis, verification, applications, reliability, industrial experience, compilers and distributed systems.

The conference also included an interesting selection of tutorials, featuring international experts who presented introductory and advanced material in the domain of the conference:

- Verification and validation for reliable software systems, *William Bail*
- The Ada 2005 Standard Container Library, *Matthew Heaney*
- Developing Web-Aware Applications in Ada with AWS, *Jean-Pierre Rosen*
- SAE Architecture Analysis and Design Language, *Joyce L. Tokar*
- Model-Driven Development with the Unified Modeling Language (UML) 2.0™ and Ada, *Colin Coates*
- Distribution in Ada 95 with PolyORB, A Schizophrenic Middleware, *Jérôme Hugues*
- Requirements Management for Dependable Systems, *William Bail*
- Real-Time Java for Ada Programmers, *Benjamin M. Brosgol*

We would like to express our appreciation to these experts, for the work on preparing and presenting this material in the conference.

Many people contributed to the success of the conference. The Program and Industrial Committees, made up of international experts in the area of reliable software technologies, spent long hours carefully reviewing all the papers, presentations and tutorial proposals submitted to the conference. A subcommittee comprising Dirk Craeynest, Michael González Harbour, Laurent Pautet, Luís Miguel Pinho, Erhard Plöedereder, Jorge Real, and Tullio Vardanega met in Porto to make the final program selection. Various Program Committee members were assigned to shepherd some of the papers. We are grateful to all those who contributed to the technical program of the conference.

We would also like to thank the members of the Organizing Committee, for their valuable effort in taking care of all the bits and pieces that must fit together for a smooth run of the conference. We would like to thank Peter Dencker for the effort in the preparation of the industrial track, to Jorge Real for the attractive tutorial program and to José Ruiz for preparing the appealing exhibition of the conference. Also to Dirk Craeynest, who worked very hard to make the conference prominently visible, and to all the members of the Ada-Europe board for helping with the intricate details of the organization. A special thanks to Sandra Almeida, who took care of all details of the local organization.

Finally, we would like to express our appreciation to the authors of the contributions submitted to the conference, and to all the participants who helped in achieving the goal of the conference: providing a forum for researchers and practitioners for the exchange of information and ideas about reliable software technologies. We hope they all enjoyed the program as well as the social events of the 11th International Conference on Reliable Software Technologies.

June 2006   Luís Miguel Pinho
                                                          Michael González Harbour

Organization

Conference Chair

Luís Miguel Pinho, Polytechnic Institute of Porto, Portugal

Program Co-chairs

Luís Miguel Pinho, Polytechnic Institute of Porto, Portugal
Michael González Harbour, Universidad de Cantabria, Spain

Industrial Committee Co-chairs

Peter Dencker, Aonix GmbH, Germany
Michael González Harbour, Universidad de Cantabria, Spain

Tutorial Chair

Jorge Real, Universidad Politécnica de Valencia, Spain

Exhibition Chair

José Ruiz, AdaCore, France

Publicity Chair

Dirk Craeynest, Aubay Belgium and K.U. Leuven, Belgium

Local Chair

Sandra Almeida, Polytechnic Institute of Porto, Portugal

Ada-Europe Conference Liaison

Laurent Pautet, Telecom Paris, France

Program Committee

Alejandro Alonso, Universidad Politécnica de Madrid, Spain
Lars Asplund, Mälardalens Högskola, Sweden
Janet Barnes, Praxis High Integrity Systems, UK
Guillem Bernat, University of York, UK
Johann Blieberger, Technische Universität Wien, Austria

Ben Brosgol, AdaCore, USA
Bernd Burgstaller, University of Sydney, Australia
Alan Burns, University of York, UK
Dirk Craeynest, Aubay Belgium and K.U. Leuven, Belgium
Alfons Crespo, Universidad Politécnica de Valencia, Spain
Raymond Devillers, Université Libre de Bruxelles, Belgium
Michael González Harbour, Universidad de Cantabria, Spain
José Javier Gutiérrez, Universidad de Cantabria, Spain
Andrew Hately, Eurocontrol CRDS, Hungary
Günter Hommel, Technische Universität Berlin, Germany
Hubert Keller, Institut für Angewandte Informatik, Germany
Yvon Kermarrec, ENST Bretagne, France
Jörg Kienzle, McGill University, Canada
Fabrice Kordon, Université Pierre and Marie Curie, France
Albert Llamosi, Universitat de les Illes Balears, Spain
Franco Mazzanti, ISTI-CNR Pisa, Italy
John McCormick, University of Northern Iowa, USA
Stephen Michell, Maurya Software, Canada
Javier Miranda, Universidad Las Palmas de Gran Canaria, Spain
Laurent Pautet, Telecom Paris, France
Luís Miguel Pinho, Polytechnic Institute of Porto, Portugal
Erhard Plödereder, Universität Stuttgart, Germany
Juan A. de la Puente, Universidad Politécnica de Madrid, Spain
Jorge Real, Universidad Politécnica de Valencia, Spain
Alexander Romanovsky, University of Newcastle upon Tyne, UK
Jean-Pierre Rosen, Adalog, France
José Ruiz, AdaCore, France
Edmond Schonberg, New York University and AdaCore, USA
Joyce Tokar, Pyrrhus Software, USA
Tullio Vardanega, Università di Padova, Italy
Andy Wellings, University of York, UK
Jürgen Winkler, Friedrich-Schiller-Universität, Germany

Reviewers

Gaetan Allaert
Alejandro Alonso
Mrio Amado Alves
Wolfram Amme
Lars Asplund
Ricardo Barbosa
Janet Barnes
Johann Blieberger
Maarten Boasson
Ben Brosgol

Bernd Burgstaller
Alan Burns
Dirk Craeynest
Alfons Crespo
Garreg Lewis Dawe
Raymond Devillers
Michael González Harbour
José Javier Gutiérrez
Andrew Hately
Günter Hommel

Stefan Kauer
Hubert Keller
Yvon Kermarrec
Jörg Kienzle
Fabrice Kordon
Albert Llamosi
Kristina Lundqvist
Franco Mazzanti
John McCormick
Stephen Michell
Javier Miranda
Gustaf Naeser
Martin Ouimet
Laurent Pautet

Luís Miguel Pinho
Erhard Plödereder
Juan A. de la Puente
Jorge Real
Alexander Romanovsky
Philippe Rose
Jean-Pierre Rosen
José Ruiz
Edmond Schonberg
Joyce Tokar
Tullio Vardanega
Andy Wellings
Jürgen Winkler

Table of Contents

Reliability

Compilers

Distributed Systems

Hierarchical Scheduling with Ada 2005[*]

José A. Pulido[1], Santiago Urueña[1], Juan Zamorano[1],
Tullio Vardanega[2], and Juan A. de la Puente[1]

[1] Departamento de Ingeniería de Sistemas Telemáticos (DIT)
Universidad Politécnica de Madrid (UPM), E28040 Madrid, Spain
{pulido, suruena, jzamorano, jpuente}@dit.upm.es
[2] Dipartimento di Matematica Pura ed Applicata
Università di Padova, I35131 Padova, Italy
tullio.vardanega@math.unipd.it

Abstract. Hierarchical scheduling is a basic technique to achieve temporal isolation between applications in high-integrity systems when an integrated approach is opted for over traditional federation. While comparatively heavyweight approaches to hierarchical scheduling have been prevailing until now, the new scheduling features of Ada 2005 enable lighter-weight techniques to be used. This will expectedly result in increasing the efficiency and flexibility of hierarchical scheduling, thus enabling new ways to developing critical applications in Ada. The paper explores the new opportunities opened by Ada 2005 and proposes some concrete techniques for implementing hierarchical scheduling in the new version of the language.

1 Introduction

High-integrity systems (HIS) are applications with stringent safety or security requirements, in which a failure can have unacceptable consequences [1]. Such systems are usually required to exhibit a fully predictable behaviour, to which end comprehensive verification and validation (V&V) processes must be deployed. The particular approach and techniques that must be used in different applications are often described in domain-specific certification standards, such as DO-178B (civil avionics), IEC 601-4 (medical systems), IEC 880 (nuclear power plants), EN 50128 (European railways), etc. These standards define different criticality levels (CL), as well as the V&V requirements that must be met by an application candidate for certification at a given level. The applications in turn must be classified into the different criticality levels, depending on the severity of the consequences of a potential failure.

Complex systems are often composed of several applications that may be classified at differing criticality levels. A common requirement for this kind of systems is to isolate the most critical applications from the less critical ones, so that a failure in the latter does not compromise the behaviour of the vital parts

---

[*] This work has been supported by the Spanish Ministry of Education, project no. TIC2002-04123-C03-01.

L.M. Pinho and M. González Harbour (Eds.): Ada-Europe 2006, LNCS 4006, pp. 1–12, 2006.
© Springer-Verlag Berlin Heidelberg 2006

of the system. Isolation has often been achieved by building systems according to a *federated* approach, i.e. by allocating different applications to different computer platforms. However, the processing power of current processors eases the adoption of more efficient, *integrated* architectures in which several applications, possibly with different criticality levels, share a common computer platform. Under this approach, alternate architectural mechanisms must be sought to provide the required degree of isolation among applications. The computer platform is divided into a number of *logical partitions*, each of which is allocated a share of the available computer resources, including processor time and memory space. Each application runs on one of the partitions, and partitions are isolated from each other both in the temporal and spatial domains:

- *Temporal isolation* means that a partition cannot use processor time allocated to other partitions as long as the applications running on them are ready to execute. Temporal isolation ensures that high criticality applications are not prevented from meeting their temporal requirements by the misbehaviour of lower-criticality applications. Indeed, the converse is also true, although not that useful in practical situations. Since high criticality applications are usually subject to strict validation and verification procedures, in most cases it can be safely assumed that they do not incur overruns.
- *Spatial isolation* means that a partition cannot access memory outside its allocated storage space. Therefore, high criticality applications can safely assume that low criticality applications will not change any data in their memory space by the effect of misbehaviour.

Temporal and spatial isolation collectively enable high criticality applications to run in the same computer platform as other, lower criticality, applications whilst preserving their integrity in the face of faults in the latter, which thus need not be developed under the same stringent validation and verification processes.

This paper is focused on temporal isolation, for which a new architectural approach making use of the new Ada 2005 scheduling features is presented. The concept of hierarchical scheduling as a general approach to temporal isolation is introduced and discussed in section 2. Section 3 introduces the proposed architecture and shows how it can be implemented using the Ada 2005 scheduling model. Temporal analysis and implementation issues are discussed in section 4.1. Finally, some conclusions are presented in section 5.

2   Hierarchical Scheduling

2.1   Temporal Isolation

Depending on the granularity of partitioning, a partition contains a number of execution tasks performing functions with the same criticality level. Appropriate scheduling and temporal analysis methods (see e.g. [2]) can be used at design time to ensure that threads running in a partition will not "steal" (by overrun) processor time budgeted to other partitions. However, since temporal analysis is based on design assumptions that may be violated at run time, some kind of run-time mechanisms (e.g. based on clocks and timers) must be used to warrant isolation in the face of a possible misbehaviour of the application threads.

2.2　Hierarchical Scheduling

Hierarchical scheduling is a technique that can be used to implement isolation between logical partitions. The main idea behind it is to use two kinds of schedulers on the same computer platform:

- A *global scheduler*, which allocates the processor to a partition in accord with a global scheduling policy. The partition that has the processor at a given instant is called the *active partition*.
- A *local scheduler*, which is used to decide which task among those that are ready to run within the active partition executes first, following a *local scheduling policy*.

Several schemes are possible for global and local scheduling policies, including static scheduling, time slicing, dynamic priorities and fixed priorities. Some architectural patterns that have been proposed in this framework are fully partitioned architectures and server-based architectures. The main properties of these architectures are described in the next paragraphs.

2.3　Fully Partitioned Architecture

This architectural pattern entails using a completely separated global scheduler, and as many local schedulers as logical partitions. When the global scheduler dispatches a partition for execution, it yields control to the local scheduler in that partition, which in turn dispatches ready tasks within the partition according to the local scheduling policy. With this approach, different partitions may have different local scheduling policies.

A well-known example of this model is the ARINC 653 standard [3] for avionics systems (figure 1). The ARINC global scheduler is a variant of a static cyclic executive, while the local schedulers are priority-based. Some proposals to build systems in Ada based on this architecture have been presented in recent years [4, 5].

The main advantage of this approach is the guarantee of timeliness and predictability. However, the approach also suffers from the same drawbacks as other static scheduling methods, for it is rigid and inflexible. It is in fact difficult to modify the configuration of a system by adding or changing partitions. Moreover, the communication scheme is very rigid and the problem of allocating sporadic tasks is hard. All in all, this model approach scales poorly to increasing levels of architectural partitioning.

Other approaches within the same overall strategy are obviously possible, however, under the fully partitioned architecture. For example, fixed priorities could be employed for global scheduling, or else dynamic priorities could be used at the local level. The strict separation between schedulers at different partitions

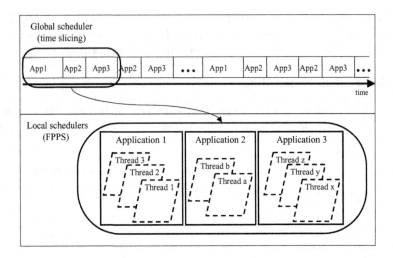

Fig. 1. Fully partitioned architecture

and the global scheduler enables a rich variety of scheduling methods to be accommodated under this architecture, although practical considerations and the apparent need for further research on temporal analysis methods for partitioned architectures may impair the development of mixed scheduling methods.

2.4   Served-Based Architecture

The server-based architecture goes one step further, adding flexibility to the fully static partitioned model while preserving a high degree of robustness and staying comparatively simple to implement. In this architecture the global scheduler is supplemented by a set of *servers* (cf. figure 2), which are specialized containers for executing application tasks. Servers have a *capacity* of processor time, which can be replenished at different times. When a server is dispatched for execution, it in turn dispatches the tasks it serves according to the local scheduling policy as long as it retains some residual processing time from its original capacity. When the server capacity is exhausted, it suspends its execution until the capacity is replenished.

An example of this approach is the FIRST architecture [6], one variant of which uses fixed-priority pre-emptive scheduling (FPPS) at the global level, and different kinds of servers to execute the application tasks:

- A *periodic server* [7] is released with a fixed period. As long as there are any tasks ready to run, they are executed until the server capacity is exhausted. If the tasks complete and there is some capacity available, the server remains idle in case a task is released that can use some of the remaining capacity. The server capacity is replenished at the beginning of the next period.
- A *deferrable server* [8] is similar to a periodic server, except that it suspends its execution if there are no ready tasks to be run. Its capacity is replenished

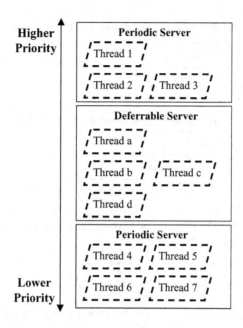

Fig. 2. Server-based architecture

at the beginning of the next period, independently of whether it has been consumed or not.

- A *sporadic server* [9] is replenished only after its capacity has been exhausted. The amount of capacity to be replenished and the time to do it depend on the particular way that the tasks are scheduled.

Unlike the fully partitioned architecture, this priority-based method improves the flexibility of the system substantially, while also keeping a reasonable degree of timeliness and predictability. An exhaustive discussion of the schedulability analysis issues arising from the approach has been made in [6]. One distinct conclusion of the cited work is that periodic servers are best equipped to warrant the deadline of hard real-time tasks, while also noting the current difficulty of choosing optimal parameters for the servers.

3   An Architecture Based on Priority Bands

3.1   General Approach

The enhancements to the Ada tasking model included in the new Ada 2005 standard [10, Annex D] enable a new approach to hierarchical scheduling in which the global and local schedulers are integrated in a single framework. The new standard keeps fixed priority pre-emptive scheduling (FPPS) as the basic scheduling mechanism, but it defines a set of new features that extend the Ada tasking model in some significant directions:

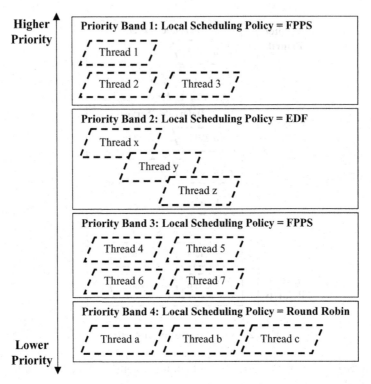

Fig. 3. Priority band architecture

- *New dispatching policies.* In addition to FIFO within priorities, the new standard includes non pre-emptive FIFO, round-robin, and earliest-deadline first (EDF) dispatching.

  The nice properties of the ceiling locking policy for protected object access are preserved when using the new dispatching policies (including EDF) by redefining it in such a way that it is equivalent to the *stack resource protocol* [11].

- *Mixed dispatching policies.* The new pragma Priority_Specific_Dispatching enables different task dispatching policies to be used within a range of priorities. Again, the new definition of the ceiling locking policy ensures bounded priority inversion even when protected objects are used by tasks running under different dispatching policies.

This tasking model suggests an integrated hierarchical architecture in which partitions are implemented as sets of tasks that are assigned priorities within a priority band. The global scheduling policy is FPPS, and the local scheduling policy is the task dispatching policy used in the priority bands assigned to the different partitions (cf. figure 3). This has the advantage of a greater simplicity and flexibility with respect to the server-based architecture.

Example 1.1. Sporadic task pattern

```
task body Event_Handler is
  -- declarations, including D of type Data
  Minimum_Separation : constant Ada.Real_Time.Time_Span
    := ... -- some appropriate value
  Next : Ada.Real_Time.Time;
begin
  -- Initialization code
  loop
    Event_Object.Wait(D);
    Next := Ada.Real_Time.Clock + Minimum_Separation;
    -- Non-suspending event handling code
    delay until Next;-- this ensures minimum temporal separation
  end loop;
end Event_Handler;
```

However, relying on scheduling only for temporal isolation between tasks belonging to different logical partitions (and possibly with different criticality levels) is not enough, as some scheduling-related assumptions might be violated at run-time. The main sources of timing errors are:

- Violations of the arrival models of sporadic tasks (e.g. a sporadic task being activated more often than stipulated).
- Overruns of execution time with respect to the WCET value considered in the off-line feasibility analysis.

Both forms of run-time misbehaviour can result in an overload situation whereby one or more tasks may miss their deadlines, which is clearly unacceptable for high-criticality tasks. However, Ada 2005 provides some mechanisms which can be used to detect overload situations at run time and react to them in an appropriate way:

- Minimum inter-arrival times for sporadic tasks can be enforced, like in Ada 95, by using a delay until statement. Example 1.1 shows a sporadic task pattern taken from [12] that follows this approach.
- Overruns of budgeted execution time can be detected by using the *execution-time timers* and *group budget timers* that have been introduced as novel features in Ada 2005 [10, D14]. Example Example 1.2 illustrates the use of these mechanisms.

Execution-time timers can be used to detect overruns at the task level, while group budget timers can be used to limit the total execution time of a group of tasks. This mechanism can be used to enforce temporal isolation between partitions, as explained in the next section.

Example 1.2. Programming example

```
-- Priority bands --

-- Band A (FPPS)
pragma Priority_Specific_Dispatching (FIFO_Within_Priorities, 18, 32);

-- Band B (EDF)
pragma Priority_Specific_Dispatching (EDF_Across_Priorities, 3, 17);

-- Band C (RR)
pragma Priority_Specific_Dispatching (Round_Robin_Within_Priorities, 1, 2);
Set_Quantum (1, Milliseconds(150));
Set_Quantum (2, Milliseconds(100));

-- Task specifications --
task Task_A1
   pragma Priority (30);   -- Set preemption level
end Task_A1;

[...]

task Task_C5
   pragma Priority (1);   -- Set preemption level
end Task_C5;

-- Group budget declarations --
Budget_A : Group_Budget;
Budget_B : Group_Budget;
Budget_C : Group_Budget;

-- Overrun handler declarations --
Handler_A : Group_Budget_Handler;
Handler_B : Group_Budget_Handler;
Handler_C : Group_Budget_Handler;

Set_Handler (Budget_A, Handler_A);
Set_Handler (Budget_B, Handler_B);
Set_Handler (Budget_C, Handler_C);

-- Attach tasks to groups --
Add_Task (Budget_A, Task_A1);
Add_Task (Budget_A, Task_A2);
[...]
Add_Task (Budget_C, Task_C5);

-- Sample protected objects --
protected B_To_A_Flow;
   -- Set preemption level
   pragma Priority (25);

   procedure Check_And_Read_Data (...);
   entry Write_Data (...);
private
   ...
end B_To_A_Flow;
```

3.2   Mapping Partitions to Ada 2005

The above approach can be used to map a system with several applications, possibly with different criticality levels, to a set of Ada 2005 tasks with inter-partition temporal isolation.

The main architectural rule is to allocate a priority band to every logical partition. The priority band for a partition should contain as many different priority levels as tasks in the partition, so that each task can have a distinct base priority if required. We assume that task priorities are static, except for priority inheritance under the ceiling locking protocol.

The way of assigning priorities to partitions should be directly linked to their criticality levels, i.e it seems reasonable that the partitions with the higher criticality levels are allocated higher priority bands than lower criticality ones. In this way, if an overrun occurs, tasks belonging to low-criticality partitions will miss their deadlines before tasks in higher criticality partitions do. Of course, this priority assignment is not optimal, in contrast with other well-known priority assignment methods [13, 14, 15]. This sub-optimality means that the achievable processor utilization may be inferior to what could be attained with an optimal priority allocation. In practical developments however the theoretical utilization limits attained by the optimal methods are seldom sought and reached.

Communication between tasks in the same partition is mediated by protected objects in the usual style. Inter-partition communication can also be realized with protected objects, but in that case the ceiling priority of the protected object used for it will always be in the priority band of the highest priority partition. This ensures that the criticality level of the latter is also preserved when executing protected operations. If any partition uses the EDF policy, the stack resource protocol (SRP) ensures a minimal amount of blocking for the highest criticality task too.

Temporal isolation is attained by design, confirmed by temporal analysis, and preserved by execution-time timers at run time. A group budget is allocated to each partition, and all tasks in the partition are added to the group. If the budget is exhausted, a handler procedure is invoked to take corrective actions, which in general are application-specific.

The main advantage of the priority bands architecture is the great flexibility it offers to the designer. Contrary to the statically partitioned architecture, modifying the system is comparatively inexpensive, while communications between partitions can be much more easily accommodated. Besides, the fact that the facilities required for its realization are all included in the Ada 2005 standard eases the development process and increases portability. Response time analysis methods for this approach are discussed in the following section.

Example 1.2 illustrates a partitioned system containing three applications with three different criticality levels. The scheduling policies are FPPS for level A, EDF for level B, and round-robin for level C. The applications are composed of several tasks which are allocated base priorities within priority bands in accord with their criticality levels. There is a group budget for each priority band, which includes tasks with the same criticality level. Each task group is attached a handler that is in charge of executing the appropriate code if any of tasks in the group should attempt to execute longer than stipulated.

4   Related Issues

4.1   Response Time Analysis

Temporal analysis is usually required as part of the verification and validation process to be performed in high-integrity systems. The best known temporal analysis methods are usually grouped under the term *Rate-Monotonic Analysis (RMA)* [16] or *Response Time Analysis (RTA)* [17]. The current form of analysis deals with periodic and sporadic tasks with arbitrary deadlines, precedence relationships, communication through shared data, as well as multiprocessor and distributed systems, using fixed-priority scheduling [18]. Similar results are available for analysing systems based on EDF scheduling [19, 20, 21].

Hierarchical scheduling, on the other hand, is comparatively new, and significant research work has still to be performed to develop or to adapt temporal analysis methods to new scheduling architectures. Some promising results have already been produced [22, 6], and especially [23], but their applicability to the proposed scheduling model is still to be explored.

4.2   Spatial Isolation

Although we regard it as outside the scope of this paper, spatial isolation is a mandatory requirement for systems that integrate mixed criticality applications. We are currently exploring two complementary approaches to spatial isolation in systems with hierarchical scheduling. The first one is using SPARK and static flow analysis, as shown in [24], to ensure that non-critical code cannot modify critical data. The other one is based on using specialized hardware mechanisms to enforce isolation between the storage spaces of the different applications at run time, as it is usually done in many operating systems. However, this technique cannot be used in some hardware platforms commonly used in the aerospace domain, that only have rudimentary mechanisms (e.g. fence registers) for memory protection.

5   Conclusions

This paper has illustrated a method for scheduling tasks with mixed criticality requirements. The proposed method can be used to enforce temporal isolation between applications with different levels of criticality. Applications are realised as groups of tasks with prescribed time budgets, which warrant that no single task group may ever overrun into the processor time allocated to another group. Each task group is assigned a band of contiguous priorities, within which specific local dispatching policies can be enforced. This method, which protects logical partitions by advanced use of current scheduling theory, permits to implement high-integrity systems following an integrated approach and therefore gain a precious extent of design flexibility.

The concrete implementation of the proposed architectural approach is greatly facilitated by the use of new real-time features of the new Ada 2005 standard, and in particular: mixed scheduling policies and group budget timers. We contend that this result is only an initial manifestation of the expressive power provided for by the Ada 2005 standard for the construction of new-generation real-time systems.

References

1. ISO/IEC: TR 15942:2000 — Guide for the use of the Ada programming language in high integrity systems. (2000)
2. Vardanega, T.: Development of on-board embedded real-time systems: An engineering approach. Technical Report ESA STR-260, European Space Agency (1999) ISBN 90-9092-334-2.
3. ARINC: Avionics Application Software Standard Interface — ARINC Specification 653-1. (2003)
4. Tokar, J.L.: Space & time partitioning with ARINC 653 and pragma profile. Ada Letters **XXIII** (2003) 52–54. Proceedings of the 12th International Real-Time Ada Workshop (IRTAW 12).
5. Dobbing, B.: Building partitioned architectures based on the Ravenscar profile. Ada Lett. **XX** (2000) 29–31
6. Davis, R., Burns, A.: Hierarchical fixed priority pre-emptive scheduling. Technical Report YCS-2005-385, University of York (2005)
7. Sha, L., Lehoczky, J., Rajkumar, R.: Solutions for some practical problems in prioritized preemptive scheduling. In: IEEE Real-Time Systems Symposium, IEEE Computer Society Press (1986)
8. Strosnider, J., Lehoczky, J., Sha, L.: The deferrable server algorithm for enhanced aperiodic responsiveness in hard real-time environments. IEEE Tr. on Computers **44** (1995)
9. Sprunt, B., Sha, L., Lehoczky, J.: Aperiodic task scheduling for hard real-time systems. Real-Time Systems **1** (1989)
10. ISO SC22/WG9: Ada Reference Manual. Language and Standard Libraries. Consolidated Standard ISO/IEC 8652:1995(E) with Technical Corrigendum 1 and Amendment 1 (Draft 15). (2005) Available on `http://www.adaic.com/standards/rm-amend/html/RM-TTL.html`.
11. Baker, T.P.: Stack-based scheduling for realtime processes. Real-Time Systems **3** (1991) 67–99
12. Burns, A., Dobbing, B., Vardanega, T.: Guide for the use of the Ada Ravenscar profile in high integrity systems. Technical Report YCS-2003-348, University of York (2003)
13. Liu, C., Layland, J.: Scheduling algorithms for multiprogramming in a hard-real-time environment. Journal of the ACM **20** (1973)
14. Leung, J., Whitehead, J.: On the complexity of fixed-priority scheduling of periodic real-time tasks. Performance Evaluation **2** (1982)
15. Audsley, N., Burns, A., Richardson, M., Tindell, K., Wellings, A.: Applying new scheduling theory to static priority preemptive scheduling. Software Engineering Journal **8** (1993)

16. Klein, M.H., Ralya, T., Pollack, B., Obenza, R., González-Harbour, M.: A Practitioner's Handbook for Real-Time Analysis. Guide to Rate Monotonic Analysis for Real-Time Systems. Kluwer Academic Publishers, Boston (1993)
17. Audsley, N., Burns, A., Richardson, M., Wellings, A.: Hard real-time scheduling: The deadline-monotonic approach. In Halang, W.A., Ramamrithan, K., eds.: Real Time Programming 1991. Proceedings of the IFAC/IFIP Workshop, Pergamon Press (1992)
18. Sha, L., Tarek Abdelzaher, Karl-Erik Årzén, Cervin, A., Baker, T., Alan Burns, Giorgio Buttazzo, Marco Caccamo, John Lehoczky, Mok, A.: Real time scheduling theory: A historical perspective. Real-Time Systems 28 (2004) 101–155
19. Baruah, S.K., Rosier, L.E., Howell, R.R.: Algorithms and complexity concerning the preemptive scheduling of periodic, real-time tasks on one processor. Real-Time Syst. 2 (1990) 301–324
20. Spuri, M., Buttazzo, G.C.: Efficient aperiodic service under earliest deadline scheduling. In: IEEE Real-Time Systems Symposium. (1994)
21. Spuri, M.: Analysis of deadline scheduled real-time systems. Technical Report RR-2772, INRIA, France (1996)
22. Shin, I., Lee, I.: Periodic resource model for compositional real-time guarantees. In: Proceedings of the 24th IEEE Real-Time Systems Symposium. (2003)
23. González-Harbour, M., Palencia, J.C.: Response time analysis for tasks scheduled under EDF within fixed priorities. In: Proceedings of the 24th IEEE Real-Time Systems Symposium, Cancún, México (2003)
24. Amey, P., Chapman, R., White, N.: Smart certification of mixed criticality systems. In Vardanega, T., Wellings, A., eds.: Reliable Software Technologies - Ada-Europe 2005. Volume 3555 of LNCS., Springer-Verlag (2005) 144–155

A Comparison of Ada and Real-Time Java™ for Safety-Critical Applications

Benjamin M. Brosgol[1] and Andy Wellings[2]

[1] AdaCore, 104 Fifth Ave., New York,
NY 10011, USA
brosgol@adacore.com

[2] Dept. of Computer Science, University of York, Heslington,
York YO10 5DD, UK
andy.wellings@cs.york.ac.uk

Abstract. Ada has long been used for developing safety-critical systems, and the upcoming Ada 2005 language revision extends this support. For various reasons Java has not been a serious choice in this domain. However, recent work based on the Real-Time Specification for Java promises to make Java technology a credible alternative. This paper discusses and compares Ada and the RTSJ with respect to the requirements for safety-critical systems, in particular how they can serve as the basis for subsets that can be used for developing safety-certified software.

1 Introduction

Software is safety-critical if a failure can directly cause loss of human life or have other catastrophic consequences. Correctness needs to be demonstrated with high assurance, and regulatory agencies in safety-critical industries typically require system providers to meet stringent certification requirements, e.g. DO-178B [1] in commercial aviation.

A major factor affecting the development of safety-critical software is the choice of programming language. But there is a dilemma: features with the expressive power to make a system easier to design, implement and maintain — e.g., Object-Oriented Programming — also bring semantic complexity that makes the resulting software harder to certify. This is especially true for features requiring run-time support.

This conflict is resolved in practice by defining language subsets (also known as profiles) that exclude features that might interfere with safety certification. But this still raises several issues. A language may have semantics with intrinsic safety certification problems that cannot be addressed by subsetting, and there is also the difficulty of deciding what should be in the subset, and who (the language designer, the compiler implementor, or the programmer) should make the choices.

In practice there have been a range of approaches. Ada has proved to be a viable basis for safety-critical subsets, as evidenced by SPARK, which emphasizes a particular approach towards demonstrating program correctness, and by various Ada compiler implementations targeted to the safety-critical community. C (and thus C++) are less safe starting points, but the guidelines in MISRA-C [2] intend to avoid C's insecurities and error-prone features. Java, in particular the enhanced platform known as

L.M. Pinho and M. González Harbour (Eds.): Ada-Europe 2006, LNCS 4006, pp. 13–26, 2006.
© Springer-Verlag Berlin Heidelberg 2006

real-time Java,[1] is currently attracting interest from both the research community and from organizations using Java in systems that have safety-critical requirements.

This paper focuses on Ada[2] and real-time Java, discussing how each can serve as the basis for safety-critical subsets (specifically with respect to the certification issues raised by the DO-178B guidelines).

2   DO-178B and Programming Language Issues

DO-178B comprises a set of 66 "guidelines" that apply to the development of software for commercial aircraft systems.[3] The document defines five increasingly stringent levels of criticality, from Level E (lowest) through A (highest). Levels A and B apply to systems whose failure may cause loss of life and are thus considered safety critical.

DO-178B's emphasis is on ensuring the soundness of the process used to build the software, as opposed to directly showing that the resulting software product is correct. Compliance with DO-178B involves the preparation of many certification artifacts (generally documentation of various kinds), adherence to configuration management and quality assurance procedures, and a focus on testing.

2.1   General Requirements

With its emphasis on process, DO-178B says very little about the programming language that is to be used. The document likewise says very little about specific features. Nevertheless, from those guidelines that relate to the software verification process it is possible to infer four main requirements that must be met by a language (or language subset) that is used for developing software for systems at levels A or B:

Reliability. The language should encourage the development of readable, reliable software (no "traps and pitfalls"). This means early error detection, compile-time checking, intuitive lexical and syntactic properties, and similar sorts of features.
Predictability. First, the programmer must be able to know the exact effect of the program's execution. Thus the language semantics needs to be precisely defined — no implementation dependences or undefined behavior. Second, it must be possible to demonstrate statically (before program execution) that time/space constraints will not be exceeded: deadlines are met, and storage is not exhausted or fragmented.
Analyzability. Several DO-178B guidelines deal with code analyzability in connection with testing. For example, requirements- and structure-based coverage analysis must guarantee that all software requirements are implemented and that there is no "dead code" that is present in the system but does not correspond to requirements. Structural coverage analysis is particularly stringent at Level A, for example requiring "modified condition decision coverage" for boolean expressions, and analysis

---

[1] We use the term *real-time Java* to mean the Java platform extended with real-time functionality and predictability, as defined in the Real-Time Specification for Java [3].

[2] Unless indicated otherwise, *Ada* in this paper refers to the Ada 2005 language revision currently in progress [4].

[3] The guidelines are not specific to aircraft systems and may be used more generally on any system where high confidence in predictability, reliability and safety is required.

at the object code level when there is not direct traceability from source to object. Language features may either help or interfere with performing such analyses.

Expressiveness. Safety-critical systems almost always have real-time constraints and deal with hardware interrupts, shared memory, and other low level issues. The programming language (or language subset) needs to support such functionality.

2.2 Language Feature Issues

The requirements just described have tradeoffs, and advances in language technology sometimes complicate compliance with DO-178B.

High-Level Features [*Predictability, Analyzability*]. Programmers use high-level constructs since it saves development time. For example, array slice assignment in Ada is better than writing a loop with element-by-element assignment. However, for the slice assignment the compiler may generate code that contains implicit loops and conditionals. This may be problematic at Level A, for structural coverage at the object-code level. Recursion can simplify some algorithms, at the sacrifice of storage predictability. Subprograms as run-time objects are often useful, but they complicate coverage analysis.

Encapsulation [*Analyzability*]. The "black box" principle — "clients" of a module can access only the module's interface and not its implementation — is a basic tenet for robust software design. However, such "information hiding" may be in conflict with the DO-178B guidelines for structural coverage analysis.

Object-Oriented Programming. OOP raises several serious issues with respect to safety certification. especially with respect to traceability. For example:

- **Inheritance [*Reliability, Analyzability*]** semantics may lead to several kinds of programming errors: accidental overloading of a method when the intent was to override, or accidental overriding when the intent was to overload or introduce a new method. Inheritance may also exacerbate data coupling (dependence of subclass on fields in superclass) and complicate analysis.
- **Polymorphism [*Predictability, Analyzability*]** requires pointers and generally involves dynamic allocation. That raises the issue of memory management / fragmentation / garbage collection. Interface types (as in Java and Ada 2005) complicate analysis since a variable of such a type can reference any object from any class that implements the interface.
- **Dynamic binding [*Analyzability*]** presents serious issues for structural coverage analysis. Unlike a case statement, where the effect (and thus the analysis) is known to be local to the statement itself, a dynamically bound method call may invoke code distant from the context of the call itself.

Generics [*Analyzability*]. Generics ("templates") are key to successful code reuse, but for safety certification each instantiation must be analyzed individually. Since a generic instance does not directly correspond to source code provided by the developer, generics can be more difficult to certify than the equivalent program with the expanded instance explicit in the source text.

Inline expansion [*Predictability, Analyzability*]. Inline expansion raises issues similar to generics and also introduces implementation dependences (the compiler may or may not expand invocations inline).

Facilities Requiring Run-Time Support [*Predictability, Analyzability*]. Exception handling, concurrency, and memory management require implementation-provided run-time libraries. Even features that are part of the "static semantics" may result in code that was not explicitly provided by the program (for example "type support" routines for assignment and equality). The generality of the language can make certifiability impractical or impossible for such libraries.

The semantics of dynamic features can significantly complicate coverage analysis for application code. With exceptions there may be "catch-all" handler code that is not easily exercised, and throwing an exception may require dynamic allocation. Concurrency features greatly increase the number of control paths in a program and may introduce timing dependences that are difficult to analyze.

Coverage issues likewise arise for the Application Program Interface. Sometimes the largest advantage of a programming language is the set of libraries that accompanies the implementation (math packages, etc.), but if these are not certifiable then they cannot be used in a safety-critical program.

Compiler Optimizations [*Predictability, Analyzability*]. In order to improve run-time performance, modern compilers may generate code that is not directly traceable to the source program. Optimization also interacts with exception handling (e.g., if an exception is raised in an expression that has been moved) and concurrency (caching of shared data in thread-local memory). These kinds of issues significantly complicate coverage analysis.

These issues are receiving attention, since there is interest (especially from developers) to use many of these features in safety-critical code, and the impact on certification must be understood by all parties. During recent years several workshops have focused on these topics; one of the results is a 4-volume handbook [5] that analyzes the issues raised by Object-Oriented Technology. The following sections show how Ada and real-time Java address such issues.

3   Safety-Critical Support in Ada

Ada addresses the requirements in Section 2.1 by including features that help, and by allowing the program to exclude features that complicate, safety certification.

3.1   Reliability

Ada was designed with an emphasis on reliability, with features such as strong typing, run-time checks, avoidance of error-prone syntax, and many others. For example:

- *Valid attribute*. With this attribute the programmer can check whether a scalar object that is set from an external device has a valid value. This seemingly simple problem was difficult to solve in Ada 83.

- *Prevention of dangling references to declared entities.* Ada's access type rules prevent creating a "pointer" to a data object or subprogram whose lifetime could be shorter than that of the pointer.
- *Specification of intent on operation inheritance.* Ada 2005 has syntax that allows the detection (at compile time) of unintended overriding or non-overriding.
- *Task activation control.* Ada 2005 has introduced rules for "atomic" elaboration; this prevents interrupts during package elaboration from invoking handlers that referenced uninitialized data.
- `pragma Assert`. Ada 2005 has defined a pragma that allows the assertion of a boolean condition, with program control over the effect when the condition is false, for example by raising an exception.

But Ada also has features that can lead to hard-to-detect errors. Providing dynamic allocation but not requiring garbage collection, Ada places storage reclamation responsibilities on the programmer. This entails either unchecked deallocation (risking dangling references) or reusable object pools (requiring careful analysis to use correctly) to avoid storage leakage.

3.2 Predictability

Any language design has to make tradeoffs among deterministic semantics, program efficiency, and implementability across a wide range of processors and operating systems. For example, if an expression can have side effects then order of evaluation is important. But if the language rules dictate order of evaluation, optimizations become more difficult. As another example, if the concurrency features have specific rules for task dispatching, ready queue placement, and the effect of priorities, then the language's implementation on some platforms may be difficult or inefficient. If it lacks such specificity, then a program may have different effects on different platforms.

Ada 95 offered a partial solution to this dilemma by separating the standard into the core language and the specialized needs annexes. For some kinds of features (e.g., tasking) the core language is intentionally permissive, with constraints added in the Systems Programming or Real-Time Annexes.

However, as a compromise, this approach left a number of areas with nondeterministic semantics. The use of various features may result in erroneous execution, bounded errors, or unspecified or implementation-defined behavior. Examples include the effect of reading the value of an uninitialized object, elaboration order choice, and dependence on the parameter passing mechanism (by copy versus by reference).

Beyond the general issue of deterministic semantics, there is also the potential problem of implementation decisions that interfere with a program's time or space predictability. An example is the possibility of implicit use of the heap for unconstrained discriminated records or functions returning unconstrained arrays.

Solving such issues requires one or more of the following:

- Analyzing the program to ensure that the effect does not arise (e.g., no reads of uninitialized data)
- Adhering to a restricted subset that does not contain the feature in question (e.g., avoiding elaboration order nondeterminism by ensuring that all library-level packages can be specified with pragma `Pure` or `Preelaborate`)

- Knowing any relevant implementation decisions so that the program effect (including time and space behavior) is deterministic

3.3 Analyzability

Given the size and generality of the full Ada language, arguably the most important feature for safety-critical systems is a pragma that indicates what a program is *not* doing: pragma Restrictions. Indeed, Ada may best be regarded not as a single language but rather as a family of languages. This is important because there is no such thing as *the* safety-critical subset of Ada; instead pragma Restrictions provides a framework that allows a programmer to define the subset needed for his or her application. Sometimes a set of restrictions collectively is useful, and Ada 2005 introduces pragma Profile as a higher level mechanism for this purpose. The now-classic Ravenscar concurrency restrictions [6] are captured in this fashion: pragma Profile(Ravenscar).

An attempt to define a "one size fits all" safety-critical subset is problematic, since the features that need to be restricted depend on the sorts of analyses that will be carried out.[4] This point is discussed and illustrated extensively in [7].

However, the utility of pragma Restrictions depends on how it is supported in practice. An implementation is permitted to "bundle" restrictions, for example by supplying some fixed number of versions of its run-time support libraries. A program that needs some but not all of the facilities in one of these libraries will end up with the entire library, including features that might not be desired. This will require extra expense for certifying software that is not needed (and will also require explanation to the certification authorities as to why such deactivated code is present).

It is much more useful if the implementation is more flexible, supplying run-time support for a feature only if the feature is actually used in the program. This *à la carte* style is provided in some current Ada implementations, for example AdaCore's High Integrity Edition of GNAT Pro.

Ada 95's Safety and Security Annex included several pragmas designed to assist with safety certification-related analysis. In practice most of these pragmas have been too weakly specified to have much of an effect, although Normalize_Scalars can help in ensuring a deterministic set of initial values.

Ada's exception handling mechanism raises certification issues regarding library complexity and unreachable handler code.

Ada's high-level nature presents specific challenges to analyzability, but again an implementation can allow the user to specify relevant restrictions. For example, since generated code may contain loops or conditionals that were only implicit in the source program, an implementation may allow the user to prevent such code from being generated. (The compiler will either generate alternative code, possibly less efficient, or reject the program if no such alternative is available.) As another example, an implementation may restrict the use of exception handling, e.g. only for "last chance" code that runs before program termination.

---

[4] This is not to argue against the utility of well-defined subsets such as SPARK, but it might be noted that the SPARK subset is derived from a particular approach to program verification. Other approaches could give rise to other subsets.

Unlike other languages, encapsulation in Ada does not conflict with coverage analysis. It is possible to define a test procedure as a child unit, whose body then has full visibility onto the "state" data encapsulated in the specification of private child package.

3.4 Expressibility

Ada provides excellent support for low-level and real-time programming, both of which are typically needed in safety-critical systems. It also is a methodology-neutral language; if OOP is needed then it is available. If OOP is not needed then traditional language features can be used. It is also possible to use Ada 83-style Object-Oriented Design, or Ada 95 tagged types with type extension, but to exclude complicating features such as polymorphism (class-wide types) and dynamic binding

Ada's concurrency model is a good fit for the requirements of safety-critical programming, as is evidenced by the Ravenscar profile.

Ada may be judged weak in the area of distribution and networking, since it lacks many built-in language features or libraries for these domains. However, Ada's Distributed Systems Annex ensures type safety across partitions, and equivalent semantics when partitioning the application. In addition, Ada has extensive standard facilities for interfacing with code in other languages. Thus if there is a certified library available in C, it can be incorporated into an Ada application.

Other Ada limitations include the absence of built-in constructs or library support for common idioms such as periodic tasks. The language also lacks a general annotation facility; SPARK, for example, uses specially interpreted comments.

3.5 Summary

Ada in its entirety is too large a language for safety critical systems, but subsetting is allowed and indeed facilitated by the Restrictions and Profile pragmas. It is strong in terms of underlying reliability features, expressibility, and its flexibility in subsetting. It has a proven track record in the safety arena and in several areas has advanced the state of the art: SPARK, which has demonstrated the practicality of applying rigorous methods to demonstrate correctness of large systems; Ravenscar, which has shown that concurrency features can be used in safety-critical code.

Ada's main potential drawback is with respect to portability in the context of certification. Although Ada in general supports portability well, a program with restrictions that allow certification in one implementation might not be certifiable in another. This is due both to Ada's flexible approach to subsets and to its various semantic implementation dependences. This may be an issue more in theory than in practice, since certification details tend to be rather implementation specific even for language features that are portable.

4   Safety-Critical Support in Java

Java [8] was certainly not designed for safety-critical programming, but it is still useful to assess the language as a whole with respect to the requirements in Section 2.1. This will identify problems that must be addressed in a safety-critical subset and will also point to intrinsic issues that will arise in subsets as well as the full language.

4.1   Reliability

Java was designed in response to known insecurities in C and C++ and has many features that support reliable programming. However, it also has some shortcomings. Its primitive numeric types are weakly typed and do not provide a mechanism for defining range constraints. The solution, to define a class with the numeric data as a field, brings run-time overhead (dynamic allocation of new objects) and some notational clumsiness. The signed integer types have "wraparound" semantics on overflow, resulting in the counterintuitive effect that the sum of two positive numbers may be negative. Java carries over the C/C++ syntactic framework almost intact, thereby inheriting a number of programming pitfalls. These include poorly human-engineered numeric literals (what is the value of 0XF000000000000000?), susceptibility to "dangling else" problems, and errors stemming from the use of "=" for assignment. In the OOP area, although Java 1.5 has an annotation, @override, that detects the error of introducing a new or over-loaded method when the intent was to override an inherited method, it lacks a facility for addressing the symmetric situation: overriding an inherited method when the intent was to define a new one. Typographical errors or spelling mistakes can result in legal programs with subtle-to-detect bugs. The semantics for class loading can lead to some unexpected effects, with a static field accessed before its explicit initialization value has been assigned. The Java concurrency model is low-level and contains many subtleties (for example with the use of synchronization and the wait / notify mechanism) that can lead to hard-to-detect errors or race conditions. Java allows a function to be invoked as a statement. If this is done unintentionally the program will compile and run but might not give the expected result.

   Most of these shortcomings are intrinsic and will apply to subsets as well as to full Java. The thread model problems are somewhat addressable through a combination of an API and a set of restrictions on thread methods (e.g., prohibiting explicit calls on wait and notify). However, the mutual exclusion mechanism – synchronized code and methods – is basic to Java semantics. Since all arrays and class instances are dynamically allocated, "locking" a data structure is more complex in Java (since the data structure may comprise discontiguous parts) than in other languages.

   These are not necessarily fatal flaws—it is, after all, possible to certify systems written in C and assembly language. However, their effect is to make the certification process more complex and thus more expensive.

4.2   Predictability

One of Java's strengths is its well-defined semantics, at least for sequential programs. Like Ada, and in contrast to C or C++, Java defines the effect of run-time conditions such as array index out of bounds and storage overflow. But Java goes much further. Decisions that are implementation dependent or unspecified in other languages—such as order of evaluation in expressions, the effect of referencing uninitialized data, the interaction between optimizations (code motion) and exceptions—are specified deterministically in Java.

   However, some issues still arise. One is the effect of finalization. Java allows the user to override the finalize method for a new class; during garbage collection for any object of this class, finalize will be invoked. However, there is no guarantee when garbage collection is performed.

The other major area where Java semantics are ill-defined is the thread model. Priorities are not guaranteed to be used for thread dispatching; priority inversions and other anomalies are possible.

Beyond these issues of deterministic semantics, there is also the issue of how the language supports programs whose run-time resources (particularly space and time requirements) must be predictable. In this area Java presents major challenges:

- *Memory Management*
  One of the major strengths of Java is its provision of automatic garbage collection. However, the presence of garbage collection does not prevent memory leaks. Moreover, a program may suffer from unexpected GC-induced interruptions that defeat analysis of time predictability.
- *Real-Time Deadlines*
  Safety-critical systems generally have real-time constraints, with hard deadlines that must be met. The Java thread model's nondeterminism, and interference from the Garbage Collector, defeat this requirement:
- *Java Virtual Machine Issues*
  Java is different from traditional languages in that its execution platform is generally a software (JVM) environment. This is not essential, and there are Java compilers that generate code for standard hardware processors. However, if a JVM is used, several issues arise. Most significant is the need to certify the JVM itself, a formidable undertaking in view of Java's rich run-time semantics. There is also the problem that some JVM instructions take an unbounded amount of time (e.g. athrow for exception propagation), complicating analysis of time predictability.

4.3 Analyzability

As a modern, highly dynamic, "pure" Object Oriented Language, Java suffers from many of the issues identified in Section 2.2.

There is no Java analog to Ada's pragma Restrictions. Thus subsetting will be decided by individual Java implementations, or perhaps as the result of a Java Community Process effort. In either case there is a potential loss of flexibility with respect to analysis techniques, if the specific subset contains features that are outside the set allowed by a user's analysis approach.

4.4 Expressibility

On the positive side, Java does provide class libraries for functionality such as networking and distribution. However, these libraries would need to be rewritten if they are to be used for safety-critical systems, with careful attention paid to memory management.

Java also supplies annotations (in V1.5), which can be useful for describing statically analyzable properties.

Java is weak with respect to "systems programming" level features. This is alleviated in part by some of the facilities provided by the RTSJ, but it is likely that low-level programming will require native code, which will complicate certification.

A more encompassing issue is that Java is a "pure" Object-Oriented Language. It is possible to program in Java without using the dynamic OO features—for example with all methods static or final—but that would result in a style that is distinctly non-Java-like. This is an intrinsic issue; it will arise for any subset.

4.5 Summary

The fact that full Java is not appropriate for safety-critical programming is no surprise. The question is whether the impediments can be removed by restricting the language features to a "safe subset", by providing a specialized API, or both.

Although there is no equivalent of SPARK for Java, this problem has to some extent been addressed in other contexts, in industries that, while not safety-critical, demand high reliability and security. As one example, a subset of the Java platform for smart cards [9] removes a number of complex features such as multithreading and garbage collection; class loading is also more restrictive. And there has been some work on formally defining Java's syntax and semantics [10].

As the Java language has evolved, features have been added that are useful for safety-critical programming (and that thus might be candidates for inclusion in a safety-critical subset). These include annotations and the `assert` statement (although, as in Ada, the `assert` statement raises issues of coverage analysis for exception handling code that is only executed when "impossible" conditions occur).

5 Safety Critical Support in the Real-Time Specification for Java

This section describes how the RTSJ addresses the safety-critical requirements presented in Section 2.1.

5.1 Safety-Critical Issues

The RTSJ was designed to address Java's shortcomings in the real-time area, and not to serve as an API for safety-critical applications. Nonetheless, many features that satisfy real-time goals also support safety-critical development, so it is useful to see how the RTSJ rates against the requirements of Section 2.1.

Reliability. The RTSJ inherits Java's semantic underpinnings and has both the advantages and disadvantages of full Java with respect to reliability. Thus most of the Java problems cited in Section 4.1 also arise in the RTSJ. An exception is the thread model; the problems in full Java have been largely solved by the RTSJ.

Predictability. The RTSJ addresses the major predictability issues with Java. It resolves the underspecified semantics of the general Java thread model, and provides a mechanism (scoped and immortal memory) that can serve as an adjunct to or replacement of the garbage collector. A few issues still arise, however. One is the presence of optional features in the RTSJ (for example, the Priority Ceiling Emulation policy for monitor control). Also, some RTSJ aspects are implementation dependent, such as the placement of preempted threads in ready queues.

Analyzability. There are obviously features that would be too complicated for certification and that would thus need to be excluded or substantially restricted, such as asynchronous transfer of control, the general scoped memory model, the full mechanism for monitor control policies, and "on line" (run-time) feasibility analysis. On the other hand, a number of RTSJ features are designed to support analyzability, such as the cost and deadline data supplied to various constructors.

Expressibility. The RTSJ supports idioms (periodic, aperiodic and sporadic real-time threads and asynchronous event handlers) that will be useful for safety-critical applications. It also adds some classes that help with low-level programming. On the other hand, the "pure" Object-Oriented nature of Java means that expressing traditional (non-OO) functionality may have a style that is awkward. And although Java is rich in support for distributed applications, distribution was outside the scope of the RTSJ.

In summary, the RTSJ has demonstrated the feasibility of solving Java's most substantive predictability challenges — thread issues and garbage collection problems — in a way that makes sense for real-time programs. It is thus reasonable to consider the RTSJ as a starting point for the design of a safety-critical profile.

6   Defining a Safety-Critical RTSJ Profile

Early work has focused on providing a Ravenscar-like profile [11] and its associated real-time JVM [12]. More recently, work within the European High-Integrity Java Applications (HIJA) project — www.hija.org — and under the auspices of The Open Group's Real-Time and Embedded Systems (RTES) Forum have begun to take this approach forward in an attempt to produce an industrial standard, which is planned for development under Sun Microsystems' Java Community Process and which, at a later stage, might be submitted to ISO. No clear agreements have yet emerged out of the RTES Forum yet, so this section will discuss the models proposed by Ravenscar-Java and the HIJA project. These are serving as input to the RTES Forum's deliberations.

The Memory Management Model. Both Ravenscar-Java and the HIJA high-integrity subset use a limited form of scoped memory in order to allow dynamic allocation with predictable reclamation and avoidance of fragmentation. Ravenscar-Java allows a single scope per schedulable object and assumes that each application program executes in two phases: an *initialization* phase and a *mission* phase. In the initialization phase, all non-time-critical activities and initializations that are required before the mission phase are carried out. This includes loading all the classes needed in the application, and running static initializers. In the mission phase the application is executed, with each schedulable object s treated as comprising a sequence of releases. Any objects allocated during one release go in s's scoped memory and are deallocated on completion of the release. Static analysis based on annotations can detect reference assignment errors.

In the HIJA proposal, a recovery phase is added, and nested scoped memory areas are allowed, but there is no sharing of scopes between the schedulable objects (except the initial-scope memory area). Recovery consists of exiting the initial scoped memory area and re-entering to re-initialize the entire system.

The Concurrency Model. Both Ravenscar-Java and the HIJA proposal support a subset of the RTSJ concurrency model. Among the restrictions:

- Each schedulable object must have either periodic or sporadic release parameters (aperiodic release parameters are not supported).
- The only scheduler is the default preemptive priority-based scheduler (FIFO within priority) with exactly 28 priorities. There is no support for dynamic priorities.
- Deadline misses are detected but there is no support for CPU-time monitoring.
- Shared objects are from classes with synchronized methods. The `synchronized` statement is not allowed. Suspension is prohibited within a synchronized method.
- Priority inversion is controlled by use of the Priority Ceiling Emulation policy. The default ceiling priority is the maximum priority supported by the default scheduler.
- Complicated features, such as asynchronous transfer of control, are prohibited.

Safety-Critical Issues with RTSJ Profiles. In summary:

- **Reliability.** These issues are the same as for the RTSJ.
- **Predictability.** The profiles supply deterministic semantics and require support for Priority Ceiling Emulation.
- **Analyzability.** The profiles remove the RTSJ features that compromise analyzability, although they do this to different degrees. Ravenscar-Java is simpler and thus easier to certify than the HIJA approach.
- **Expressibility.** The essence of a subset is reduced functionality, so an issue that will be open until there is actual application experience is whether the profiles' restrictions introduce unacceptable stylistic complexity. For example, Ravenscar-Java's assumes that an application comprises an initialization phase and a mission phase. This may be overly constraining (it is sometimes useful to have a "warm restart" with initialization repeated; this is allowed in the HIJA profile).

7   Comparison and Conclusions

Table 1 (page 25) summarizes the main points of comparison between Ada and Real-Time Java with respect to their suitability as the basis for safety-critical subsets.

Ada and Java represent rather different starting points for the definition of safety-critical subsets. Ada has an established history in this domain, as illustrated by SPARK and vendor-supplied profiles. The Ravenscar profile showed that Ada's concurrency features could be used for certifiable systems; there was no need to use the methodologically fragile cyclic executive style. Pragma `Restrictions` may be a real breakthrough in safety-critical technology, offering the programmer the opportunity to develop systems with precise control over which features are needed and to choose the subset based on the planned analysis techniques. Ada has reliable underpinnings; there are few if any intrinsic issues that cause problems for a subset. And being methodologically neutral, Ada supports traditional development techniques as well as OOP at whatever level the programmer needs (for example it is possible to use type extension but not polymorphism or dynamic binding).

Table 1. Comparison of Ada and Real-Time Java for Safety-Critical Systems

	Ada Advantages	Real-Time Java Advantages
Reliability	• Secure syntactic foundation, avoiding Java's C-based pitfalls • Stronger typing, especially for the numeric types • Specific features such as named associations, Valid attribute • Intuitive semantics for signed integer arithmetic overflow	• Prevention of dangling references (no explicit deallocation) • Prevention of references to uninitialized values • Prevention of unreachable code
Predictability	• Specific features with predictable time/space behavior, such as non-blocking protected operations, and Suspension_Objects • Absence of Garbage Collector	• Avoidance of implementation dependences and unspecified behavior • Provision of automatically reclaimed non-heap memory areas
Analyzability	• General framework (Restrictions, Profile pragmas) for defining analyzable subsets • Child unit as test procedure for package with hidden "state"	• Built-in framework for feasibility analysis
Expressibility	• Support for classical (non-OO) development • Support for low-level programming, interfacing with other languages	• Support for common real-time idioms and release characteristics • Useful features in Java 1.5, such as annotations

Ada also has some disadvantages. The flexibility of pragma Restrictions brings possible portability issues, and there are a number of cases in Ada where the semantics is not completely specified (e.g., bounded errors or implementation defined behavior).

Java is a much newer technology for the safety-critical domain, and the Real-Time Specification for Java serves as a possible starting point. Its advantages include protection against dangling references, and explicit support for idioms such as asynchronous event handlers and periodic realtime threads. Work in progress (on the Ravenscar-Java and HIJA profiles) thus far shows that safety-critical profiles of real-time Java are feasible. On the other hand, there are intrinsic Java issues with any subset. The C-oriented syntactic framework can lead to errors, and Java's status as a "pure" OO language can result in clumsy style for programs that do not need OOP. The RTSJ's scoped memory mechanism, even in its simple forms, is new and will require a different style of programming than what Java and real-time developers are accustomed to.

Ada is certainly expected to continue as a language of choice for safety-critical systems. It has a proven track record, and its issues are well understood and manageable.

A real-time Java profile may be attractive for a system where Java is the chosen technology and which has safety-critical components. The potential demand for such systems means that research and development on safety-critical real-time Java will likely continue well into the future. Given Ada 2005's interfacing capabilities with Java, a system with a mix of safety-critical code in Ada and real-time Java would not an be unrealistic development.

References

1. RTCA SC-167 / EUROCAE WG-12. *RTCA/DO-178B – Software Considerations in Airborne Systems and Equipment Certification*, December 1992.
2. The Motor Industry Software Reliability Association. *MISRA-C:2004 – Guidelines for the use of the C language in critical systems*, October 2004.
3. Peter Dibble (spec. lead), Rudy Belliardi, Benjamin Brosgol, David Holmes, and Andy Wellings. *Real-Time Specification for Java^{TM}*, V1.0.1, June 2005. www.rtsj.org.
4. ISO/IEC JTC1/SC 22/WG 9. *Ada Reference Manual – ISO/IEC 8652:1995(E) with Technical Corrigendum 1 and Amendment 1 (Draft 13) – Language and Standard Libraries*, 2005.
5. *Handbook for Object-Oriented Technology in Aviation (OOTiA)*, October 2004. www.faa.gov/aircraft/air_cert/design_approvals/air_software/oot.
6. Alan Burns, Brian Dobbing, and George Romanski. The Ravenscar profile for high-integrity real-time programs. In *Reliable Software Technologies – Ada Europe '98*, number 1411 in Lecture Notes in Computer Science, Uppsala, Sweden, June 1998. Springer-Verlag.
7. ISO/IEC JTC1/SC 22/WG 9. *ISO/IEC DTR 15942: Guide for the Use of the Ada Programming Language in High Integrity Systems*, July 1999.
8. James Gosling, Bill Joy, Guy Steele, and Gilad Bracha. *The Java Language Specification*. Addison-Wesley, third edition, 2005.
9. E. Poll, J. van den Berg, and B. Jacobs. Formal specification of the JavaCard API in JML: the APDU class. *Computer Networks (Amsterdam, Netherlands: 1999)*, 36(4):407–421, 2001.
10. Jim Alves-Foss, editor. *Formal Syntax and Semantics of Java*, volume 1523 of *Lecture Notes in Computer Science*. Springer, 1999.
11. J. Kwon, A. Wellings, and S. King. Ravenscar-Java: a high-integrity profile for real-time Java. *Concurrency and Computation: Practice and Experience*, 17(5-6):681–713, April/May 2005.
12. Hao Cai and Andy Wellings. A real-time Isolate specification for Ravenscar-Java. In *Proceedings of the Seventh IEEE International Symposium on Object-Oriented Real-Time Distributed Computing*, May 2004.

POSIX Trace Based Behavioural Reflection

Filipe Valpereiro and Luís Miguel Pinho

Polytechnic Institute of Porto, Porto, Portugal
{fvalpereiro, lpinho}@dei.isep.ipp.pt

Abstract. Traditional Real-Time Operating Systems (RTOS) are not designed to accommodate application specific requirements. They address a general case and the application must co-exist with any limitations imposed by such design. For modern real-time applications this limits the quality of services offered to the end-user. Research in this field has shown that it is possible to develop dynamic systems where adaptation is the key for success. However, adaptation requires full knowledge of the system state. To overcome this we propose a framework to gather data, and interact with the operating system, extending the traditional POSIX trace model with a partial reflective model. Such combination still preserves the trace mechanism semantics while creating a powerful platform to develop new dynamic systems, with little impact in the system and avoiding complex changes in the kernel source code.

1 Introduction

Traditional Real-Time Operating Systems (RTOS) are designed to support a generic real-time environment. In this scenario, *a priori* assumptions are made on the tasks characteristics, resource utilization requirements and platform. Consequently, the decisions made in the RTOS design narrow the range of possible applications. However, the need to support a new rich set of applications, maybe running on embedded devices, such as multimedia and real-time telecommunication, introduce more stringent requirements on the dynamicity of the underlying operating system.

Although these applications still present real-time requirements, the characteristics of tasks and resource utilisation patterns vary considerably. Typically, multimedia applications demand resources in a non-deterministic way. Under such scenario, the application should deliver the best possible service while respecting the real-time requirements. To achieve such functionality, the application may need to change its own behaviour, for which it is important to be perceptive of the system's current state.

One particular strategy that fits well with dynamic behaviour is Reflection [1], a well know technique in the object-oriented world. Nevertheless, the use of the reflection paradigm to acquire (and control) the state of the system is hindered by the lack of support for reflection in current RTOS. In this scenario we present a flexible framework to reify operating system data using the POSIX trace [2] as a meta-object protocol. Research in the field has already addressed the problem of adapting a reflective approach to an RTOS kernel. Systems like ApertOS [3]; the Spring kernel [4] and more recently DAMROS [5] are attempts to provide reflective capabilities to operating systems. Our approach differs from previous works, since it is intended to be used in general purpose RTOS.

L.M. Pinho and M. González Harbour (Eds.): Ada-Europe 2006, LNCS 4006, pp. 27–39, 2006.

We consider the use of a partial reflection model [6] to establish behavioural reflection, integrating this model with the POSIX trace mechanism to achieve an efficient reflective framework. It is our belief that such combination can create a powerful tool on non-reflective RTOS, giving the developer freedom to implement new dynamic support on current and well know systems. This will allow providing feedback from the operating system to applications running in parallel with the system application. By providing such feedback, it will then be possible to support quality of service requirements evaluation [7] using real data from the system and to collect valuable metrics on the overall system behaviour.

In this paper, we focus on the reification of data through the use of the POSIX trace mechanism [2] and on its implementation in the MarteOS operating system [8], to validate its usefulness and analyse its impact in the latency and determinism of the system. The paper is structured as follows. Section 2 presents a brief notation on computational reflection and previous approaches on using this paradigm in RTOS. Section 3 presents a brief discussion of the POSIX tracing mechanism, and on the benefits of its use, whilst Section 4 presents the proposed framework and discusses some of the strategies used to reify data using the POSIX trace mechanism. Finally, Section 5 presents some conclusions and future work.

2   Computational Reflection

Reflection can be described as the ability of a program to become 'self-aware'. Self-aware programs can inspect themselves and possibly modify their behaviour, using a representation of themselves [1] (the meta-model). The meta-model is said to be causally connected with the real system in such a way that any changes in the meta-model will be reflected in the system behaviour. In the same way, any changes in the system are reflected in the meta-model. This "inter-model connection" is performed through the use of a meta-interface (often termed as meta-object protocol: MOP).

A reflective system is thus composed by the meta-interface and two levels: a base level where normal computation takes place and a meta-level where abstract aspects of the system are being computed. Through the use of a meta-interface the meta-level can gather information from the base-level (a process termed *reification*) and compute the non-functional aspects of the system, eventually interfering in the system and changing the behaviour (a process termed *reflection*). This principle clearly separates the normal system computation from non-functional aspects of the system.

There are mainly two models of computational reflection [1]. The structural reflection model is focused on the structural aspects of a program (e.g. data types and classes). In contrast, behavioural reflection exposes the behaviour and state of the system (e.g. methods call execution). These models can also be classified as being partial if any form of selection can be performed on the entities being reflected. Partial behavioural reflection [6] is an efficient approach that balances flexibility vs. efficiency by allowing a tight control over the spatial and/or temporal selection of entities that need reification. While spatial control can be applied at compile time by selecting the objects and methods to be reflected, temporal selection requires an efficient runtime support which goes beyond the scope of our framework.

Meta-level

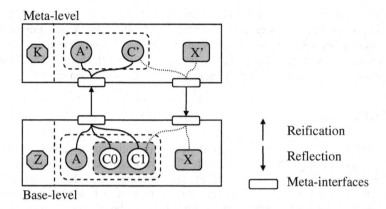

Reification

Reflection

Meta-interfaces

Base-level

Fig. 1. A reflective system

Figure 1 illustrates a partial behavioural reflective system. Entities can be reflective as A, C, and X and non-reflective as Z. Not all entities may need to reflect into a unique meta-object. C0 and C1 have a common base class and thus in this example are reflected by a single meta-object C' which represents a generalization of class C. Entities A, C0 and C1 belong to a group with related functionality (or behaviour) and thus the meta-model may explore that relation.

2.1 Reflection in Real-Time Operating Systems

RTOS systems are usually designed to support a wide range of applications. It is common for such design to assume no specific knowledge on the target application. However, this approach is not suitable for some class of applications. Some applications may require a real-time response yet they present factors of non-deterministic behaviour. Thus, the dynamic behaviour must adapt to new system (or functional) constraints. It is clear that an interface between the OS and the application needs to exist. The system must allow the application to be aware of system constraints and resources, eventually it may even allow valuable data to be accessed (read only) by the application. In return, the application is responsible to determine the best strategy for its behaviour, and ask the system to incorporate this new strategy. It is also clear that this interface should allow different strategies to be available simultaneously in the target OS.

Computational reflection is a promising solution since it allows us to expose key OS data and computational behaviour into the meta-level where the application non-functional concerns can be expressed and evaluated [9]. Early works on reflective RTOS (such as ApertOS [3] and Spring [4]) have addressed these concerns, incorporating the reflection mechanism in the design and programming language. In Spring, reflection has been used for task management and scheduling, and to support on-line timing requirements analysis, exposing tasks requirements data. The ApertOS approach relies heavily in the object-oriented model and proposed a complete reflective kernel. While these approaches certainly offer some advantages, they rely on the development of completely new operating systems.

A more recent approach has been done in DAMROS [5] which augments a μ-kernel with a reflection mechanism. This approach allows the application to install user-defined policies in the form of executable source code under certain restrictions. Applications, for example, may not access certain data from the kernel. This limits the implementation of some functionality exclusively in the application space.

3 POSIX Trace

The POSIX trace [2] is a mechanism to collect information on a running system and related process through the use of events. The standard defines a portable set of interfaces whose purpose is to collect and present trace logs over selected functionality in the OS such as: internal kernel activities or faults, system calls, I/O activity and user defined events. A major advantage on the POSIX trace is the ability to monitor (or debug) the kernel and applications during execution.

Another important feature in the trace mechanism is the ability to record events as a stream, allowing the OS to store the traced data on a file system or upload it to a remote server via a network link. The ability to read this stream back again gives the developer a powerful tool to monitor, analyse and understand the application behaviour in a post-mortem analysis. There are few restrictions on standard usage; applications are free to use the trace streams for any particular purposes. Trace streams can be shared across the operating system, with each traced system call placing trace events in one or more streams. It is up to the developer to choose the event calls/stream configuration used in the operating system. For example, several trace streams can be used simultaneously and shared by the operating system and running applications. It is easy to think of an application that can take simultaneous advantage of this architecture to log data into a server while performing system metrics and do some self-monitoring using the trace mechanism.

3.1 The Trace Mechanism

The trace mechanism is composed by two main data types: the trace event and the trace stream. The trace activity is defined as the period between stream activation and deactivation where events are recorded/processed from the trace stream. Traces events are a convenient way to encapsulate data with meta-attributes that refer to the actual instance, conditions and event record status within the trace stream. This information defines (up to some time resolution) the exact moment where the trace event has occurred in the traced process. During this activity, the standard identifies three different roles [2]: the trace controller process, the traced process and the analyser process (also called monitor process). The trace stream establish a link (eventually controlled) that connects the traced process and the analyser process.

There are no restrictions in the standard forbidding a merge between the trace controller process and the analyser process and thus we can view the traced system as being composed by two levels: the observed level where the trace occurs, and the observer level where the streams are controlled and data is analysed. It is also clear that no auto-feedback should occur in the observer level which could influence the actual observation.

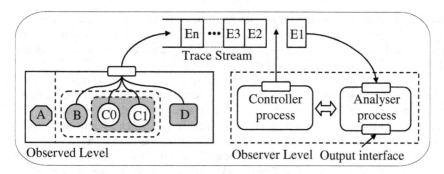

Fig. 2. A system with the trace mechanism

Figure 2 exemplifies the different roles that take part in the traced system. Not all objects in the system may be traced (or needed to be traced). The analyser process presents an output interface which can be used by the application (or system) to obtain information derived from the traced data. As an example, the quality of server managers of [7] requires access to information concerning the actual resource utilization of the system. This information can be provided by analysing the events generated by the operating system.

3.2 Flexibility

The POSIX standard defines the trace mechanism as a monolithic component. There is no room for customization, and thus, this component can not be used with the RTOS targeted for the Minimum Real-time System Profile (MRSP) [10]. Nevertheless, features required by the standard such as filesystem and process inheritance are of no use in this profile and do not compromise the trace functionality. Our work intends to supply a flexible, customizable trace implementation with a small memory footprint, toward the application requirements, in a way that only the necessary trace functionality will be present in the final application.

4 Framework Design

Several techniques have emerged in the RTOS research to address the lack of proper support for dynamic applications behaviour. Our main motivation for the development of this framework is the need of a common, portable platform for data collection and system actuation where these and future techniques can be evaluated. The goal is to support reflection on static application-oriented RTOS, allowing soft real-time applications to change behaviour in response to the system's state, therefore becoming more adaptive. Moreover, the framework will allow to separate the application development from the development of system state analysis mechanisms, and to minimize the system interference.

The need of a portable interface to collect and reify system data led us to consider the POSIX trace mechanism [2] as the basis component of our framework. However, the standard requires the operating system to support functionality which is not required for the role played by the trace mechanism in our framework. The standard rationale defines a monolithic trace mechanism, creating dependencies between the individual trace components. To overcome this limitation we consider a trace mechanism based on modular components, avoiding unnecessary code dependencies while preserving the functional semantics.

We do not consider the use of computational reflection as a whole. Instead a partial reflection model [6] is used; where data is reified without direct transfer of control to the meta-level (an asynchronous reflection model). Traditionally, computational reflection belongs to the language domain, usually implemented into the language run-time environment. This approach does not explore the advantages of concurrent systems and thus reflection occurs as a linear transition between the base-level to the meta-level and vice-versa. The framework takes direct advantage of our problem domain, redefining the transition between the base and meta-level. This is supported by extending the controller and analyser process roles within the POSIX trace mechanism. We also introduce a third process to reify data from the trace streams and create/modify the meta-objects (see figure 3). Under this extended model, the meta-objects act as a "consciousness memory" of the system state, while the analyser process performs some "consciousness" analysis. Eventually, the analyser process may intercede asynchronously in the system, introducing non-functional aspects.

In this paper we focus on the data reification and meta-objects construction; the analyser interface and intercede mechanism (necessary to complete the framework model) will be the focus of further work.

4.1 Modular POSIX Trace

The main reason why the trace standard is not available in the MRSP profile is the lack of filesystem support which is a required feature for the implementation of the POSIX trace interface. The organization of the tracing rationale text for the trace interface defines the trace as a monolithic component, thus leaving no flexibility in the usage. Yet, there are distinct individual components composing the trace mechanism.

A detailed examination of the standard and the trace use cases show us that filesystem support is only useful for offline analysis, a feature used by the trace logs to record data into a permanent storage (a use case not addressed in this paper). On contrast, online analysis is a useful tool to reason on the current system state and does not require filesystem support. This component works as an extension to the main trace functionality, adding new features that support other trace scenarios.

We can explore the inter-component relations to avoid non-functional and unnecessary code in the final binary image, thus reducing the application memory footprint and minimizing the impact on the traced system. Modularity can be achieved if each component is implemented as a separate package in such a way that the main tracer component does not require linking against other component packages. All the remaining trace components must depend strictly on the main package which contains the base definitions, unless a dependency exists between different modules.

The modularity goal is to preserve the functional semantics while eliminating inter-component dependencies. To break these dependencies we need to work on the trace implementation. The application may not use some of the trace components; however the existence of these code dependencies will create a link between the application code and the implementation code. An example of a usage scenario for the trace mechanism is the ability to perform system metrics. Such example may not require the filtering or trace log features. Consider the steps performed on every call to the `posix_trace_event` function to successfully trace an event:

- Find an available trace stream or return.
- Discards the event and return if the event does not pass the filter.
- If it is a user event and data is larger than maximum value, truncate the data.
- Store the event
- Adjust the stream properties (trace policy).
- Flush the stream into the trace log if required.

The function semantics will require the filter component due to the existence of a function call, even if it the function result is irrelevant for the usage scenario, thus a link to this code will be established at compile time. To implement the desired modularity we are currently using a dispatch table that invokes the requested function if the table entry is not null. This solution minimizes the amount of compiler work, since it only needs to recompile the main component. It introduces a new indirection level, but that does not generate any measurable delay in the trace execution.

4.2 The Extended Trace Model

In this extended model, we introduce some principles of partial reflection using the POSIX trace. In the model, the trace streams are used as the meta-interface that allows the meta-level to reify information from the base-level. We also introduced a new process in the trace observer level (the meta-level), the reify process, that acts upon instructions from the controller process. Its main role is to read events from the trace stream and to create and modify the corresponding meta-objects. These objects will be used by the analyser process to perform some "consciousness" analysis, thus the analyser process works exclusively with reified data. The amount of data and analysis type depends only on the developer purpose. For this reason the framework defines the task type but not the task body and properties, giving the developer the freedom to manage the meta-objects.

To avoid possible data inconsistencies any meta-object access is performed using a protected type and the associated interface (see figure 5). The base interface for meta-objects is a procedure to replace a meta-object, a procedure to commit changes in the meta-object and a function to obtain a full copy of the meta-object. However it might be useful to extend this interface with specialized read functions to access some data in the meta-object, improving the access time by avoiding a full object copy. Figure 3 illustrates the extended trace model and the relation between the various entities.

To use the framework the developer must define the analyser task body, completing the meta-model. This activates the framework, triggering the code inclusion in the application; otherwise the compiled code will be trace free. Note that from the traced call point of view no transfer of control from the base-level to the meta-level takes place during the traced call execution; hence the reflection model behaves asynchronously. This is a powerful property, since the meta-level will behave

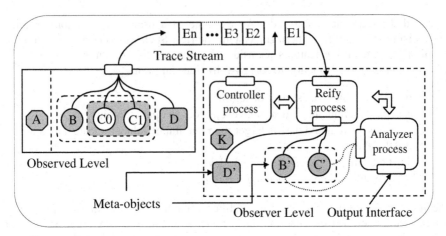

Fig. 3. The extended trace model

as a central state of the operating system that can be queried by higher abstract concerns that can not be expressed with traditional reflection. Note that at present we do not define the output interface which is beyond the scope of this paper.

4.3 Implementation Details

The first step to implement the extended model is to determine which functionality offers interesting data to be reified. Examples of possible information to reify are: memory usage per process (or task), mutex operations including some internal details (accessing task ID, blocked task list, mutex policy …) and CPU bandwidth used, but different types of information can be also be gathered. Figure 4 presents some simplified examples of event definitions used to reify data from the mutex functions. The Data_Envelop type as been defined to ensure that trace events with size larger than the maximum data size allowed in the trace stream can flow without loosing information. However, this option pays heavily and must be avoided whenever possible. Note that we omitted some type info just for clarity's sake.

Some of the reified information exhibits patterns of similarity and thus we can group it, creating a convenient way of express the application "reflective" requirements. With this purpose, we define four sets of functionality that can also be expressed in terms of sub-sets for convenience and further fine-grain control over the data. The sets of functionality are: internal kernel structures; scheduler, locking mechanism and signals; system calls; and I/O triggering (data transmitted/received).

Each set of functionality is also connected to a unique trace stream, leaving the remaining streams free to other purposes. This simplifies the data reification process, avoiding intersection of data events from different functionality sets which would result in a larger and complex decoding task. We also define the events used for each functional unit in each traced set and the corresponding meta-objects and the event(s) associated, creating a map that links the reified units and the meta-objects. This information is vital to the "reify process", to create the meta-objects whenever a related event is received. A second map is created dynamically that binds the created

```
package Trace_Events_Data is

    type Data_Envelop is record
       Info : Data_Info;
       Data : Data_Buffer;
    end record;

    type Mutex_Init_Event is record
       Op               : Op_Code;
       Mutex_Id         : Integer;
       Policy           : Locking_Policy;
       Prio             : Task_Priority;
       Preemption_Level : Task_Preemption_Level;
    end record;

    type Mutex_Event is record
       Op          : Op_Code;
       Mutex_Id    : Integer;
       Task_Id     : Integer;
       Task_Status : Task_Status;
       Prio        : Task_Priority;
    end record;

    -- ...
end Trace_Events_Data;
```

Fig. 4. Events definition

```
with Trace_Events_Data;
package Meta_Objects is

    type Meta_Mutex is record
       Owner            : Integer;
       Mutex_ID         : Integer;
       Policy           : Locking_Policy;
       Preemption_Level : Task_Preemption_Level;
       Blocked_Tasks    : Tasks_Lists;
       Status           : Boolean;
    end record;

    procedure Init_Meta_Object (Event : in Mutex_Init_Event);

    protected type Meta_Mutex_Access is
       procedure Store_Object (Mutex : in Meta_Mutex);
       procedure Commit_Changes (Event : in Mutex_Event);
       function  Get_Copy return Meta_Mutex;

    private
       Mutex : Meta_Mutex;
    end Meta_Mutex_Access;

    -- ...
end Meta_Objects;
```

Fig. 5. Meta-objects definition

meta-objects to the meta-object ID and type. This step ensures that any update information arriving in further events is committed to the corresponding meta-object.

Figure 5 present a simplified meta-object definition and the protected object used to ensure that no data inconsistency occurs whenever an update operation is performed in the meta-object. The protected interface was kept simple, but can be extended to support faster access to individual fields on the meta-object to improve the access time. This option might be useful for testing some properties without requiring access to the whole object.

Figure 6 presents some maps definitions and task types. This package also defines the controller, the reify and the analyser tasks. Bodies for the first two tasks will be defined within the framework. The third task must be defined by the application developer to perform the desired analysis using the meta-objects.

```
with Trace_Events_Data;
with Meta_Objects;
package Meta_Level is

    type Mutex_ID is Integer;
    type Mutex_List_Access is
        new Map (Mutex_ID, Meta_Mutex_Access);

    Mutex_List : Mutex_List_Access;

  task type Controller_Task (Prio : Task_Priority);
  task type Reify_Task (Prio : Task_Priority);
  task type Analyser_Task (Prio : Task_Priority);


  -- ...
end Meta_Level;
```

Fig. 6. Meta-level definition

4.4 Performance Metrics and Results

We have done some experiments in order to find the impact of the framework both on the size of the code and on the execution times of the traced functions. Table 1 presents the overhead on the code size of a traced system. The results allow determining that, depending in the number and type of trace events embedded in the traced

Table 1. Comparison of code size

Description	Size in Bytes
Simple procedure (sum of one integer)	480
Simple procedure with a single trace event	780
Mutex unit without trace events	15884
Mutex unit with eight trace events	17692
Scheduler unit without trace events	13032
Scheduler unit with eleven trace events	15088
Trace implementation with all dependable units	38056
Hello World without trace	341936
Hello World with trace unit	379088

unit, an overhead of approximately 10% is created in the overall code size. This presents a considerable impact, but it is an expected side effect of the increased functionality.

Tables 2 and 3 show the execution times for some of the traced functions, with and without the trace functionality. The tests were performed on a Pentium-III at 930 MHz. The time values are measured by the time-stamp counter (TSC), and mean values were obtained after 5000 measures. The test application sets up a trace stream with sufficient space for all the events generated during the simulation.

Table 2 presents the results of a test setup, where events related to the mutex unit were generated by a loop performing several calls to obtain a lock on the mutex. The results show an increase of execution time by a factor of approximately 0.8 μs for each traced function. The last test also shows the average trace time for regular events versus events using the data envelop capability. As expected they are heavier but offer a more flexible solution to trace large amounts of data.

Table 2. Execution times for the mutex unit

Function	Trace	Min	Max	Mean cycles	Mean μs
Pthread_Mutex_Lock	No	137	221	179	0.19
	Yes	840	1031	900	0.97
Pthread_Mutex_Unlock	No	251	362	296	0.32
	Yes	931	1133	1024	1.1
Event Trace		699	962	740	0.8
Event Trace with envelop		1317	1640	1396	1.5

Table 3. Execution times for the scheduler unit

Function	Trace	Min	Max	Mean cycles	Mean μs
Ready_Task_Reduces_Active_Priority	No	124	286	156	0.17
	Yes	741	983	833	0.90
Running_Task_Gets_Blocked	No	92	167	118	0.13
	Yes	702	1242	774	0.83
Running_Task_Gets_Suspended	No	174	494	270	0.29
	Yes	612	1624	821	0.88
Task_Gets_Ready	No	100	305	130	0.20
	Yes	739	2108	825	0.89
Do_Scheduling	No	116	573	202	0.22
	Yes	744	1286	853	0.92
Event Trace		495	958	650	0.7

Table 3 shows the execution times for the scheduler unit. They were performed with the same configuration, except that the events generated by the scheduler unit were obtained using four simultaneous tasks with different periods, execution time and priority, to create some scheduler activity.

In this case, the experiments showed an increase of approximately 0.7 μs for each traced function, which is in the same order of magnitude of other kernel to user mechanisms available in the MarteOS kernel [11,12]. Considering the gained functionality, this overhead is more than acceptable, since it allows applications to have access to "fresh" kernel data.

5 Conclusion

Soft real-time multimedia applications tend to present factors of non-deterministic behaviour. Developing applications in this domain requires the study and development of dynamic strategies which allow the system and application to adapt, improving the quality of the output generated by the application. This requires, however, applications to have access to the current state of the system, particularly in what resource availability (CPU included) is concerned.

In this paper we present a framework, which uses the POSIX trace mechanism as a Meta-Object Protocol, to implement a partial asynchronous reflection model. Using this framework, applications can query the system state by accessing a meta-level which presents reified information of the system. The design requirement for the framework is the use of standard functionality available (or easily incorporated) in current real-time operating systems. The framework is not tied to any particular operating system, thus making further ports straightforward. We hope that this work can open new perspectives into the use of reflection in real-time operating systems.

Acknowledgements

The authors would like to thank the anonymous reviewers for their helpful comments and suggestions. This work was partially supported by FCT, through the CISTER Research Unit (FCT UI 608) and the Reflect project (POSI/EIA/60797/2004).

References

1. P. Maes. "Concepts and Experiments in Computational Reflection", in. Proceedings of the 2nd Conference on Object-Oriented Programming Systems, Languages and Applications (OOPSLA'87), Orlando USA, 1987, pp. 147–155.
2. IEEE Std. 1003.1, Information technology – Portable Operating System Interface (POSIX), Section 4.17 – Tracing, 2003.
3. Y. Yokote, "The ApertOS Reflective Operating System: The concept and its implementtation", in Proceedings of the 7th Conference on Object-Oriented Programming Systems, Languages and Applications (OOPSLA'92). ACM Press, 1992, pp. 414–434.
4. J. A. Stankovic, "Reflective Real-Time Systems", University of Massachusetts, Technical Report 93-56, June 28, 1993.
5. A. Patil, N. Audsley, "Implementing Application Specific RTOS Policies using Reflection", Proceedings of the 11th IEEE Real-Time and Embedded Technology and Applications Symposium, San Francisco, USA, 2005, pp. 438–447.
6. E. Tanter, J. Noye, D. Caromel, and P. Cointe, "Partial behavioural reflection: Spatial and temporal selection of reification" Proceedings of the 18th Conference on Object-Oriented Programming Systems, Languages and Applications (OOPSLA 2003), October 26-30, 2003, Anaheim, USA, pp. 27–46.

7. Luís M. Pinho, Luís Nogueira and Ricardo Barbosa, "An Ada Framework for QoS-Aware Applications", Proceedings of the 10th International Conference on Reliable Software Technologies (Ada-Europe 2005), York, UK, June 2005, pp. 25–38.

8. M. Aldea and M. González. "MaRTE OS: An Ada Kernel for Real-Time Embedded Applications". Proceedings of the 6th International Conference on Reliable Software Technologies (Ada-Europe-2001), Leuven, Belgium, May, 2001, pp. 305–316.

9. S. Mitchell, A. Wellings, A. Burns, "Developing a Real-Time Metaobject Protocol", Proc. of the 3rd IEEE Workshop on Object-Oriented Real-Time Dependable Systems, Newport Beach, USA, February 1997, pp. 323–330.

10. IEEE Std. 1003.13, Standardized Application Environment Profile – POSIX Realtime and Embedded Application Support, 2003

11. M. Aldea and M. González, "Evaluation of New POSIX Real-Time Operating Systems Services for Small Embedded Platforms", Proc. of the 15th Euromicro Conference on Real-Time Systems, ECRTS 2003, Porto, Portugal, July, 2003, pp. 161–168.

12. M. Aldea and J. Miranda and M. González , "Integrating Application-Defined Scheduling with the New Dispatching Policies", Proceedings of the 10th International Conference on Reliable Software Technologies (Ada-Europe 2005), York, UK, June 2005, pp. 220–235.

Static Detection of Access Anomalies in Ada95*

Bernd Burgstaller[1], Johann Blieberger[2], and Robert Mittermayr[3]

[1] School of Information Technologies, The University of Sydney, Australia
bburg@it.usyd.edu.au
[2] Institute for Computer-Aided Automation, TU Vienna
Treitlstr. 1, A-1040 Vienna, Austria
blieb@auto.tuwien.ac.at
[3] ITS Softwaresysteme, ARC Seibersdorf research GmbH, TechGate Vienna
Donau-City-Str. 1, A-1220 Vienna, Austria
robert.mittermayr@arcs.ac.at

Abstract. In this paper we present data flow frameworks that are able to detect access anomalies in Ada multi-tasking programs. In particular, our approach finds all possible non-sequential accesses to shared non-protected variables. The algorithms employed are very efficient. Our approach is conservative and may find false positives.

1 Introduction

Concurrent programming is a complex task. One reason for this is that scheduling exponentially increases the possible program states. Thus a dynamic execution order of the statements executed in parallel is introduced. In general this leads to different behavior between different runs of a program, even on the same input. Because of the nondeterministic behavior, faults are difficult to detect. Static program analysis, which has been used since the beginning of software, can be a valuable aid for the detection of such faults.

One of the major problems with concurrent programming are *access anomalies*, also called *data races*. In this paper we study the problem of detecting non-sequential access to global shared variables. We employ data flow frameworks in order to solve sub-problems of this general problem. In detail, we set up a data flow framework to find all tasks which potentially run in parallel and we set up a second data flow framework to handle the interprocedural problems of determining variables being "global" to a certain entity. In joining the solutions of these data flow problems, we are able to detect access anomalies in a conservative manner, i.e., if there actually is a non-sequential access to a shared non-protected variable, our approach will detect it. On the other hand, we may also detect false positives.

---

* Bernd Burgstaller has been supported by the ARC Discovery Project Grant "Compilation Techniques for Embedded Systems" under Contract DP 0560190, and the University of Sydney R&D Grants Scheme "Speculative Partial Redundancy Elimination" under Contract L2849 U3229.

L.M. Pinho and M. González Harbour (Eds.): Ada-Europe 2006, LNCS 4006, pp. 40–55, 2006.

The remainder of the paper is organized as follows. In Section 2 our data flow frameworks to find tasks running in parallel and to determine the set of variables "global" to a program entity are presented. Examples are used to illustrate our framework. In Section 3 we survey related work, before we conclude the paper and describe future work in Section 4.

2 Data Flow Framework

In the following we first define a data flow framework to determine which task objects run in parallel to other task objects. This information is used later on to determine if tasks running in parallel access the same global variables.

2.1 Setting Up Data Flow Equations for Relation ∥

We define a relation ∥ on task objects such that for task objects t_1 and t_2: $t_1 \parallel t_2$ if task objects t_1 and t_2 run in parallel. Note that ∥ commutes, i.e., $t_1 \parallel t_2 \iff t_2 \parallel t_1$.

A control flow graph (CFG) $G = (N, E, r)$ consists of a set N of nodes, and a set $E \subseteq N \times N$ of edges. Node r is the designated root node of the CFG.

Given a $\mathrm{CFG}(t) = (N, E, r)$ of a task body t, the basis for the data flow framework are standard equations [21] of the form

$$S_{\text{out}}(n) = \text{Gen}(n) \cup (S_{\text{in}}(n) \setminus \text{Kill}(n))$$

$$S_{\text{in}}(n) = \bigcup_{n' \in \text{Pred}(n)} S_{\text{out}}(n'),$$

where n denotes a node of a CFG, $\text{Gen}(n)$ is the set of task objects generated (declared or allocated via a new-statement) in node n, and $\text{Kill}(n)$ denotes the set of task objects terminating in node n. All Gen and Kill sets can be empty. Note that Gen sets also include task objects generated indirectly via subprogram or entry calls and via calls of protected operations. Note also that we only take into account the static structure of the underlying multi-tasking program. Thus a task object t is considered to be generated in unit u if there is a statement contained in u that allocates t or u starts with the begin-statement that immediately follows the declarative part containing the declaration of t.

The execution of a handled sequence of statements of a package body is considered to be part of the activation of its *master* task [14]. Thus the CFG of such code is prepended to the CFG of its master task. If there are several such code pieces the corresponding CFGs can be prepended in arbitrary order because if task are generated in these code pieces, their order of activation does not affect the ∥-relation.

Since these are sets a compiler has to determine in order to guarantee that a multi-tasking program is executed correctly, we assume that both Gen and Kill sets can be found automatically (and are available for our analysis).

A detailed description of sets $S_{\text{out}}(n)$ is as follows: If a task object t is generated, it is part of the Gen set, i.e., $t \in \text{Gen}(n)$. If an array of task objects of type

tt is declared, several task objects of type tt may run in parallel. We model this by writing $t^* \in \text{Gen}(n)$. In addition, we extend the usual set operations such that $\{t^*\} \cup \{t\} = \{t^*\}$. A similar notation is used for the Kill sets.

We propose to use elimination methods to solve this data flow framework (see e.g. [21] for a survey of elimination methods). As a preliminary step we need a *normal form* for our equations. We note that the equation for $S_{in}(n)$ can be eliminated by inserting it into $S_{out}(n)$. From here on we write $S(n)$ instead of $S_{out}(n)$ to keep notation short.

Let A, B, C be sets. For set operations "$\cup$" and "$\setminus$" we have

$$(A \cup B) \setminus C = (A \setminus C) \cup (B \setminus C) \tag{1}$$

and

$$(A \setminus B) \setminus C = A \setminus (B \cup C). \tag{2}$$

Let $I \subseteq N$ be a subset of the set of nodes. We define the following normal form for our equations:

$$S(n) = \bigcup_{i \in I} \left((S(i) \setminus \text{Kill}'(i)) \cup \text{Gen}'(i) \right).$$

Elimination methods require two rules:

Insertion Rule. One equation has to be substituted into another one. This is straight-forward to do and by repeated application of Eq. (1) and (2) the resulting equation can be brought to normal form again.

Loop Breaking Rule. Given an equation

$$S(n) = \bigcup_{i \in I} \left((S(i) \setminus \text{Kill}'(i)) \cup \text{Gen}'(i) \right),$$

where $n \in I$, the task of loop breaking is to find an equivalent equation [20]

$$S'(n) = \bigcup_{i \in I'} \left((S(i) \setminus \text{Kill}''(i)) \cup \text{Gen}''(i) \right) \tag{3}$$

such that $n \notin I'$.

We define our loop breaking rule as follows. Let

$$S(n) = \bigcup_{i \in I \setminus \{n\}} \left((S(i) \setminus \text{Kill}'(i)) \cup \text{Gen}'(i) \right) \cup \left((S(n) \setminus \text{Kill}'(n)) \cup \text{Gen}'(n) \right).$$

Then

$$S'(n) = \left(\left(\bigcup_{i \in I \setminus \{n\}} \left((S(i) \setminus \text{Kill}'(i)) \cup \text{Gen}'(i) \right) \right) \setminus \text{Kill}'(n) \right) \cup \text{Gen}'''(n) \tag{4}$$

where $\text{Gen}'''(n) = \{t^* \mid t \in \text{Gen}'(n) \text{ or } t^* \in \text{Gen}'(n)\}$. The definition of Gen''' ensures that t^* is present in the set if task objects t are generated in the loop body. This implies that task objects of this type are running in parallel if the loop body is executed at least two times. If the loop is iterated less than two times, this is not the case. Since however we do not know the number of loop iterations statically, we assume that the loop is iterated more than once.

Bringing Eq. (4) into normal form yields Eq. (3).

We would like to note that it is not possible to solve our data flow framework via iterative methods [15] because iterative methods require a too simple loop breaking rule.

In order to determine the $\|$-relation from the solution of the data flow framework, we use the following algorithm.

```
CONSTRUCT‖ ()
1   for each task CFG do
2       for each node n do
3           for each t* ∈ S(n) do
4               DEFINE t ‖ t
5           endfor
6           for each pair t₁, t₂ ∈ S(n) do
7               DEFINE t₁ ‖ t₂
8           endfor
9       endfor
10  endfor
```

Since our data flow framework is defined on CFGs, and since a multi-tasking program consists of several CFGs (one for each task body), the data flow framework has to be applied to all of them. This, however, has to be done in a certain order because $CFG(t)$ can only be processed if all task bodies corresponding to task objects generated in t have been processed before. This order on task objects can be modeled by a directed acyclic graph (DAG). Thus we apply our data flow framework in reverse topological order (cf. e.g. [19]) to this DAG. The last CFG to be analyzed is that of the environment task (main procedure). Hence, we do not handle mutual task declarations such as those depicted in Fig. 1, even if the declaration is performed only conditionally.

```
1    procedure Mutual is

2        task type B is end B;

3        task type C is end C;

4        task body B is
5           T_Var : C;
6        begin null; end B;

7        task body C is
8           T_Var : B;
9        begin null; end C;

10       The_Task : B;

11   begin null; end Mutual;
```

Fig. 1. Example: Unconditional Mutual Task Declarations

2.2   Determining Sets of Used and Modified Variables

In this section we develop a method to determine the global variables read and written by a task. For this we need the notion of a variable being *global* to a given entity, according to the scoping rules of Ada95. For a declared entity the scope of the declaration denotes those places in the code where it is legal to refer to it. The Ada95 programming language is based on static scoping (cf. [22, p. 176]), which means that visibility of entities at a given program point follows solely from the lexical structure of the program, and not from dynamic aspects (such as the point of invocation of a procedure). Section 8.2 of the language reference manual [14] defines the scope of a declaration; a crucial aspect of these scoping rules is that the scope of a declaration that occurs immediately within the visible part of an outer declaration extends to the end of the scope of the outer declaration.

```
                                          1   package G is
                                          2       Global : Integer;
1   with G; use G;                        3       procedure P (X : in out Integer);
                                          4   end G;

2   procedure Main is
3       Local : Integer := 0;             1   package body G is
4   begin                                 2       U : Integer;
5       P (Global);                       3       procedure P (X : in out Integer) is
6       declare                           4       begin
7           task B is end B;              5           X := X + 1;
8           task body B is                6           declare
9               Another : Integer := 0;   7               task C is end C;
10          begin                         8               task body C is
11              Global := Global + 1;     9               begin
12          end B;                        10                  X := X + 1; U := U + 1;
13      begin null; end;                  11              end C;
14  end Main;                             12          begin null; end;
                                          13      end P;
                                          14  end G;
```

Fig. 2. Example Demonstrating Global and Owned Variables

With Ada95, the following constructs act as scopes: blocks, class subtypes and types, entries, functions, loops, packages, subprograms, protected objects, record types and subtypes, private types, task types and subtypes.

Definition 1. *A declaration is local to a declarative region if the declaration occurs immediately within the declarative region. An entity is local to a declarative region if the entity is declared by a declaration that is local to the declarative region [14, Section 8.1(14)].*

Definition 2. *Given a subprogram, task body, a protected entry, procedure or function, or a dispatching operation u (in the following termed unit u), we say that u owns an entity e, if e is local to the declarative region of u. In addition, task entries constitute units; they own the union of the entities owned by their corresponding accept statements. The ownership relation is reflexive and transitive. Moreover, we extend it to the dynamic case in the sense that u owns* *all entities owned by entities called by u. Entities which are* visible *to an entity owned by u, but which are not owned by u, are said to be* global *to u. We write* $\mathcal{O}(u)$ *to denote the set of entities owned by u, and* $\mathcal{G}(u)$ *to denote the set of entities that are global to u.*

It should be noted that our definition of "globalness" is related to up-level addressing, under incorporation of call-chains.

As an example, consider Fig. 2. Variables `Local` and `Another` are owned by procedure `Main`, variable `Another` is also owned by task B, and variables `Global` and `U` are global to `Main`, B, C, and P. In this example the formal parameter X of procedure P is an alias for variable `Global`; we will treat aliasing in the latter part of this section.

For every unit u that is a task body, and for the subprogram body corresponding to the environment task (the "main" program), our analysis determines

1. the sets $\mathcal{O}_r$ and $\mathcal{O}_w$ of read/written variables owned by u,
2. the sets $\mathcal{G}_r$ and $\mathcal{G}_w$ of read/written variables global to u, and
3. the sets $\sigma_r = \mathcal{O}_r \cup \mathcal{G}_r$, $\sigma_w = \mathcal{O}_w \cup \mathcal{G}_w$, $\sigma_G = \mathcal{G}_r \cup \mathcal{G}_w$, and $\sigma_{rw} = \sigma_r \cup \sigma_w$.

Given now two task objects t_1 and t_2 with their corresponding task bodies B_1 and B_2. If $t_1 \parallel t_2$, and the intersection of the corresponding sets $\sigma_{rw}(B_1) \cap \sigma_{rw}(B_2)$ is non-empty, then we are facing a potential conflict. If an entity e from the intersection is global to at least one of the participating task bodies B_1 and B_2, and if e is modified in at least one of the participating task bodies (as opposed to just being used), then the conflict is "real". (We will formalize this condition in Section 2.3.)

We are now faced with the problem of determining for each unit u the corresponding quadruple $\langle \mathcal{O}_r, \mathcal{O}_w, \mathcal{G}_r, \mathcal{G}_w \rangle$. This can be related to interprocedural data flow analysis which is concerned with the determination of a conservative approximation of how a program manipulates data at the level of its call graph. In our case we are interested in the owned and global variables read and written by a given unit. Our problem is *flow-insensitive* as we currently do not incorporate control flow information encountered in a unit; as a consequence, a single read or update operation on a given variable v in a unit u is already sufficient to place v in the respective set of u's quadruple.

It is shown in [8] how alias-free flow-insensitive side-effect analysis can be carried out for procedure call graphs and call-by-reference parameter passing. In [9] it is shown how interprocedural flow-insensitive may-alias information can be factored into this result to account for aliases due to call-by-reference parameter passing, for procedures of arbitrary lexical nesting level. This approach assumes however the absence of pointer aliases. In the following we investigate to what extent [8, 9] apply to Ada95 and how those approaches can be adapted to determine the sought quadruples.

Parameter passing: Ada95 employs two types of parameter passing, namely by copy (aka copy-in/copy-out), and by reference. When a parameter is passed by copy, any information transfer between formal and actual parameter occurs only before and after execution of the subprogram (cf. [12], [14, 6.2]). From the point of view of our analysis method both parameter passing mechanisms are equivalent, because we screen the source code only at the granularity of whole tasks (and subprograms).

Pointer aliases: [8,9] does not include pointer aliases. Moreover, the may-alias problem for $k > 1$ level pointers is undecidable (cf. e.g., [5]). Hence we chose a conservative analysis strategy with respect to pointer aliasing which assumes that every entity possibly targeted by a pointer is modified during a procedure call. Due to the induced complexity we had to exclude access to subprogram types altogether from our analysis.

Calculation of $\langle \mathcal{O}_r, \mathcal{O}_w, \mathcal{G}_r, \mathcal{G}_w \rangle$: The only statement aggregation in [8] are *procedures*. In the following we write GMOD(p) to denote the set of *all* variables that may be modified by an invocation of procedure p. Furthermore, we write IMOD(p) to denote those variables that may be modified by executing procedure p without executing any calls within it.

In order to compute GMOD(p), [8] sets up a data flow problem that is based on the procedure call graph and consists of equations of the form

$$\text{GMOD}(p) = \text{IMOD}(p) \cup \Big[\bigcup_{e=(p,q)} b_e\big(\text{GMOD}(q) \cap \text{Nonlocals}(q)\big)\Big]. \qquad (5)$$

Therein function b_e maps names from procedure q into names from procedure p according to the name and parameter binding at the call site $e = (p,q)$. Specifically, b_e maps the formal parameters of q to the actual parameters at the call site. The intersection of GMOD(q) with the set of nonlocal variables Nonlocals(q) ensures that variables local to q are factored out beforehand.

To compute our sought quadruples for Ada95, we can set up a system of equations similar to Eq. (5). Doing so we split the set GMOD into the sets of owned and global variables, and we move from *procedures* to *units* in terms of statement aggregation. (Hence the procedure call graph becomes a unit call graph.) In this way, IMOD(u) denotes those variables that may be modified by executing unit u without executing any calls to subprograms or entries within it, and without executing any task objects owned by it. We do not count a modification that is due to an initialization expression of a declaration in the declarative_part (cf. [14, 3.11]) of unit u; this is a measure to reduce false positives and will be explained in Section 2.5.

$$\mathcal{G}'_w(u) = \bigcup_{e=(u,u')} b_e\big(\mathcal{G}_w(u')\big) \qquad (6)$$

$$\mathcal{G}_w(u) = [\text{IMOD}(u) \cap \mathcal{G}(u)] \cup [\mathcal{G}'_w(u) \setminus \mathcal{O}(u)] \qquad (7)$$

$$\mathcal{O}_w(u) = [\text{IMOD}(u) \cap \mathcal{O}(u)] \cup \Big[\bigcup_{e=(u,u')} \mathcal{O}_w(u')\Big] \cup (\mathcal{G}'_w(u) \cap \mathcal{O}(u)) \qquad (8)$$

Eq. (6) denotes the set of variables which are modified by called units of u and which are global to those called units. In Eq. (7) we determine the set $\mathcal{G}_w$

of unit u, which consists of the locally modified global variables of u and those variables of Eq. (6), which are global to u. Finally, the set $\mathcal{O}_w$ of u consists of the locally modified owned variables of u as well as the modified variables owned by called units and those modified global variables of called units which are owned by u. In replacing IMOD by IUSE as the set of used variables, a system of equations similar to Eq. (6)–(8) can be defined to determine the sets $\mathcal{G}_r$ and $\mathcal{O}_r$.

The sets $\text{IMOD}(u)$ and $\text{IUSE}(u)$ themselves can be computed by a single linear scan of the statements of u. Therein we do not consider variables which are marked by pragmas Atomic or Volatile, or protected variables, as none of them can give raise to access anomalies. In addition we treat accesses to array components as accesses to the whole array. The same applies to records and their components.

Dispatching operations of tagged types require additional thinking — if we cannot determine the target of a *dispatching call* (cf. [14, 3.9.2]) at compile-time, we have to assume calls to all dispatching operations that might be the target of the dispatching call at run-time.

A further source of complication are generic packages, for which we defer analysis to the point of instantiation.

FACTOR_SET $(u, \text{ALIAS}, \textbf{in out } S_{\text{in}})$
1    $S_{\text{out}} ::= S_{\text{in}}$
2   -- add formal parameter aliases:
3   **for** *each* $v \in \text{Ext\_Formals}(u)$ **do**

FACTOR_IN (ALIAS, U)
1   **for** *each* $u \in U$ **do**
2   FACTOR_SET$(u, \text{ALIAS}, \mathcal{O}_r)$
3   FACTOR_SET$(u, \text{ALIAS}, \mathcal{O}_w)$
4   FACTOR_SET$(u, \text{ALIAS}, \mathcal{G}_r)$
5   FACTOR_SET$(u, \text{ALIAS}, \mathcal{G}_w)$
6   **endfor**

4   **if** $v \in S_{\text{in}}$ **then**
5            $S_{\text{out}} ::= S_{\text{out}} \cup \text{ALIAS}(v, u)$
6   **endif**
7   **endfor**
8   -- add global variable aliases:
9   **for** *each* $v \in \text{Nonlocals}(u) \cap S_{\text{in}}$ **do**
10        $S_{\text{out}} ::= S_{\text{out}} \cup \text{ALIAS}(v, u)$
11   **endfor**
12    $S_{\text{in}} ::= S_{\text{out}}$

Fig. 3. Algorithm to Factor In Aliasing Information

The data flow problem defined above computes alias-free data flow information. Regarding the example given in Fig. 2, this means that e.g., with task body C, we are not aware that the formal parameter X of procedure P is an alias for variable Global[1]. To factor in aliasing information, we employ the interprocedural may-alias analysis method from [9]. Let $\text{ALIAS}(v, u)$ denote the set of aliases for variable v within unit u. Due to [9] we can compute $\text{ALIAS}(v, u)$, for each formal parameter v and for each global variable v for a unit u. We depict in Fig. 3 how this aliasing information can be factored into our alias-free quadruple-based data flow information; this algorithm is an adaption of an algorithm from [9] to our data flow problem at hand.

[1] An alias from the perspective of our analysis method, which is by necessity insensitive to the copy-in/copy-out parameter passing mechanism of Ada95.

We assume that the driver algorithm FACTOR_IN receives as arguments the sets of aliases (ALIAS) and the units (U) of the program under consideration. For each unit u and each set of its associated quadruple $\langle \mathcal{O}_r, \mathcal{O}_w, \mathcal{G}_r, \mathcal{G}_w \rangle$, FAC-TOR_IN calls the factoring algorithm FACTOR_SET in order to factor in aliasing information. This algorithm proceeds in two steps. The first loop addresses the set Ext_Formals of extended formal parameters of u, which consists of all formal parameters visible within u, including those of units that u is nested in, that are not rendered invisible by intervening declarations[2]. In the second loop we add the aliases of variables that are non-local to u. Note that FACTOR_SET only adds aliases to variables that are contained in its input-set S_{in}.

In the following section we define operations on our quadruple-based data flow information which allows us to record information on program variables being read or updated non-sequentially.

2.3 Potential Non-sequential Variable Access

We have shown in Section 2.1 how we can compute relation $\parallel$ in order to determine task objects that may execute in parallel. Moreover, in Section 2.2 we have devised an algorithm to compute the sets of global and owned variables used/modified by a task body.

Let $B(t)$ denote the task body of a task object t; with this notation we regard the environment task also as a task object, with its task body being the main procedure of the program. A variable v is used by a task object t, if v is in the set[3] of read variables of the task body of t, that is, $\mathrm{use}(v,t) \Leftrightarrow v \in \sigma_r(B(t))$. Likewise for modifications of v by t, written as $\mathrm{mod}(v,t) \Leftrightarrow v \in \sigma_w(B(t))$. We have now everything in place to formulate the condition for a potential non-sequential variable access between two task objects t_1 and t_2 which may execute in parallel, that is, $t_1 \parallel t_2$.

Definition 3. *Predicate $\sigma(t_1, t_2)$ is true if some variable v is non-sequentially accessed by task objects t_1 and t_2, false otherwise. It is formally defined as*

$$\sigma(t_1, t_2) = \bigwedge_{v \in S} \left[\left[(\mathrm{use}(v, t_1) \wedge \mathrm{mod}(v, t_2)) \right. \right. \tag{9}$$

$$\vee \left(\mathrm{mod}(v, t_1) \wedge \mathrm{use}(v, t_2) \right) \tag{10}$$

$$\left. \vee \left(\mathrm{mod}(v, t_1) \wedge \mathrm{mod}(v, t_2) \right) \right] \tag{11}$$

$$\left. \wedge \left(v \in \sigma_G(B(t_1)) \cup \sigma_G(B(t_2)) \right) \right], \tag{12}$$

where $S = \sigma_{rw}(B(t_1)) \cap \sigma_{rw}(B(t_2))$ are the variables accessed by both, $B(t_1)$ and $B(t_2)$, and (12) ensures that variable v is global to at least one of the involved task bodies.

---

[2] It is shown in [9] how Ext_Formals can be computed from the so-called binding graph of procedure parameters.

[3] Cf. Section 2.2 for the definition of these sets.

Note that $t_1 = t_2$ is not excluded by this definition. In order to see that this is useful consider two tasks of the same task type tt being allocated via new statements (e.g. in a loop-body). Thus we have $t_1 = t_2$, say, and $t_1 \parallel t_2$. Now, if both t_1 and t_2 modify variable v which is locally declared in tt, $\sigma(t_1, t_2)$ evaluates to false only because Eq. (12) becomes false in this case.

2.4   Complexity Issues

The data flow problem described in Section 2.1 can be solved via elimination methods in $O(|E| \cdot \log |N|)$ time [25], where $|N|$ denotes the number of nodes in a CFG and $|E|$ the number of edges in a CFG.

As shown in [8, 9], the data flow problem stated in Section 2.2 can be solved in $O(|E| \cdot |N| + |N|^2)$, with $|N|$ and $|E|$ being the number of call graph nodes and edges.

Summing up, our method performs very efficiently in analyzing Ada multi-tasking programs for detecting access anomalies.

2.5   A Simple Example

For purposes of demonstration we have chosen a simple concurrent Ada program without aliasing effects. It is the well know Producer/Consumer pattern, with its source code depicted in Figure 4. In procedure **Erroneous** (which is also the main subprogram of this example), variable a and two tasks, **Producer p** and **Consumer c**, are declared. Both of them are using variable a (the producer is even modifying it) ten times in an unsynchronized way.

```
procedure Erroneous is
    a : Integer := 0;                              -- Node 1
    task type Producer(Count : Natural) is         -- Node 1
    end Producer;                                  -- Node 1
    task type Consumer(Count : Natural) is         -- Node 1
    end Consumer;                                   -- Node 1
    task body Producer (Count : Natural) is
    begin
        for i in 1..Count loop                     -- Node 2
            a := i;                                 -- Node 3
            -- do something else in the meantime    - Node 3
        end loop;
    end Producer;
    task body Consumer (Count : Natural) is
    begin
        for j in 1..Count loop                     -- Node 4
            -- read global variable a              -- Node 5
        end loop;
    end Consumer;
    p : Producer(10);                              -- Node 1
    c : Consumer(10);                              -- Node 1
begin
    null;                                          -- Node 1
end Erroneous;
```

Fig. 4. Example: Source Code

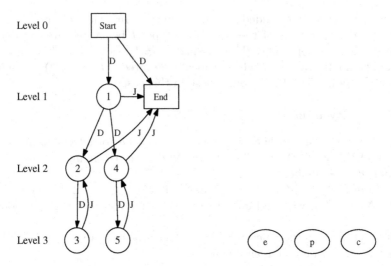

Fig. 5. Example: DJ-Graph   **Fig. 6.** Example: Unit Call Graph

The data flow equations for the example shown in Figure 5 are set up as follows (for simplicity we abbreviate **Erroneous** by "e"):

$$S(\text{Start}) = \{e\},$$
$$S(1) = (S(\text{Start})\backslash\text{Kill}(1)) \cup \text{Gen}(1) = (\{e\}\backslash\emptyset) \cup \{p, c\} = \{e, p, c\},$$
$$S(2) = ((S(1) \cup S(3))\backslash\text{Kill}(2)) \cup \text{Gen}(2) = S(1) \cup S(2),$$
$$S(3) = (S(2)\backslash\text{Kill}(3)) \cup \text{Gen}(3) = S(2),$$
$$S(4) = ((S(1) \cup S(5))\backslash\text{Kill}(4)) \cup \text{Gen}(4) = S(1) \cup S(5),$$
$$S(5) = (S(4)\backslash\text{Kill}(5)) \cup \text{Gen}(5) = S(4),$$
$$S(\text{End}) = ((S(\text{Start}) \cup S(1) \cup S(2) \cup S(4))\backslash\text{Kill}(\text{End})) \cup \text{Gen}(\text{End})$$
$$= S(\text{Start}) \cup S(1) \cup S(2) \cup S(4).$$

We employ the eager elimination method due to [25] to solve the data flow equations of our example. This method is based on DJ graphs, the union of a CFG and its dominator tree (cf. [25]). It requires to distinguish between d- and j-edges (cf. Fig. 5). For details the reader is referred to [25]. First the bottom-up join edge elimination phase (and simultaneous insertion in the data flow equations) of the eager elimination method is started at level 3: $5 \rightarrow 4$: $S(4) = S(1) \cup S(4)$; $3 \rightarrow 2$: $S(2) = S(1) \cup S(2)$.

At level 2 loop breaking is necessary: $\emptyset$ 4: $S(4) = S(1)$, $\emptyset$ 2: $S(2) = S(1)$. During the second phase of the eager elimination method the solution is propagated along d-edges in a top down manner: $S(2) = S(3) = S(4) = S(5) = \{e, p, c\}$; $S(\text{End}) = \{e, p, c\}\backslash\{e, p, c\} = \emptyset$.

According to the algorithm for constructing the $\|$-relation from Section 2.1, we get $e \parallel p$, $e \parallel c$, and $p \parallel c$.

In the following e, p, and c denote the nodes of the unit call graph of our example, which is depicted in Fig. 6. (Note that since our simple example does not contain any calls, the unit call graph is in fact trivial). According to the data flow framework given in Section 2.2 we obtain the sets

$$\mathcal{O}(p) = \{i\},$$
$$\mathcal{O}(c) = \{j\},$$
$$\mathcal{O}(e) = \{a, i, j, p, c\}.$$
$$\mathcal{G}'_w(p) = \emptyset,$$
$$\mathcal{G}_w(p) = [\text{IMOD}(p) \cap \mathcal{G}(p)] \cup [\mathcal{G}'_w(p) \setminus \mathcal{O}(p)] = [\{a, i\} \cap \{a\}] \cup \emptyset = \{a\},$$
$$\mathcal{O}_w(p) = [\text{IMOD}(p) \cap \mathcal{O}(p)] \cup \emptyset \cup (\mathcal{G}'_w(p) \cap \mathcal{O}(p))$$
$$= [\{a, i\} \cap \{i\}] \cup \emptyset \cup (\emptyset \cap \{i\}) = \{i\},$$
$$\mathcal{G}'_w(c) = \emptyset,$$
$$\mathcal{G}_w(c) = [\text{IMOD}(c) \cap \mathcal{G}(c)] \cup [\mathcal{G}'_w(c) \setminus \mathcal{O}(c)] = [\{j\} \cap \{a\}] \cup \emptyset = \emptyset,$$
$$\mathcal{O}_w(c) = [\text{IMOD}(c) \cap \mathcal{O}(c)] \cup \emptyset \cup (\mathcal{G}_w(c) \cap \mathcal{O}(c)) = [\{j\} \cap \{j\}] \cup \emptyset = \{j\},$$
$$\mathcal{G}'_w(e) = \emptyset,$$
$$\mathcal{G}_w(e) = [\text{IMOD}(e) \cap \mathcal{G}(e)] \cup [\mathcal{G}'_w(e) \setminus \mathcal{O}(e)] = [\emptyset \cap \emptyset] \cup [\emptyset \setminus \{a, i, j, p, c\}] = \emptyset,$$
$$\mathcal{O}_w(e) = [\text{IMOD}(e) \cap \mathcal{O}(e)] \cup (\mathcal{G}'_w(e) \cap \mathcal{O}(e))$$
$$= [\emptyset \cap \{a, i, j, p, c\}] \cup (\emptyset \cap \{a\}) = \emptyset.$$
$$\mathcal{G}'_r(p) = \emptyset,$$
$$\mathcal{G}_r(p) = [\text{IUSE}(p) \cap \mathcal{G}(p)] \cup [\mathcal{G}'_r(p) \setminus \mathcal{O}(p)] = [\{i\} \cap \{a\}] \cup \emptyset = \emptyset,$$
$$\mathcal{O}_r(p) = [\text{IUSE}(p) \cap \mathcal{O}(p)] \cup \emptyset \cup (\mathcal{G}'_r(p) \cap \mathcal{O}(p)) = [\{i\} \cap \{i\}] \cup (\emptyset \cap \{i\}) = \{i\},$$
$$\mathcal{G}'_r(c) = \emptyset,$$
$$\mathcal{G}_r(c) = [\text{IUSE}(c) \cap \mathcal{G}(c)] \cup [\mathcal{G}'_r(c) \setminus \mathcal{O}(c)] = [\{a, j\} \cap \{a\}] \cup \emptyset = \{a\},$$
$$\mathcal{O}_r(c) = [\text{IUSE}(c) \cap \mathcal{O}(c)] \cup \emptyset \cup (\mathcal{G}'_r(c) \cap \mathcal{O}(c))$$
$$= [\{a, j\} \cap \{j\}] \cup (\emptyset \cap \{j\}) = \{j\},$$
$$\mathcal{G}'_r(e) = \emptyset,$$
$$\mathcal{G}_r(e) = [\text{IUSE}(e) \cap \mathcal{G}(e)] \cup [\mathcal{G}'_r(e) \setminus \mathcal{O}(e)] = \emptyset \cup [\emptyset \setminus \{a, i, j, p, c\}] = \emptyset, \text{ and}$$
$$\mathcal{O}_r(e) = [\text{IUSE}(e) \cap \mathcal{O}(e)] \cup (\mathcal{G}'_r(e) \cap \mathcal{O}(e)) = \emptyset \cup (\emptyset \cap \{a, i, j, p, c\}) = \emptyset.$$

As already mentioned in Section 2.2, we do not count a modification that is due to an initialization expression of a declaration in the declarative part of unit u. This is justified by the fact that declarations in declarative part D are (1) not visible/accessible outside the scope of this task, and (2) the elaboration order ensures that tasks declared in D are activated after the declaration and initialization of the variables in D. This effectively serializes the modifications due to initialization with possible accesses from within child tasks. Thus in our example variable a is not a member of $\text{IMOD}(e)$.

Furthermore we get $\sigma_{rw}(e) = \emptyset$, $\sigma_{rw}(p) = \{a, i\}$, and $\sigma_{rw}(c) = \{a, j\}$. We have now $\sigma_{rw}(e) \cap \sigma_{rw}(p) = \emptyset$, and $\sigma(e, p) = false$. Because of $\sigma_{rw}(e) \cap \sigma_{rw}(c) = \emptyset$

and $\sigma(e, c) = \mathit{false}$, the same applies to tasks e and c. From $\sigma_{rw}(p) \cap \sigma_{rw}(c) = \{a\}$ and $\sigma(p, c) = \mathit{true}$ we conclude that there is an access anomaly concerning tasks c and p with respect to variable a.

3   Related Work

In [10, 18, 17] a detailed survey of possible erroneous executions in Ada (especially unsynchronized accesses to unprotected variables and how unpredictable the results are) is presented. Although there are protected types in Ada 95, unprotected variables can be and are used. *". . . we do not wish to jump to the simple conclusion that unprotected non-local variables should not be used. . . . although the need for them has now been greatly reduced . . . perform a mechanical verification of the fact that they are used correctly"* [17].

One way to cope with unpredictability is to allow just a strict (safe) subset of the Ada programming language [7, 4]. The Ravenscar Profile [6] removes non-deterministic tasking features from Ada and thus provides a statically analyzable subset of tasking facilities of Ada 95. This enables the development of high-integrity systems even in conjunction with tasks. *"The avoidance of unprotected shared variables is generally a requirement of high integrity systems, although detection of this erroneous case is not mandated by the Ravenscar Profile definition"* [7]. Thus, even in combination with the Ravenscar Profile, an additional check is needed to make sure that unprotected data is never shared between tasks. The Ravenscar Profile is an opportunity to allow concurrency within SPARK [4, 1].

A variety of approaches dealing with the detection of tasking anomalies in multi-tasking (Ada) programs have been proposed. These approaches include *static analysis, post-mortem trace analysis, on-the-fly monitoring*, and combinations. In [13] an overview of available techniques is presented. The goal of static analysis is to detect access anomalies prior to execution. On-the-fly monitoring is a dynamic approach and usually combined with a debugging tool. Post-mortem methods include all techniques used to discover errors in an execution following its termination.

Static Concurrency Analysis, presented in [26], is a method for determining concurrency errors in parallel programs. The class of detectable errors includes infinite waits, deadlocks, and concurrent updates of shared variables. Potentially concurrent sections of code are identified. Shared variable operations in these sections are potential anomalies. The algorithm is however exponential in the number of tasks in the program.

Detecting access anomalies by monitoring program execution is proposed in [23]. A general on-the-fly algorithm is presented, which can be applied to programs containing both nested fork-join and synchronization operations. In [11] the dynamic approach is further explored, nested parallel loops are considered, and experimental results are given. The retrospective in [24] gives a good survey of on-the-fly techniques. In general these techniques are fundamentally different to our static analysis approach. To reduce the amount of run-time checking, static program analysis can be used in combination with an on-the-fly approach (cf. e.g., [13]).

AdaWise [3] is a set of program analysis tools that performs automatic checks to verify the absence of common run-time errors affecting correctness or portability of Ada code. AdaWise checks at compile-time for potential errors such as incorrect order dependence or erroneous execution due to improper aliasing. Like our approach, it operates in a conservative way. That is, the absence of a warning guarantees the absence of a problem. If AdaWise produces a warning, there is a potential error that should be investigated by the developer.

A good survey of available tools detecting races in Java (e.g. rccjava, Java Pathfinder, ESC/Java, Bandera) or C (e.g. Warlock and RacerX) can be found in [27].

4   Conclusion and Future Work

In this paper we have presented data flow analysis frameworks for detecting non-sequential access of shared non-protected variables, so-called access anomalies. Our framework can handle most programs of practical importance. It is computationally efficient and easy to implement by modifying the source code of an existing compiler like GNAT. Toolkits for constructing data flow analyzers [16] can also be employed. Our method is conservative and may therefore raise false positives. It should be easily adaptable for the Ravenscar profile [6, 7].

Our approach is also well-suited for other programming languages like Java [2], although a Java program is not even termed erroneous if it accesses global shared variables in a non-sequential way.

In the future we plan to develop a symbolic analysis framework that is aimed at the detection of non-sequential global shared variable access. Symbolic analysis is capable of incorporating flow-sensitive side-effects of a program, which will make it less susceptible to the detection of false positives. A refinement of relation $\parallel$ to model parallelism in a more fine-grained (i.e., intra-task) manner is an orthogonal measure to reduce the number of false positives. At the moment our analysis considers parallelism only on a per-task basis, which is a safe approximation of the actual potential for parallelism between variable accesses. There are however many cases where task objects executing in parallel access a common variable, but the intra-task structure of the program reveals that the actual access operations cannot occur in parallel (e.g., due to involved synchronization primitives).

References

1. SPARK Examiner, The SPARK Ravenscar Profile,
   http://www.praxis-his.com/sparkada/pdfs/examiner_ravenscar.pdf, 2004.
2. K. Arnold, J. Gosling, and D. Holmes. *The Java Programming Language*. Addison-Wesley, Reading, MA, 3$^{\rm rd}$ edition, 2000.

3. C. Barbasch and D. Egnor. Always one more bug: applying AdaWise to improve Ada code. In *Proceedings of the conference on TRI-Ada '94*, pages 228–235, New York, NY, USA, 1994. ACM Press.
4. J. Barnes. *High Integrity Software - The SPARK Approach to Safety and Security.* Addison-Wesley, Harlow, England, 2003.
5. J. Blieberger, B. Burgstaller, and B. Scholz. Interprocedural Symbolic Evaluation of Ada Programs with Aliases. In *Proc. of the Ada-Europe International Conference on Reliable Software Technologies*, pages 136–145, Santander, Spain, June 1999.
6. A. Burns. The Ravenscar Profile. *Ada Lett.*, XIX(4):49–52, 1999.
7. A. Burns, B. Dobbing, and T. Vardanega. Guide for the use of the Ada Ravenscar Profile in high integrity systems. *Ada Lett.*, XXIV(2):1–74, 2004.
8. K. D. Cooper and K. Kennedy. Interprocedural side-effect analysis in linear time. In *PLDI '88: Proceedings of the ACM SIGPLAN 1988 conference on Programming Language design and Implementation*, pages 57–66, New York, NY, USA, 1988. ACM Press.
9. K. D. Cooper and K. Kennedy. Fast interprocedural alias analysis. In *Conference Record of the 16th ACM SIGPLAN-SIGACT Symposium on Principles of Programming Languages*, pages 49–59, 1989.
10. P. Delrio and F. Mazzanti. The risk of destructive run-time errors. *Ada Lett.*, XI(1):102–113, 1991.
11. A. Dinning and E. Schonberg. An empirical comparison of monitoring algorithms for access anomaly detection. In *PPOPP '90: Proceedings of the second ACM SIGPLAN symposium on Principles & practice of parallel programming*, pages 1–10, New York, NY, USA, 1990. ACM Press.
12. W. Gellerich and E. Ploedereder. Parameter-induced aliasing and related problems can be avoided. In *Proc. of the Ada-Europe International Conference on Reliable Software Technologies*, pages 161–172, 1997.
13. R. Hood, K. Kennedy, and J. Mellor-Crummey. Parallel program debugging with on-the-fly anomaly detection. In *Supercomputing '90: Proceedings of the 1990 ACM/IEEE conference on Supercomputing*, pages 74–81, Washington, DC, USA, 1990. IEEE Computer Society.
14. ISO/IEC 8652. *Ada Reference manual*, 1995.
15. G. Kildall. A unified approach to global program optimization . In *Proc. of the First ACM Symposium on Principles of Programming Languages*, pages 194–206, New York, NY, 1973.
16. J. H. E. F. Lasseter. Toolkits for the automatic construction of data flow analyzers. Technical report, "University of Oregon, Computer & Information Sci. Dept.", 2005.
17. C. Marzullo and F. Mazzanti. Towards the static detection of erroneous executions in Ada 95. Technical report, "Ninth International Software Quality Week '96 (QW'96)", Sheraton Palace Hotel, San Francisco, California USA, 1996.
18. F. Mazzanti. Guide to erroneous executions in Ada 95. Technical report, Centre National de la Recherche Scientifique, Paris, France, France, 1997.
19. K. Mehlhorn. *Graph Algorithms and NP-Completeness*, volume 2 of *Data Structures and Algorithms*. Springer-Verlag, Berlin, 1984.
20. M. C. Paull. *Algorithm Design – A Recursion Transformation Framework*. Wiley Interscience, New York, NY, 1988.
21. B. G. Ryder and M. C. Paull. Elimination algorithms for data flow analysis. *ACM Computing Surveys*, 18(3):277–316, 1986.
22. D. A. Schmidt. *Denotational Semantics — A Methodology for Language Development*. Allyn and Bacon, 1986.

23. E. Schonberg. On-the-fly detection of access anomalies. In *PLDI '89: Proceedings of the ACM SIGPLAN 1989 Conference on Programming language design and implementation*, pages 285–297, New York, NY, USA, 1989. ACM Press.

24. E. Schonberg. On-the-fly detection of access anomalies. *SIGPLAN Not.*, 39(4): 313–327, 2004.

25. V. C. Sreedhar, G. R. Gao, and Y.-F. Lee. A new framework for elimination-based data flow analysis using DJ graphs. *ACM Trans. Program. Lang. Syst.*, 20(2): 388–435, 1998.

26. R. N. Taylor. A general-purpose algorithm for analyzing concurrent programs. *Commun. ACM*, 26(5):361–376, 1983.

27. F. Zhou. Survey: Race Detection and Atomicity Checking, CS263 Course Project, 2003.

One Million (LOC) and Counting: Static Analysis for Errors and Vulnerabilities in the Linux Kernel Source Code

Peter T. Breuer and Simon Pickin

Universidad Carlos III de Madrid, Leganes, Madrid, 28911 Spain
ptb@inv.it.uc3m.es, spickin@it.uc3m.es

Abstract. This article describes an analysis tool aimed at the C code of the Linux kernel, having been first described as a prototype (in this forum) in 2004. Its continuing maturation means that it is now capable of treating millions of lines of code in a few hours on very modest platforms. It detects about two uncorrected deadlock situations per thousand C source files or million lines of source code in the Linux kernel, and three accesses to freed memory. In distinction to model-checking techniques, the tool uses a configurable "3-phase" programming logic to perform its analysis. It carries out several different analyses simultaneously.

1 Introduction

Two years ago, our group had developed a prototype static analysis tool for the Linux kernel and described it in this forum ([1]). At that time, it was a matter of some pride that the prototype could efficiently deal with some thirty thousand lines or so of source code at a time, that being about the size that a small kernel driver source code of some five hundred lines or so of C code would expand to once referenced header files had been included and all macros expanded.

Taking the development onwards to deal with first hundreds of thousands and then millions of lines of (unexpanded) source code has not been merely a question of linear improvement. The tool had to be (a) coupled with a logic compiler in order to allow the programming logic to be reconfigured for different analyses and (b) the way the tool applied the logic to a parsed program syntax tree was made configurable via a user-defined set of trigger/action rules, again compiled into the tool on demand. The coverage had to be extended again and again to deal with the many unexpected C code constructions that the GNU C compiler allows and the Linux kernel makes use of, as they were discovered, the order of complexity of the algorithms involved had to be reduced greatly to deal with more than toy cases, an efficient parse had to be created for expressions which in places reach to 5000 lexical tokens, and logical predicates needed to be normalised on the fly in order to avoid the buildup of repetitious and redundant contributions that increase the complexity of the analysis task.

We take the opportunity in this article to state with specificity the analytic logic applied to every C code construct, as refined over the past two years. The analysis

L.M. Pinho and M. González Harbour (Eds.): Ada-Europe 2006, LNCS 4006, pp. 56–70, 2006.

copes with the mix of C and assembler in the Linux kernel source and the tool is written wholly in C, making it easy to compile and distribute in an open source environment, and it is licensed under an open source license.

Abstract interpretation [2] plays a fundamental rôle in the analysis, causing a simplification in the description of state that is propagated through a program code; for example, there is a literal (written "NAN") meaning "don't know" in the abstract domain, and thus a program variable which may take any of the values 1, 2, or 3 may be described as having the abstract value "don't know", leading to a state described by one atomic proposition, not a disjunct of three.

By way of orientation, note that static analysis is in general difficult to apply to C code because of C's pointer arithmetic and aliasing, but some notable efforts to that end have been made. David Wagner and collaborators in particular have been active in the area (see for example [5], where Linux user space and kernel space memory pointers are given different types, so that their use can be distinguished, and [6], where C strings are abstracted to a minimal and maximal length pair and operations on them abstracted to produce linear constraints on these numbers). That research group often uses model-checking to look for violations in possible program traces of an assertion such as "chroot is always followed by chdir before any other file operations". In contrast, the approach in this article assigns a (customisable) approximation semantics to C programs, via a (customisable) program logic for C. It is *not* model-checking, but a more lightweight approach, part-way between model-checking and Jeffrey Foster's work with CQual [3, 4], which extends the type system of C in a customisable manner. In particular, CQual has been used to detect "spinlock-under-spinlock", a sub-case of the analysis here.

The remainder of this article is structured as follows: an example run of the analysis will be presented in Section 2, the theory of the analytic logic used will be described in Section 3, and the detail of the treatment of C will be given in Section 4, along with the definitions that customise the analysis. Then configurations of the analyser for a small variety of problems and the results are discussed in Section 5.

2   First Example: Sleep Under Spinlock

In [1] we focused on checking for a particular problem in SMP systems – "sleep under spinlock". A function that can sleep (i.e., that can be scheduled out of the CPU) ought never to be called from a thread that holds a "spinlock", the SMP locking mechanism of choice in the Linux kernel. Trying to take a locked spinlock on one CPU provokes a busy wait ("spin") in that thread that occupies the CPU completely until the same spinlock is released on another CPU. If the thread that has locked the spinlock is scheduled out of its CPU while the lock is held, then the only thread that likely has code to release the spinlock again is not running. If by chance it is rescheduled into the CPU before any other thread tries to take the spinlock, then all is well. But if another thread tries for the spinlock first, then it will spin, occupying the CPU and keeping out the

files checked: 1055
 alarms raised: 18   (5/1055 files)
 false positives: 16/18
 real errors: 2/18 (2/1055 files)
 time taken: ~24h
 LOC: ~700K (unexpanded)
	1 instances of sleep under spinlock
	     in sound/isa/sb/sb16_csp.c
	 1 instances of sleep under spinlock
	     in sound/oss/sequencer.c
	 6 instances of sleep under spinlock
	     in net/bluetooth/rfcomm/tty.c
	 7 instances of sleep under spinlock
	     in net/irda/irlmp.c
	 3 instances of sleep under spinlock
	     in net/irda/irttp.c

Fig. 1. Testing for sleep under spinlock in the 2.6.3 Linux kernel

thread that would have released the spinlock. If yet another thread tries for the spinlock, then on a 2-CPU system, the machine is dead, with both CPUs spinning waiting for a lock that will never be released. Such opportunities are denial of service vulnerabilities that any user can exploit to take down a system. 2-CPU machines are also common – any Pentium 4 of 3.2GHz or above has a dual "hyper-threading" core. Detecting sleep under spinlock is one application of the abstract logic applied by the analyser.

That analysis may now be applied at almost industrial scales – Table 1 shows the results of checking for spinlock abuse in 1055 of the 6294 C source files in the Linux 2.6.3 kernel. This particular run took about 24 hours running in a single thread on a 550MHz (dual) SMP PC with 128MB ram (nowadays the analysis runs about two to three times as fast as that). About forty more files failed to parse at that time for various reasons (in one case, because of a real code error, in others because of the presence of GNU C extensions for the gcc compiler that the analyser could not cope with at that time, such as __attribute__ declarations in unexpected positions, case statement patterns matching a range instead of just a single number, array initialisations using "{ [1,3,4] = x }" notation, etc.). Five files showed up as suspicious under the analysis, as listed in Fig. 1.

Although the flagged instances are indeed calls of the kernel memory allocation function kmalloc (which may sleep) under spinlock, the arguments to the call sometimes make it safe. The function will not sleep with GFP_ATOMIC there, and that is the case in several instances, but not in the two shown in Fig. 2.

The first of these two is in code that writes microcode from user-space to the sound processor chip on the sound card; in the 2.6.11 Linux kernel source, that section of code has been replaced entirely. The second, however, is still present in 2.6.11 and 2.6.12 Linux kernels. Alan Cox owned up to it at 2.6.12.5 (Linux kernel mailing list, in thread *sleep under spinlock, sequencer.c, 2.6.12.5*, dated 19 Aug 2005): *Yep thats* (sic) *a blind substitution of lock_kernel in an old tree it seems. Probably my fault. Should drop it before the sleep and take it straight after.* The vulnerability might be exercised by evoking system sounds on an SMP machine (e.g. by triggering many "you have mail" notifications at once).

File & function	Code fragment
sb/sb16_csp.c: snd_sb_csp_load	619 `spin_lock_irqsave(&p->chip->reg_lock, flags);` ... ... 632 `unsigned char *kbuf, *_kbuf;` 633 `_kbuf = kbuf = kmalloc (size, GFP_KERNEL);`
oss/sequencer.c: midi_outc	1219 `spin_lock_irqsave(&lock,flags);` 1220 `while (n && !midi_devs[dev]->outputc(dev, data)) {` 1221 `interruptible_sleep_on_timeout(&seq_sleeper,HZ/25);` 1222 `n--;` 1223 `}` 1224 `spin_unlock_irqrestore(&lock,flags);`

Fig. 2. Sleep under spinlock instances in kernel 2.6.3

3   Analytic Program Logic

The analysis works by sweeping an initial description of state (for example, "the count of spinlocks taken so far is zero"), forward through the code, constructing descriptions of all the possible states reachable at every point.

The "descriptions" are *predicates* from a very restricted set, consisting of disjunctions and conjunctions of simple propositions of the form $x \leq a$, $x = b$, and so on, where a and b may only be constant values (including the abstract literal meaning "don't know", written "NAN"). These predicates correspond to shapes that are the unions of cubes in n-dimensional integer space and we can check for inclusion of one such "cuboid" p in another q via a linear-programming algorithm, thus determining mechanically (and efficiently) whether the implication $p \rightarrow q$ holds or not. The variables that appear in the predicates are not program but *condition* variables, introduced purely for the purpose of the analysis and manipulated by the logic configured for the individual statements of C.

At the same time as the predicate descriptions are propagated, an approximate state (different in all likelihood from the predicate constructed, but not incompatible with it) is calculated at each point and swept through the program, in order to give some guidance. It is not necessary to construct this approximation but it is helpful in detecting dead code and forced branches. It is not uncommon to write "if (0)", for example, and the abstraction would calculate the value 0 for the "0" and guide the analysis to drop the block.

The "approximate state" (currently) consists of the assignment of a range of integer values to program (not condition) variables (Fig. 3). This approximation is intended to capture all the possible values that the variable may take at that point. For example, if x is assigned the range $[-1, 1]$ just prior to the statement x=x+1; then it is assigned the range $[0, 2]$ after it.

To take account of the effect of loops in the guiding approximation, changes made by the loop body to variables outside the loop are evaluated broadly. So, for example, if the loop enters with the external program variable x set to $[-1, 1]$, but the body transforms it to $[0, 2]$, it may be assigned the value NAN after the loop, on the basis that repeat iterations change it unpredictably. The aim is

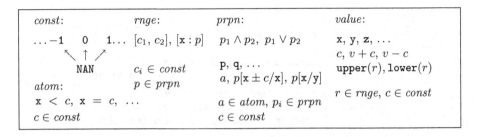

Fig. 3. The semantic domains for the specification language. Arrows show refinement

to generate a *loop invariant* abstract state. At present we do not try harder to find an accurate invariant state, though in principle we could try again with $[-1,1] \cup [0,2] = [-1,2]$ as the putative invariant, and again for any desired number of repetitions. We currently move directly to NAN as the assigned value for any variant program variable, and stop the procedure as soon as we have an invariant approximation state. Assigning NAN for every variable always gives an invariant, so the procedure stops in at most #variables steps.

At each point in the program code, the predicate (not the state approximation) description of the reachable states is evaluated to see if it may permit a violation of an objective that has been set. If it does, the line is flagged. Thus if we get "number of spinlocks taken may be in the range [0,2]" at a point where a function f that may sleep is called, the flag is set; it is set because the analysis says that sleepy function f *may* be called under spinlock there and the objective is that sleepy functions not be called under spinlock. In particular, if the uniformative statement "true" (T) were all that we had as the predicate description of state at that point, the alarm flag would be set because the state could be anything at all, and thus the objective may not be met there.

The predicate description of the reachable states at each point is propagated through the code by a compositional program logic called NRBG [1] (for "normal", "return", "break", "goto", reflecting its four principal components). The four components, N, R, B, G, represent different kinds of control flow: a "normal" flow, N, and several "exceptional" flows.

Program fragments are thought of as having three phases of execution: *initial*, *during*, and *final*. The initial phase is represented by a condition p that holds as the program fragment is entered. The only access to the internals of the during phase is via an exceptional exit (R, B, G; return, break, goto) from the fragment. The final phase is represented by a condition q that holds as the program fragment terminates normally (N).

The N part of the logic represents the way code "falls off the end" of one fragment and into another. That is, if p is the precondition that holds before program $a; b$ runs, and q is the postcondition that holds afterwards, then

$$p \; N(a;b) \; q \quad = \quad p \; N(a) \; r \; \wedge \; r \; N(b) \; q \tag{1}$$

To exit normally with q, the program must flow normally through fragment a, hitting an intermediate condition r, then enter fragment b, exiting it normally.

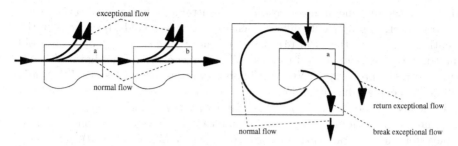

Fig. 4. (L) Normal and exceptional flow through two program fragments in sequence; (R) the exceptional break flow from the body of a forever loop is the normal flow exit from the loop composite.

The R part of the logic represents the way code flows exceptionally out of the parts of a routine through a "return" path. If r is the intermediate condition that is attained after normal termination of a, then:

$$p \, R(a;b) \, q \quad = \quad p \, R(a) \, q \, \vee \, r \, R(b) \, q \qquad (2)$$

That is, one may either return from program fragment a, or else terminate a normally, enter fragment b and return from b.

The logic of break is (in the case of sequence) exactly equal to that of return:

$$p \, B(a;b) \, q \quad = \quad p \, B(a) \, q \, \vee \, r \, B(b) \, q \qquad (3)$$

where again r is the intermediate condition that is attained after normal termination of a. One may either break out of a, or wait for a to terminate normally, enter b, and break out of b (see Fig. 4(L)).

Where break and return logic do differ is in the treatment of loops. First of all, one may only return from a forever `while` loop by returning from its body:

$$p \, R(\texttt{while}(1) \, a) \, q \quad = \quad p \, R(a) \, q \qquad (4)$$

On the other hand, (counter-intuitively at first reading) there is no way (F, "false") of leaving a forever `while` loop via a break exit, because a break in the body of the loop causes a normal exit from the loop itself, not a break exit:

$$p \, B(\texttt{while}(1) \, a) \, \text{F} \qquad (5)$$

The normal exit from a forever loop is by break from its body (see Fig. 4(R)):

$$p \, N(\texttt{while}(1) \, a) \, q \quad = \quad p \, B(a) \, q \qquad (6)$$

To represent the loop as cycling possibly more than once, rather than the "almost once" of the above. one would extend (4), for example, to:

$$p \, R(\texttt{while}(1) \, a) \, q \quad = \quad p \, R(a) \, q \, \vee \, r \, R(\texttt{while}(1)a) \, q \qquad (7)$$

where r is the intermediate condition that is attained after normal termination of a. However, in practice it suffices to check that $r \rightarrow p$ holds, because then the equation reduces to the form (4) given originally. In case $r \rightarrow p$ does not hold immediately, p is *relaxed* until it does. What is meant by this is that a $p' \geq p$ is found with the property $p'\ N(a)\ p'$. There always is such a p' since T ("true") will do. We explain further below.

Typically the precondition p is the claim that the spinlock count ρ is below or equal to n, for some n: $\rho \leq n$. In that case the logical components N, R, B have for each precondition p a strongest postcondition $p\ SP_N(a)$, $p\ SP_R(a)$, $p\ SP_B(a)$, compatible with the program fragment a in question. For example, in the case of the logic component N:

$$p\ N(a)\ q \quad \leftrightarrow \quad p\ SP_N(a) \leq q \qquad (8)$$

Each logic component X can be written as a function rather than a relation by identifying it with a postcondition generator no stronger than SP_X. For example:

$$(\rho \leq n)\ N\left(\begin{array}{c} \texttt{spin\_lock(\&}x\texttt{)} \\ \texttt{spin\_unlock(\&}x\texttt{)} \end{array}\right) = \left(\begin{array}{c} \rho \leq n+1 \\ \rho \leq n-1 \end{array}\right) \qquad (9)$$

Or in the general case, the action on precondition p is to substitute ρ by $\rho \pm 1$ in p, giving $p[\rho-1/\rho]$ (for $\texttt{spin\_lock}$) and $p[\rho+1/\rho]$ (for $\texttt{spin\_unlock}$) respectively:

$$p\ N\left(\begin{array}{c} \texttt{spin\_lock(\&}x\texttt{)} \\ \texttt{spin\_unlock(\&}x\texttt{)} \end{array}\right) = \left(\begin{array}{c} p[\rho-1/\rho] \\ p[\rho+1/\rho] \end{array}\right) \qquad (10)$$

The functional action on sequences of statements is then described as follows:

$$p\ N(a;b) = (p\ N(a))\ N(b) \qquad (11)$$

$$p\ R(a;b) = p\ R(a) \ \vee \ (p\ N(a))\ R(b) \qquad (12)$$

$$p\ B(a;b) = p\ B(a) \ \vee \ (p\ N(a))\ B(b) \qquad (13)$$

Returning briefly to how we *relax* a predicate p to $p' \geq p$ with $p'\ N(a)\ p'$, we first look at $p' = p \vee pSP_N(a)$. If this implies p, we are done, since p itself is an invariant. We next check if $p' > p$ is an invariant by seeing if $p' \vee p'SP_N(a)$ implies p'. If it does, we are done. If not, there is a dimension (a variable x appearing in p') in which the lack of fit of the one cuboid in the other is manifest, because $x = k$ for some particular k is permitted by p' but not by $p' \vee p'SP_N(a)$. We erase atomic propositions referring to x from p', thus obtaining a $p'' \geq p' > p$ (p' is a positive dis/conjunctive form in the atomic ordering propositions, so erasing part of it makes it less restricting) and then check to see if $p'' \vee p''SP_N(a)$ is contained in p''. If it is, we are done. If not we remove references to one more variable and repeat. The procedure terminates in at most #variables steps. At worst it gives T.

The G component of the logic is responsible for the proper treatment of $\texttt{goto}$ statements. To allow this, the logic – each of the components N, R, B and G – works within an additional *context*, e. A context e is a set of labelled conditions, each of which are generated at a `goto` x and are discharged/will take effect at a corresponding labelled statement x: .... The G component manages this context, first storing the current pre-condition p as the pair (x, p) (written $x{:}p$) in the context e at the point where the `goto` x is encountered:

$$p\ G_e(\texttt{goto } x) = \{x{:}p\} \uplus e \tag{14}$$

The $\{x{:}p\}$ in the equation is the singleton set $\{(x, p)\}$, where x is some label (e.g. the "foo" in "`foo: a = 1;`") and p is a logical condition like "$p \leq 1$".

In the simplest case, the operator $\uplus$ is set theoretic disjunction. But if an element $x{:}q$ is already present in the context e, signifying that there has already been one `goto` x statement encountered, then there are now two possible ways to reach the targeted label, so the union of the two conditions p and q is taken and $x{:}q$ is replaced by $x{:}(p \cup q)$ in e.

Augmenting the logic of sequence to take account of context gives:

$$p\ N_e(a; b) = (p\ N_e(a))\ N_{pG_e(a)}(b) \tag{15}$$

$$p\ R_e(a; b) = p\ R_e(a)\ \lor\ (p\ N(a)_e)\ R_{pG_e(a)}(b) \tag{16}$$

$$p\ B_e(a; b) = p\ B_e(a)\ \lor\ (p\ N(a)_e)\ B_{pG_e(a)}(b) \tag{17}$$

The N, R, B semantics of a `goto` statement are vacuous, signifying one cannot exit from a `goto` in a normal way, nor on a break path, nor on a return path.

$$p\ N_e(\texttt{goto } x) = p\ R_e(\texttt{goto } x) = p\ B_e(\texttt{goto } x) = \text{F} \tag{18}$$

The only effect of a `goto` is to load the context for the logic with an extra exit condition. The extra condition will be discharged into the normal component of the logic only when the label corresponding to the `goto` is found (e_x is the condition labelled with x in environment e, if any):

$$p\ N_{\{x:q\}\cup e}(x{:}) = p \lor q \qquad p\ R_e(x{:}) = \text{F} \tag{19}$$

$$p\ B_e(x{:}) = \text{F} \qquad p\ G_e(x{:}) = e - \{x{:}e_x\} \tag{20}$$

This mechanism allows the program analysis to pretend that there is a "short-cut" from the site of the `goto` to the label, and one can get there either via the short-cut or by traversing the rest of the program. If label `foo` has already been encountered, then we have to check at `goto foo` that the current program condition is an invariant for the loop back to `foo:`, or raise an alarm.

False positives are possible, but false negatives (in the sense of detectable cases that are somehow missed) are not, provided only that the code does not contain backward-going `goto`s, which we do not currently treat with full genericity (in the future that may change). This is not a claim for omniscience in the technology, just an observation that the predicate description that is calculated at each point is intentionally broad enough to encompass (1) every value that may be obtained in (2) every state that may be reached there.

That is subject to several provisos; the code must not do something odd like call an opaque subroutine that modifies its own code or data, because that is a possibility not modelled in the logic. And the analysis cannot know if `int *x=123456789; (*x)++;` modifies a memory location that is significant other than as data; perhaps it is the stack return address. The logic detailed in the next section ignores possible accesses other than by name to the data in variables, and indeed, as configured, takes no note of what value is stored.

4   The Analyser

The static analyser allows the program logic of C to be configured in detail by the user. The motive was originally to make sure that the logic was implemented in a bug-free way – writing the logic directly in C made for too low-level an implementation for what is a very high-level set of concepts. A compiler into C for specifications of the program logic was written and incorporated into the analysis tool. The *logic compiler* understands specifications of the format

$$\text{ctx } \textit{pre-context, precondition } :: \textit{name(arguments)} =$$
$$\textit{postconditions} \text{ with ctx } \textit{post-context ;}$$

where the *precondition* is an input argument, the entry condition for a code fragment, and *postconditions* is an output, a tuple consisting of the N, R, B exit conditions according to the logic. The *pre-context* is the prevailing `goto` context. The *post-context* is the output `goto` context, consisting of a set of labelled conditions. For example, the specification of the empty statement logic is:

$$\text{ctx e, p::empty() = (p, F, F) with ctx e;}$$

signifying that the empty statement preserves the entry condition `p` on normal exit (`p`), and cannot exit via return (`F`) or break (`F`). The context (`e`) is unaltered.

The analysis propagates a specified initial condition forward through the program, developing postconditions after each program statement that are checked for conformity with a specified objective. The full set of logic specifications is given in Table 1. To relate it to the logic presentation in Section 3, keep in mind:

$$\text{ctx } e, p :: k() = (n, r, b) \text{ with ctx } e';$$

means
$$p\, N_e(k) = n \qquad p\, R_e(k) = r$$
$$p\, B_e(k) = b \qquad p\, G_e(k) = e'$$

written out in the mathematical notation of Section 3.

The treatment of `spin_unlock` calls, `write_unlock` calls, `read_unlock` calls, etc. in Linux kernel code is managed by the `unlock` entry in the table. These all decrement the spinlock counter `n`. The argument `label l` to the call is an identifier for the spinlock address that appears as an argument to the call. Similarly the `lock` entry in the table represents the logic of the `spin_lock`, `write_lock`, `read_lock`, etc. calls. These calls all increment the spinlock counter `n`.

Note that function calls act like spinlock no-ops. That is, other functions are assumed to be balanced with respect to their effect on spinlocks. That is a good heuristic, because the only function that is explicitly unbalanced in that respect

Table 1. The single precondition/triple postcondition program logic of C

```
ctx e, p::for(stmt)            = (n∨b, r, F) with ctx f
                                 where ctx e, p::stmt = (n,r,b) with ctx f;
ctx e, p::empty()              = (p, F, F) with ctx e;
ctx e, p::unlock(label l)      = (p[n+1/n], F, F) with ctx e;
ctx e, p::lock(label l)        = (p[n-1/n], F, F) with ctx e;
ctx e, p::assembler()          = (p, F, F) with ctx e;
ctx e, p::function()           = (p, F, F) with ctx e;
ctx e, p::sleep(label l)       = (p, F, F) with ctx e
                                 { if (objective(p) ≥ 0) setflags(SLEEP); };
ctx e, p::sequence(s₁, s₂)     = (n₂, r₁∨r₂, b₁∨b₂) with ctx g
                                 where ctx f, n₁::s₂ = (n₂,r₂,b₂) with ctx g
                                 and   ctx e, p::s₁ = (n₁,r₁,b₁) with ctx f;
ctx e, p::switch(stmt)         = (n∨b, r, F) with ctx f
                                 where ctx e, p::stmt = (n,r,b) with ctx f
ctx e, p::if(s₁, s₂)           = (n₁∨n₂, r₁∨r₂, b₁∨b₂) with ctx f₁∨f₂
                                 where ctx e, p::s₁ = (n₁,r₁,b₁) with ctx f₁
                                 and   ctx e, p::s₂ = (n₂,r₂,b₂) with ctx f₂;
ctx e, p::while(stmt)          = (n∨b, r, F) with ctx f
                                 where ctx e, p::stmt = (n,r,b) with ctx f;
ctx e, p::do(stmt)             = (n∨b, r, F) with ctx f
                                 where ctx e, p::stmt = (n,r,b) with ctx f;
ctx e, p::goto(label l)        = (F, F, F) with ctx e∨{l::p};
ctx e, p::continue()           = (F, F, p) with ctx e;
ctx e, p::break()              = (F, F, p) with ctx e;
ctx e, p::return()             = (F, p, F) with ctx {};
ctx e, p::labeled(label l)     = (p∨e.l, F, F) with ctx e\\l;
```

Legend			
assembler	– *gcc inline assembly code;*	if	– *C conditional statement;*
sleep	– *calls to C functions which can sleep;*	switch	– *C case statement;*
function	– *calls to other C functions;*	while	– *C while loop;*
sequence	– *two statements in sequence;*	do	– *C do while loop;*
		labelled	– *labelled statements.*

in the Linux kernel is the call `spin_trylock`, which takes the spinlock if it is free and returns 0, or else cannot take it and returns 1. And if any (other) function were unbalanced it would be noticed during the analysis of that function.

An "objective" function for the analysis is specified by an `objective` specification in the same format as the logic specifications (see Table 1). The term `upper[n:p]` gives the estimated upper limit of the counter n subject to the constraints in the precondition p. The limit is $+\infty$ if p is "true" (T). The predicate must contain information that bounds n away from positive values if the objective is not to generate a positive value, and less information in the predicate will cause a more positive value to be calculated as the spinlock count upper bound.

The objective is computed at each node of the syntax tree. Positive values of the objective function are reported to the user (with the trigger/action rules that are currently in force and which will be described in the following part of

Table 2. Trigger/action rules which propagate information through the syntax tree

1.	SLEEP! & OBJECTIVE_SET & OBJECTIVE $\geq$ 0	$\rightarrow$ aliases |= SLEEP,
		callers |= SLEEP
2.	REF! & SLEEP	$\rightarrow$ callers |= SLEEP, ~REF
3.	(SLEEP & OBJECTIVE_SET & OBJECTIVE $\geq$ 0)!	$\rightarrow$ output()

this section). In particular, calls to functions which can sleep at a node where the objective function is positive are reported (this indicates where a call to a sleepy function might occur under spinlock).

The initial specification ($n \leq 0$) shown in Table 3 describes the initial program state at runtime. It says here that the spinlock counter n is less than or equal to zero (actually, zero, but the inequality is just as good and simpler).

The analysis also assumes that the tested value in conditionals, case statements and loops contains no significant program code (break, continue, etc.) – GNU C allows it but it does not appear in practice in the Linux kernel source.

The logic propagation through the syntax tree is complemented by a trigger/action system which acts whenever a property changes on a node. As the analysis tool is currently configured, the rules in Table 2 are applied. Their principal aim is to construct the list of sleepy functions, checking for calls by name of already known sleepy functions and thus constructing the transitive closure of the list under the call (by name) graph.

Rule (1) applies whenever a function is newly marked as sleepy (SLEEP!). Then if the objective function (here the maximal value of the spinlock count n) has already been calculated on that node (OBJECTIVE_SET) and is not negative (OBJECTIVE $\geq$ 0, indicating that the spinlock count is 0 or higher) then all the known *aliases* (other syntactic nodes which refer to the same semantic entity) are also marked sleepy, as are all the known *callers* (by name) of this node (which will be the current surrounding function, plus all callers of aliases of this node).

The reason why sleepiness is not propagated under negative spinlock is quite subtle. Consider function f called from function g called from function h. If the spinlock count is negative at the call of f in g, then g is intended to be called under spinlock (releasing an already released spinlock is a design error). If f is sleepy then g would ordinarily be marked sleepy too and that would be marked as an error when g is called under spinlock in h. But that is wrong when f is under negative spinlock in g, because then f is not under spinlock when g is called under spinlock in h and it is not a problem in h that f chooses to sleep inside g. So, under these conditions, g should not be marked as sleepy.

Rule (2) in Table 2 is triggered when a known sleepy function is referenced (REF!). Then all the callers (including the new referrer) are marked as sleepy if they were not so-marked before. The REF flag is removed as soon as it is added so every new reference triggers this rule. The effect of rules (1) and (2) together is to efficiently create the transitive sleepy call (by name) graph.

Table 3. Defining initial conditions, and an objective function to be calculated at every node of the syntax tree

```
::initial()   = (n≤0);
p::objective() = upper[n:p];
```

A list of all calls to functions that may sleep under a positive spinlock count is created via rule (3) in Table 2. Entries are added when a call is (a) sleepy, and (b) the spinlock count at that node is already known and (c) is nonnegative (positive counts will be starred in the output list, but all calls will be listed).

The analyser is called with the same arguments as the gcc compiler would have used. That enables the kernel to be compiled once, the calls to gcc recorded, and then the analyser to be run using the same arguments as were used for gcc.

The parser handles both the code of the 2.4 series Linux kernel and the 2.6 series. The lexer is user-configurable and needs seeding with the names of those functions which are known a priori to sleep, and the names of the spinlock lock and unlock calls. Less than twenty seed functions have been used.

5   More Targets

Spinlock-under-spinlock can be detected by first constructing the transitive graph of functions which call functions which take spinlocks, and sounding the alarm at a call of such a function under spinlock.

Making that graph requires attaching the code

setflags(SPINLOCK)

into the logic of the spin lock function calls in Table 1, just as for the sleep function calls. The trigger/action rules in Table 2 are then duplicated, substituting SPINLOCK for SLEEP in the existing rules, so that the rules propagate the SPINLOCK flag as well as the SLEEP flag from callee to caller. Then a single trigger/action rule is added which outputs an alert when a function marked with SPINLOCK (i.e. a function which calls a function which ... takes a spinlock) is called under spinlock:

(SPINLOCK & SPIN_SET & SPIN > 0)! → output()

Why is taking a spinlock twice dangerous? Taking the same spinlock twice is deadly, as Linux kernel spinlocks are not reentrant. The result will be to send the CPU into a busy forever loop. Taking two different spinlocks one under the other in the same thread is not dangerous, unless another thread takes the same two spinlocks, one under the other, in the reverse order. There is a short window where both threads can take one spinlock and then busy-wait for the other thread to release the spinlock they have not yet taken, thus spinning both CPUs simultaneously and blocking further process. In general, there is a deadlock

```
files checked:   1151
alarms raised:   426        (30/1151 files)
false positives: 214/426
real errors:     212/426 (3/1151 files)
time taken:      ~6h
LoC:             650K       (unexpanded)
```

Fig. 5. Testing for access to kfreed memory in the 2.6.3 Linux kernel

File & function	Code fragment

fm801-gp.c:
  fm801_gp_probe
	101 `kfree(gp);`
	102 `printk("unable to grab region 0x%x-0x%x\n",`
	          `gp->gameport.io, gp->gameport.io + 0x0f);`

aic7xxx_old.c:
  aic7xxx_detect
	9240 `while(current_p && temp_p)`
	9241 `{`
	9242 `    if (((current_p->pci_bus==temp_p->pci_bus)&&...){`
	       `    ...`
	9248 `      kfree(temp_p);`
	9249 `      continue;`

Fig. 6. Access to kfreed memory in kernel 2.6.3

window like this if there exists any spinlock cycle such that A is taken under B, B is taken under C, etc. Detecting double-takes flags the potential danger.

We have also been able to detect *accesses to freed memory* (including frees of freed memory). The technique consists of setting the logic of a kfree call on a variable containing a memory address to increment a counter variable $a(l)$ unique to the (integer index label l generated by the analysis for the) variable. Assigning the variable again resets the counter to zero ($p[!a(l)]$ means proposition p relaxed to remove references to the counter $a(l)$; a is treated like a vector where appropriate, so initial condition $a \leq 0$ has $a(l) \leq 0$ too):

```
ctx e, p ::kfree(label l)      = (p[a(l)-1/a(l)], F, F) with ctx e;
ctx e, p ::assignment(label l) = (p[!a(l)], F, F) with ctx e;
```

The alarm is sounded when the symbol with label l is accessed where the counter $a(l)$ may take a positive value – variable with index l may point to freed memory.

A survey of 1151 C source files in the Linux 2.6.3 kernel reported 426 "alarms" but most of these were clusters with a single origin. Exactly 30 of the 1151 files were reported as suspicious in total (see Table 5). One of these (aic7xxx_old.c) generated 209 of the alarms, another (aic7xxx_proc.c) 80, another (cpqphp_ctrl.c) 54, another 23, another 10, then 8, 7, 5, 4, 2, 2, 2, 2, and the rest 1 alarm each. Three (3) of the flagged files contained real errors of the type searched for. Two of the error regions are shown in Fig. 6. Curiously, drivers/scsi/aic7xxx_old.c is flagged correctly, as can be seen in the second code segment in the figure.

All the false alarms were due to a bug in the postcondition logic of assignment at the time of the experiment, which caused a new assignment to x closely following on the heels of a kfree(x) to be (erroneously) flagged.

A repeat experiment on 1646 source files (982K LOC, unexpanded) of the Linux 2.6.12.3 kernel found that all the errors detected in the experiment on kernel 2.6.3 had been repaired, and no further errors were detected. There were 8 false alarms given on 7 files (all due to a parser bug at the time which led to a field dereference being treated like reference to a variable of the same name).

6   Software

The source code of the software described in this article is available for down-load from ftp://oboe.it.uc3m.es/pub/Programs/c-1.2.13.tgz under the conditions of the GNU Public Licence (GPL), version 2.

7   Summary

A practical C source static analyser for the Linux kernel has been described, capable of dealing with the millions of lines of code in the kernel on a reasonable time-scale, at a few seconds per file. The analysing logic is configured to obtain different analyses (and several are performed at once).

The particular logical analysis described here has detected about two uncorrected deadlock situations per thousand files in the Linux 2.6 kernel, and about three per thousand files which access already freed memory.

Acknowledgements

This work has been partly supported by funding from the EVERYWARE (MCyT No. TIC2003-08995-C02-01) project, to which we express our thanks. We are also grateful to the shepherding member of the program committee for his helpful guidance in the final preparation.

References

1. Peter T. Breuer, Marisol Garciá Valls: Static Deadlock Detection in the Linux Kernel, pages 52-64 In *Reliable Software Technologies - Ada-Europe 2004, 9th Ada-Europe International Conference on Reliable Software Technologies, Palma de Mallorca, Spain, June 14-18, 2004*, Eds. Albert Llamosí and Alfred Strohmeier, ISBN 3-540-22011-9, Springer LNCS 3063, 2004
2. P. Cousot, R. Cousot: Abstract interpretation: A unified lattice model for static analysis of programs by construction or approximation of fixpoints. In *Proc. 4th ACM Symposium on the Principles of Programming Languages*, pages 238–252, 1977
3. Jeffrey S. Foster, Manuel Fähndrich, Alexander Aiken: A Theory of Type Qualifiers. In *Proc. ACM SIGPLAN Conference on Programming Language Design and Implementation (PLDI'99)*, Atlanta, Georgia, May 1999

4. Jeffrey S. Foster, Tachio Terauchi, Alex Aiken: Flow-Sensitive Type Qualifiers. In *Proc. ACM SIGPLAN Conference on Programming Language Design and Implementation (PLDI'02)*, pages 1–12. Berlin, Germany. June 2002
5. Rob Johnson, David Wagner: Finding User/Kernel Pointer Bugs With Type Inference. In *Proc. 13th USENIX Security Symposium, 2004* August 9–13, 2004, San Diego, CA, USA
6. David Wagner, Jeffrey S. Foster, Eric A. Brewer, Alexander Aiken: A First Step Towards Automated Detection of Buffer Overrun Vulnerabilities. In *Proc. Network and Distributed System Security (NDSS) Symposium 2000*, February 2-4 2000, San Diego, CA, USA

Bauhaus – A Tool Suite for Program Analysis and Reverse Engineering

Aoun Raza, Gunther Vogel, and Erhard Plödereder

Universität Stuttgart
Institut für Softwaretechnologie, Universitätsstraße 38
70569 Stuttgart, Germany
{raza, vogel, ploedere}@informatik.uni-stuttgart.de

Abstract. The maintenance and evolution of critical software with high requirements for reliability is an extremely demanding, time consuming and expensive task. Errors introduced by ad-hoc changes might have disastrous effects on the system and must be prevented under all circumstances, which requires the understanding of the details of source code and system design. This paper describes Bauhaus, a comprehensive tool suite that supports program understanding and reverse engineering on all layers of abstraction, from source code to architecture.

1 Introduction

This paper presents an overview of the program understanding and reverse engineering capabilities of Bauhaus [1], a research project at the universities of Stuttgart and Bremen. The importance of understanding program source code and of being able to reverse engineer its components derives both from the costly effort put into program maintenance and from the desire to create and preserve the reliability of the code base even under extensive change. The quality of software under maintenance is crucially dependent on the degree to which the maintainers recognise, observe, and occasionally modify the principles of the original system design.

Therefore, tools and techniques that support software understanding and reverse engineering have been developed by industry and academia as a vehicle to aid in the refurbishment and maintenance of software systems. Especially critical systems with high requirements for reliability benefit from the application of such tools and techniques. For example, it becomes possible to automatically prove the absence of typical programming errors, e.g., uninitialised variables, to raise the internal source code quality, e.g., by detecting dead code, and to improve the understanding of the software on all layers of abstraction from source code to architectural design.

The details of these techniques will be described later in this document. The rest of the document is organised as follows: section 2 provides the motivation and background of Bauhaus. Section 3 discusses the program representations used in Bauhaus. Section 4 and 5 describe the low- and high-level

L.M. Pinho and M. González Harbour (Eds.): Ada-Europe 2006, LNCS 4006, pp. 71–82, 2006.
© Springer-Verlag Berlin Heidelberg 2006

analyses implemented in Bauhaus. Trace analysis techniques are introduced in section 6. Some other analyses are discussed in section 7. Section 8 describes the development process and summarises experiences with Ada as the main implementation language of Bauhaus. The paper ends with some conclusions in section 9.

2   Background

The project Bauhaus is motivated by the fact that programmer efforts are mostly (60% - 80%) devoted to maintain and evolve rather than to create systems [2]. Moreover, about half of the maintenance effort is spent on understanding the program and data [3], before actual changes are made. Therefore, helping maintainers to understand the legacy systems they have to maintain could greatly ease their job. A better understanding of the code and of its design will undoubtedly also contribute to the reliability of the changed software. An important step in assisting the maintainers is to provide them with a global overview comprising the main components of the system and their interrelations and with subsequent refinements of the main components. Therefore, our initial goal for Bauhaus was the development of means to semi-automatically derive and describe the software architecture, and of methods and tools to represent and analyse source code of legacy systems written in different languages. At present, Bauhaus is capable to analyse programs in Ada, C, C++, and Java. Bauhaus is implemented mainly in Ada and interfaces to software in C, C++, and an assortment of other languages. Figure 1 provides basic data about the composition of the 2005 Bauhaus system.

Language	Handwritten	Generated	Total
Ada95	589'000	291'000	880'000
C	106'000	0'000	106'000
C++	115'000	177'000	292'000
...	...	...	...
Total	843'000	469'000	1'312'000

Fig. 1. The Bauhaus project: number of non-commented lines of code, categorised by programming language

The primary challenges that the Bauhaus infrastructure addresses are the support for multiple source languages and the creation of a common framework, in which advanced compiler technologies for data- and control-flow analyses offer foundation support engineered to allow the analysis of multi-million lines of user code. User-oriented analyses with ultimate benefits to the maintainers of systems achieve their goals by building on the results of these basic analyses. In the realm of tools for program understanding, Bauhaus is one of very few toolsets that takes advantage of data- and control-flow analyses.

3   Program Representations

3.1   Requirements for Program Representations

The particular program representation has an important impact on what analyses can be performed effectively and efficiently. Fine-grained analyses, e.g., of data- and control-flow, require more low-level information than coarse-grained analyses. Some of the Bauhaus tools utilise compiler techniques, which produce rich syntactic and semantic information, often referred to as the detailed, low-level representation of a program. Unlike compilers, all Bauhaus tools analyse and know the system as a whole. The Bauhaus analyses used for reverse- and re-engineering the architecture of a system, on the other hand, build on a much coarser, high-level program representation. To reduce the size of the information being operated upon by these analyses, the detailed information is first condensed into this coarser, more suitable high-level representation. An additional design goal for our program representations was to keep them independent from the source programming languages and, in particular, to allow for the analysis of mixed-language systems.

In Bauhaus two separate program representations exist, catering to the need of detailed low-level and coarser high-level analyses, respectively. The *InterMediate Language* (IML) representation contains information at the syntactical and semantical levels. Resource flow graphs (RFG) are used to represent information about global and architectural aspects of the analysed systems.

3.2   IML

The IML representation is defined by a hierarchy of classes. Each class undertakes to represent a certain construct from a language, as for instance a while loop. Instances of these classes model the respective occurrences in a program. Within the hierarchy, a specialisation takes place: child classes model the same semantic construct as their parent class, however in a more specialised pattern, e.g., the While_Loop class is a child of the more general Loop_Statement class. By enforcing certain rules on the generation of the sub-nodes of such an instance, a semantic equivalence is ensured, so that analyses not interested in the fact that the loop was indeed a While_Loop will function correctly when operating on the instance merely as a general Loop_Statement. This modelling strategy allows us in many cases to add a construct from a particular language as instance of a more general common notion present in many languages. E.g., the for-loops of Ada and C are represented by two distinct classes. Both share the same base class that models the common aspects of all loops. In this regard, IML is quite unique among the known Intermediate Languages [4].

Objects in IML possess attributes, which more specifically describe the represented constructs. Often such an attribute is a pointer, or a list, or a set of pointers to other objects. Thus, IML forms a general graph of IML objects and their relationships. IML is generated by compiler frontends that support C and C++. Frontends for Ada and Java are under development. Foundation support for the persistence of IML automates the writing and reading of IML to and from a file. Prior to advanced analyses, the IML parts of a program are linked by a Bauhaus tool into a complete representation of the entire program to be analysed.

3.3   RFG

As described earlier, different abstraction levels are used in Bauhaus for the recognition of the architecture of a software system. While IML represents the system on a very concrete and detailed level, the abstraction levels for global understanding are modelled by means of the RFG. An RFG is a hierarchical graph, which consists of typed nodes and edges. Nodes represent architecturally relevant elements of the software system, e.g., routines, types, files and components. Relations between these elements are modelled with edges. The information stored in the RFG is structured in views. Each view represents a different aspect of the architecture, e.g., the call graph or the hierarchy of modules. Technically, a view is a subgraph of the RFG. The model of the RFG is fully dynamic and may be modified by the user, i.e., by inserting or deleting node/edge attributes and types. For visualising the different views of RFGs, we have implemented a Graphical Visualiser(Gravis) [5]. The Gravis tool facilitates high-level analysis of the system and provides rich functionality to produce new views by RFG analyses or to manipulate generated views.

For C and C++, an RFG containing all relevant objects and relationships for a program is automatically generated from IML, whereas for Ada and Java the RFG is generated from other intermediate representations or compiler supported interfaces, e.g., the Ada Semantic Interface Specification (ASIS) or Java classfiles.

This RFG is then subjected to and augmented by additional automated and interactive analyses.

4   Analyses Based on IML

This section describes the Bauhaus analyses that can be performed on the IML representation to help maintain the reliability and quality of the operational code.

4.1   Base Analyses for Sequential Code

In Bauhaus we have implemented the fundamental semantic analyses of control- and data-flow as well as different known and adapted points-to analysis techniques. The results of all these analyses are conservative in the sense that they produce overestimations in the presence of situations that are known to be undecidable in the general case. Examples are unrealizable paths or convoluted patterns of points-to aliasing on the heap. A different class of conservative inaccuracy comes from analyses which generate less precise results in favour of a better run time behaviour in space and time consumption. As we strive to analyse large systems, these engineering tradeoffs are highly relevant.

Over the years, several pointer analyses with different characteristics have been implemented and evaluated in the context of the Bauhaus project. The focus of the first set of analyses was the production of highly precise points-to information for the data-flow analyses. The experiences with an implementation of the algorithm by Wilson [6] showed that the accurate results come at a high price. The run time and memory requirements of this analysis are often prohibitive. This cost as well as pronounced variations in timing behaviour prevented its application to large programs; even for smaller programs the runtime performance was too unpredictable. To be able to analyse programs with more than 200.000 lines of code, we have implemented flow insensitive analyses as developed by Steensgaard, Das, or Andersen [7, 8, 9]. These analyses show a much better and acceptable run time behaviour, but are considerably less precise than the analysis by Wilson. We presently investigate how those imprecise results can still be improved and the balance optimised between the cost of tighter results and their benefit to subsequent analyses.

The control-flow analysis in Bauhaus computes traditional intraprocedural control-flow graphs for all routines of a program. Together with the call-relationships, the set of intraprocedural control-flow graphs form an interprocedural control-flow graph that can be traversed by interprocedural data-flow analyses. The control-flow analysis is based on basic blocks which are a sparse representation of control-flow graphs. Besides the information of the possible flow of control between the basic blocks, derived information like dominance- and control-dependency information is available and subsequently used in architectural analyses.

A thorny issue for the analysis of C++, Java, and Ada is the representation of exception handling in control-flow graphs. Our model is similar to the modelling that was shown by Sinha and Harrold in [10]. As exceptions generate complex control-flow graphs and implicit exceptions might be raised at any time during an execution (e.g., the virtual machine error in Java), we compromised and consider only explicitly thrown exceptions in our analyses.

Data-flow relations are represented by the SSA-form (Static Single Assignment form). The SSA generation of Bauhaus is derived from the algorithm proposed by Cytron in [11]. The algorithm operates on locators which are an abstraction of variables or of parts of variables. The analysis itself does not know about the specific characteristics of the locators. Through this, it is possible to have analyses with different precision by just changing the locators, e.g., from one locator for each variable to one locator for each part of a structured variable. Also, it is possible to incorporate arbitrary pointer analyses by generating locators for the specific memory elements of each analysis. The data-flow analysis is performed interprocedurally in two phases. The first phase determines side effects, the second phase performs a local SSA generation for each routine and incorporates the side effects. The generation is context-sensitive, i.e., it takes multiple calling contexts for each routine into account. Each calling context might result in different data-flow patterns and side effects.

Manifold applications for the results of the data-flow analysis exist. Simple tests for error detection like finding uninitialised variables, or the location of redundant or unread assignments, are truly trivial algorithms once the SSA form is available. Escape analysis for C pointer arguments is a slightly more elaborate but still simple algorithm.

Similarly, the results are the basis for applications of slicing or tracing for program understanding, all the way to applications on the architecture level like the recovery of glue code that implements the interactions between two components, or the classification of components within the architecture based on their external data-flow behaviour.

4.2   Base Analyses for Parallel Programs

In parallel programs, different tasks often need to communicate with each other to achieve their assigned job. Different communication methods are available for these interactions, such as message passing, use of shared memory or encapsulated data objects. Furthermore, tasks may need to claim other system resources that cannot be shared with others. As multiple threads try to access shared resources, their access must be protected by some synchronisation mechanism. Otherwise, their interaction could lead to data inconsistencies, which can further lead to abnormal program behaviour. Two important classes of inter-process anomalies are race conditions and deadlocks. A race condition occurs when shared data is read and written by different processes without prior synchronisation, whereas deadlock is a situation where the program is permanently stalled waiting for some event such as the freeing of a needed resource. Both these classes of errors tend to be very difficult to detect or to recreate by test runs; they arise in real-life execution as an inexplicable, sudden, and not recreatable, sometimes disastrous malfunction of the system. For reliable systems it is literally a "must" to impose coding restrictions and to perform a static analysis of the code to ensure the absence of race conditions and deadlocks. Tools can help to discover the situations and can assist programmers in locating the culprit source code.

There has been considerable research on defining different static and dynamic analysis techniques and building tools for race detection [12, 13, 14]. Tools based on static approaches need good base analyses, i.e., points-to and alias analyses [12]. In Bauhaus different points-to, control- and data-flow analysis techniques are implemented as discussed in 4.1. To overcome the deficiencies in previously proposed solutions we are now exploiting the Bauhaus base analyses for the implementation of race detection and deadlock analysis tools. A tool LoRad for the detection of data races in parallel programs has been implemented and is in its testing phase. LoRad uses the Bauhaus control-flow and points-to analyses to detect competing concurrent read and write accesses of variables shared by multiple threads or tasks, but executed without proper mutual exclusion. While not always an error, such accesses at best may cause non-deterministic program results, at worst are truly disastrous if multiple, functionally related variables are updated and read without proper synchronisation.

It is worth mentioning that none of the already implemented race detection approaches have included rich points-to information, which is surprising, as the prevalent OS-interfaces are invariably based on pointer semantics for their arguments. Additionally, we are also implementing a deadlock detection technique, which uses a data-flow analysis based technique to check for necessary conditions to enable dangerous cyclic waiting situations.

4.3 Dead Code Analysis

Many systems contain code that is never executed because the corresponding subprograms are never reached. Despite being not necessary, the so-called dead code complicates the analysis and evaluation of the software and should be eliminated.

Bauhaus provides tools for the automatic detection of dead code. Those tools test the reachability of routines in the call graph. For safe and precise approximations of the effects of indirect calls, our tools consider the results of the points-to analyses described in section 4.1.

5 Analyses Based on RFGs

This section describes some Bauhaus analyses performed on the high-level RFG representation.

5.1 Component Recovery

The IEEE standard for recommended practice for architectural description of software-intensive systems [15] defines architecture as the fundamental organisation of a system embodied in its components, their relationships to each other, and to the environment, and the principles guiding its design and evolution. Bauhaus focuses on the recovery of the structural architecture that consists of components and connectors. 12 automatic component recovery techniques were evaluated, none alone has a sufficient recovery coverage [16]. To overcome the limitations exhibited by automated component recovery techniques, a semi-automatic approach was developed and implemented that combines automatic techniques in an interactive framework. The effectiveness of the method was validated through a case study performed on xfig [5]: In the limited time of five hours an analysis team was able to gain a 50% coverage of the source code, which was sufficient to understand the full architecture of xfig. Later the team could validate the acquired knowledge by solving three typical maintenance tasks.

5.2 Reflexion Analysis

Reverse engineering large and complex software systems is often very time consuming. Reflexion models allow software engineers to begin with a hypothetical high-level model of the software architecture, which is then compared with the actual architecture that is extracted from source code. We extended the reflexion model defined by [17] with means for hierarchical decomposition [18], i.e., now the entities of the hypothetical and the actual architecture may contain other entities. The reflexion starts with a coarse model of the architecture which is iteratively refined to rapidly gain deeper knowledge about the architecture. Most importantly, the reflexion analysis flags all differences of the two models with respect to dependencies among entities. Thus, unintentional violations of the hypothetical model can be easily recognised or the model adjusted, respectively. Two major case studies performed on non-trivial programs with 100 and 500 KLOC proved the flexibility and usefulness of this method in realistically large applications. These systems, maintained and evolved over a long time, contained many deviations from the hypothetical architecture which were detected by our tool. In many cases, the deviations are not flaws, but rather a result of a too idealistic model. Thus, our tools help to find reality and avoid surprises by unrecognised dependencies. An interesting side-result of the case studies was that the quality of the results depended heavily on the availibility of points-to information.

5.3 Feature Analysis

Features are the realisation of functional requirements of a system. In trying to understand a program and its architecture, maintainers often want to know where in the code base a set of features has been implemented. For Bauhaus, we have developed a new technique for feature location [19]. A set of scenarios (test cases) invokes the features of interest and a profiler records the routines called by each test case. The relations between test cases and features and between test cases and routines is then analysed by concept analysis [20]. The output of the analysis is a lattice that allows a classification of the routines with respect to their specificity for the implementation of a particular feature or groups thereof. This assessment is of significant value in judging the effects of changes or the ability to extract a component from a system for reuse. The maintainer can additionally augment the concept lattice with information learned from the static call graph in Bauhaus. The very nature of deriving the lattice from test case profiles implies that important cases might be missed, but are guaranteed to be present in the static call graph. Inversely, the static call graph may include calls that implement cross-cutting concerns and hence are not specific to a feature.

5.4 Protocol Analysis

Despite being important aspects of interface documentation, detailed descriptions of the valid order of operations on components are often missing. Without such a specified protocol, a programmer can only guess about the correct use of the component.

The component recovery implemented in Bauhaus is able to discover the exported interface of components which serves as a starting point for further analysis. The protocol recovery described by Haak [21] can be applied to discover the actually used protocol of the component. It is based on information derived from dynamic and static trace analyses (see section 6). The retrieved traces are transformed into finite automata which are later used in a unification process to form the protocol of the component.

The protocol validation [21] automatically detects infringements of protocol, e.g., if a component was accessed before it was initialised. The validation is based on an existing protocol which is compared with the actual use.

6   Static and Dynamic Traces

6.1   Static Trace Extraction

Traces are records of a program's execution and consist of sequences of performed operations [22]. Static trace graphs cover all possible executions and are derived directly from IML. In Bauhaus those graphs have many applications and are important input to further analyses, e.g., protocol recovery and validation (see section 5.4) and the recovery of information about component interaction. Static trace graphs are extracted with respect to an object that may be located on stack or heap [22] and contain all operations that might affect the object, including accesses, modifications and subroutine calls. In general, static trace graphs are projections of the interprocedural control flow graph and must cover all possible dynamic traces. Again, a key factor for the precision of the analysis is the quality of the base analyses. In four case studies performed using the Bauhaus implementation we further investigated these effects and showed that the extraction of trace graphs is feasible for programs with more than 100kLOC [22].

6.2   Dynamic Trace Extraction

As dynamic traces generally depend upon input, test cases have to be prepared that require a certain component for the derivation. Then, the source or object code program has to be instrumented [23], and executed on the specific input. The advantage of this dynamic analysis is that it yields precisely what has been executed and not an approximation. The problem of aliasing, where one does not exactly know at compile time what gets indirectly accessed via an alias, does not occur for dynamic analysis. Moreover, infeasible paths, i.e., program paths for which a static analysis cannot decide that they can never be taken, are excluded by dynamic analysis, too. On the other hand, the dynamic analysis lacks from the fact that it yields results only for one given input or usage scenario. In order to find all possible dynamic traces of the component, the use cases have to cover every possible program behaviour. However, full coverage is generally impossible because there may be principally endless repetitions of operations.

The Bauhaus dynamic analyses use IML for code instrumentation and further enhancements. The resulting IML graph is used to obtain a semantically equivalent C code. After its compilation, the execution of the program additionally generates traces in RFG representation. The generated traces are used in component and protocol analysis.

7   Other Analyses

7.1   Clone Detection

A widely used way of re-use is to copy a piece of code to some other place and possibly modify it slightly there. When an error is discovered in one of the copies, all other copies ought to be corrected as well. However, there is no trace of where the clones reside. Consequently, the same error gets rediscovered, reanalysed and fixed in different ways in each clone. Code quality suffers and the cost of maintenance rises. Studies have claimed that 20% and more of a system's code is duplicated in this fashion. The Bauhaus clone detection [24] identifies code clones of three categories: *type-I* clones are truly identical; *type-II* clones are copies in which identifiers or literals are consistently changed; *type-III* clones are modified by insertions or deletions and thus hardest to detect.

The evaluation of existing clone detection tools by Bellon [24] determined that a detection based on an abstract syntax graph has a better precision than a token-based clone detection. Consequently, the Bauhaus clone detection operates on IML.

7.2   Metrics

Metrics are quantitative methods to assess the overall quality of the software system and provide objective numbers for present and future software development plans. The metrics implemented in Bauhaus operate on different levels of a software system, i.e., source code or architecture level, and are computed on IML and RFG, respectively:

- **Source code level:** lines of code, Halstead, maximal nesting, cyclomatic complexity
- **Architecture level:** number of methods, classes and units, coupling, cohesion, derived metrics e.g., number of methods per class, classes per unit

The calculated results can be used in many ways, for instance, to estimate software complexity, to detect code smells, or to provide parameters to maintenance effort models. Most importantly, they can be used to observe trends while the software evolves.

8   Bauhaus Development and Experiences with Ada

We chose Ada as the main implementation language of Bauhaus, because we knew that few other languages would allow us to evolve and maintain a very large system in such a controlled and guided manner. The platform-independence of Ada allowed us to configure Bauhaus very easily to run on a variety of different platforms like x86-Linux, Microsoft Windows, and Sun Solaris.

The long term development and maintenance of Bauhaus in the research context is done by the researchers of the Universities of Stuttgart and Bremen.

Since the beginning, various student projects were performed on the Bauhaus infrastructure to implement new software components [25]. While most students would have preferred Java or C++ in the beginning, in retrospective (and after having worked on Java or C++ projects), they appreciated the features of Ada and it often seems to have become their language of choice.

Since all collaborators of the Bauhaus project have different backgrounds and are more or less experienced programmers, the adherence to common rules and standards is crucial. Since the introduction of the GNAT Coding Style, all developers share the same conventions which increased the readability and hence the quality of source code tremendously.

9 Conclusion

Bauhaus provides a strong and generic base for low- and high-level program understanding using advanced code- and data-flow analyses, pointer analyses, side-effect analyses, program slicing, clone recognition, source code metrics, static tracing, query techniques, source code navigation and visualisation, object recovery, re-modularisation, and architecture recovery techniques. In the near future we plan to extend Bauhaus with more analyses and error finding techniques for parallel programs. We have plans to implement deadlock and race detection analysis for Ada and Java. Bauhaus is growing as a large scale research initiative. Besides the University of Stuttgart we now have another Bauhaus working group at Bremen University. We have introduced portions of Bauhaus as a commercial product to deal with growing industrial response. Very recently, a company was created, focused on Bauhaus as a product.

Looking into the future, it is interesting to note that many program properties that were reasonably easy to analyse in procedural languages, because they were statically decidable, were moved in more modern languages into the realm of undecidability. For example, polymorphism makes determination of the called routine much more imprecise. Similarly, the efficiently decidable aliasing among reference parameters has now been mapped onto the undecidable and very difficult reference-value based aliasing. In short, object-oriented languages have significantly increased the need to obtain accurate points-to information, where in the past simple static semantic knowledge still sufficed. It is reassuring to know that, within Bauhaus, all tools can easily query the results of the IML base analyses to obtain this information.

References

1. Eisenbarth, T., Koschke, R., Plödereder, E., Girard, J.F., Würthner, M.: Projekt Bauhaus: Interaktive und inkrementelle Wiedergewinnung von SW-Architekturen. In: 1. Workshop Software-Reengineering, Bad Honnef, Germany (1999)
2. Nosek, J.T., Palvia, P.: Software Maintenance Management: Changes in the Last Decade. Journal of Software Maintenance **2** (1990) 157–174
3. Fjeldstadt, R.K., Hamlen, W.T.: Application Program Maintenance Study: Report to Our Respondents. In: Proc. of GUIDE 48, Philadelphia, PA (1983)

4. Rainer Koschke, J.F.G., Würthner, M.: An Intermediate Representation for Reverse Engineering Analyses. In: Working Conference on Reverse Engineering, Hawaii, USA, IEEE Computer Society Press (1998) 241–250
5. Czeranski, J., Eisenbarth, T., Kienle, H., Koschke, R., Simon, D.: Analyzing xfig Using the Bauhaus Tool. In: Working Conference on Reverse Engineering, Brisbane Australia, IEEE Computer Society Press (2000) 197–199
6. Wilson, R.P., Lam, M.S.: Efficient Context-Sensitive Pointer Analysis for C Programs. In: PLDI. (1995)
7. Steensgaard, B.: Points-to Analysis in Almost Linear Time. In: POPL '96: Proceedings of the 23rd ACM SIGPLAN-SIGACT Symposium on Principles of Programming Languages, New York, NY, USA, ACM Press (1996) 32–41
8. Das, M.: Unification-based Pointer Analysis with Directional Assignments. In: PLDI. (2000) 35–46
9. Andersen, L.O.: Program Analysis and Specialization for the C Programming Language. PhD thesis, DIKU, University of Copenhagen (1994)
10. Sinha, S., Harrold, M.J.: Analysis and Testing of Programs with Exception Handling Constructs. IEEE Trans. Softw. Eng. 26 (2000) 849–871
11. Cytron, R., Ferrante, J., Rosen, B.K., Wegman, M.N., Zadeck, F.K.: Efficiently Computing Static Single Assignment Form and the Control Dependence Graph. ACM Transaction on Programming Languages and Systems 13 (1991) 451–490
12. Engler, D., Ashcraft, K.: RacerX: Effective, Static Detection of Race Conditions and Deadlocks. In: SOSP '03: Proceedings of the 19th ACM Symposium on Operating Systems Principles, New York, NY, USA, ACM Press (2003) 237–252
13. Savage, S., Burrows, M., Nelson, G., Sobalvarro, P., Anderson, T.: Eraser: A Dynamic Data Race Detector for Multi-Threaded Programs. In: SOSP '97: Proceedings of the 16th ACM Symposium on Operating Systems Principles, New York, NY, USA, ACM Press (1997) 27–37
14. Helmbold, D.P., McDowell, C.E.: A Taxonomy of Race Detection Algorithms. Technical report, University of California, Santa Cruz, CA, USA (1994)
15. IEEE Standards Board: IEEE Recommended Practice for Architectural Description of Software-intensive Systems—Std. 1471-2000 (2000)
16. Koschke, R.: Atomic Architectural Component Detection for Program Understanding and System Evolution. PhD thesis, University of Stuttgart (2000)
17. Murphy, G.C., Notkin, D., Sullivan, K.J.: Software Reflexion Models: Bridging the Gap between Design and Implementation. IEEE Computer Society Transactions on Software Engineering 27 (2001) 364–380
18. Koschke, R., Simon, D.: Hierarchical Reflexion Models. In: Working Conference on Reverse Engineering, IEEE Computer Society Press (2003) 36–45
19. Eisenbarth, T., Koschke, R., Simon, D.: Locating Features in Source Code. IEEE Computer Society Transactions on Software Engineering 29 (2003)
20. Lindig, C., Snelting, G.: Assessing Modular Structure of Legacy Code Based on Mathematical Concept Analysis. In: Proceedings of the 19th International Conference on Software Engineering, IEEE Computer Society Press (1997)
21. Haak, D.: Werkzeuggestützte Herleitung von Protokollen. Diplomarbeit (2004)
22. Eisenbarth, T., Koschke, R., Vogel, G.: Static Object Trace Extraction for Programs with Pointers. Journals of Systems and Software (2005)
23. Larus, J.R.: Efficient Program Tracing. Computer 26 (1993) 52–61
24. Bellon, S., Koschke, R.: Comparison and Evaluation of Clone Detection Tools. IEEE Computer Society Transactions on Software Engineering 21 (2004) 61–72
25. Vogel, G., Simon, D., Plödereder, E.: Teaching Software Engineering with Ada95. In: Proc. Reliable Software Technologies, Ada-Europe 2005, York, LNCS (2005)

SPARK Annotations Within Executable UML

Damian Curtis

AWE plc, Aldermaston, Reading, Berkshire, RG7 4PR, United Kingdom
damian.curtis@awe.co.uk

Abstract. The emergence in the software industry of the Unified Modelling Language (UML) has led to the question as to whether it may be used to complement existing development techniques for high integrity systems. Work is in progress to develop a code generator for SPARK Ada from the executable UML (xUML) subset. This paper concentrates on the work completed, which enables the utilisation of SPARK annotations within xUML models for a prototype code generator. The code generated by this prototype has been successfully analysed using the SPARK toolset.

1 Introduction

There are a number of well established approaches to designing software for dependable systems. In the defence industry the approach chosen has been historically guided by standards such as UK Def-Stan 00-55 [1], which prescribed suitable methods for developing high integrity software. This mandated the use of formal methods for the highest integrity systems and the use of the SPARK toolset was strongly recommended.

The recent revision of Def-Stan 00-56 [2] (which also superseded 00-55) has reduced the emphasis on prescribing particular approaches and allows greater flexibility of software development, as long as there is a suitable justification for the approach taken. Given this new "goal based" approach, as well as the understanding that the wider software industry has advanced considerably in recent years, it has been recognised that there are new approaches possible, which would be of benefit when developing high integrity software.

In particular, it has been noted that there has been a move towards the development of what can be described as "semi-formal" methods, such as the use of the Unified Modelling Language (UML) to design software systems. UML suffers from the lack of a precise definition, which makes it impossible to execute as it stands, but there is a movement within the Object Management Group (OMG) to establish an executable subset of UML (xUML), which does not suffer from this problem [3].

The work described in this document concerns a project to develop an xUML to SPARK code generator. This project aims to demonstrate that the benefits of xUML can be combined with those of more formal approaches such as SPARK to provide a new approach for high integrity software development.

L.M. Pinho and M. González Harbour (Eds.): Ada-Europe 2006, LNCS 4006, pp. 83–93, 2006.

The tools used within this project are the iUML Modeller and iCCG Configurable Code Generator tools from Kennedy Carter [4] and the SPARK toolset from Praxis High Integrity Systems (Praxis-HIS)[5].

This paper concentrates on the work that has been undertaken to identify a suitable strategy for utilising the SPARK annotations within this project.

1.1 Existing UML to SPARK Code Generators

It was recognised prior to commencing this work that there are other tool vendors who also support SPARK code generation from UML. However, there are some key differences between these approaches and that of the Kennedy Carter tools. The models developed using iUML are completely independent of the target language, as all the action semantics are written using an implementation independent language. There is no Ada or other target language code embedded in the models created with iUML, unless "inline" code is required to interface with legacy code and/or low level operating system primitives. Most other "executable UML" tool vendors only generate the structure of the code from their models and use embedded target language (e.g. Ada, C etc.) code to specify the actions [6]. This results in the models losing their platform independence. It is the ability to generate 100% of the target SPARK code from the xUML models, with the actions coded using an implementation independent language, that is a *unique* feature of our chosen approach.

1.2 Executable UML and the iUML Toolset

xUML is a precisely defined subset of UML. xUML has the concept of domains (or subject areas) which allow a system to be divided into subsystems. Each domain has a class diagram. The class diagram is used to define the static structure of the model, using classes, attributes and relationships. The dynamic behaviour is captured using state charts, along with operations. However, this alone is insufficient to produce a fully executable model and so an action semantic language is added. This action language operates at a higher level of abstraction than a conventional programming language; it is designed to model interactions between model elements and thus it is used to provide the detailed description of the model's behaviour. It is this which makes the model executable.

The action language used with the iUML toolset is Action Specification Language (ASL) [7]. Most ASL code appears in operations in the class diagram and state actions. It is also used to specify bridge operations, which are used to link different domains together; initialisation code, which is used to start-up the model; and test methods, which are used to stimulate the model during simulation.

Amongst its additional features that support programming at the modelling level, ASL has the ability to access all data contained in the class diagram. This includes supporting relationship navigation, and the ability to generate signals, which trigger state transitions in classes with associated state charts.

When a signal is generated by a segment of ASL, it is placed in a queue. The signal queue is serviced regularly, and if a signal is present it will be removed and processed. A processed signal causes a state transition in the state machine of the class instance to which the signal is targetted.

The iUML tool allows models to be built and executed either as a single-domain build, where just one subsystem is executed, or as a multi-domain build, where the whole system or just a collection of subsystems can be executed.

The iUML tool also allows the user to create other diagrams including: use case, sequence and collaboration diagrams. These are not used, however, as a source of data for code generation. Other UML diagrams (e.g. activity, component and deployment diagrams) are not currently supported by the iUML tool.

This project is using the iCCG to automatically generate SPARK code from xUML models produced using iUML. The iCCG itself is a meta-model of xUML and the ASL language, written using xUML. Further ASL code is added to this meta-model to tailor code generation to the target language (i.e. in this case SPARK).

1.3   SPARK Ada and the SPARK Toolset

The SPARK Ada language [8, 9] is a subset of the Ada language, suitable for use in high integrity systems. It features a set of annotations which are used by the programmer to specify the intended behaviour of the code. The annotations appear in the form of Ada comments, and are therefore invisible to an Ada compiler. They therefore have no effect on the compilation and execution of the code. Their purpose is to provide an expression of the code designers intent. The existence of annotations in the code means that it is possible to use the static analysis capability provided by the SPARK toolset (developed by Praxis-HIS [5], comprising three main tools: the Examiner, Simplifier and Proof Checker) on that code. It is the development of a method to utilise these annotations, with an xUML to SPARK Ada automatic code generator, that is the subject of this paper.

2   Proposed Modelling Process

The SPARK INFORMED Process [10] emphasises the importance of considering the detailed structure of the design prior to implementing the code. The SPARK toolset supports this, as it is possible to analyse the specifications of the code packages without having a full implementation of the package bodies.

The xUML approach is similar, although less formal, and encourages extensive analysis of the system design. The system design is first broken down into domains, each of which deals with one complete subject area. These domains are populated with classes, some of which may have state machines. Coupling between domains is minimised and the domains can be developed independently.

Therefore much consideration was given to a modelling process which would merge the benefits of using a graphical notation such as UML, with those of the more formal approach offered by SPARK. The process is outlined in Figure 1. The concept is that a skeleton xUML model is developed on the basis of the system requirements; however no action language is inserted at this stage.

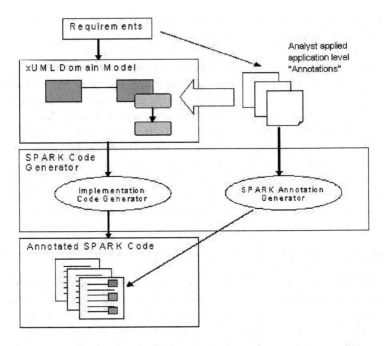

Fig. 1. Model Development Process

The analyst will annotate this model with SPARK-like annotations, which will indicate their design intent. At this point code can be generated, and the SPARK Examiner used to analyse the generated package specifications. The analyst will then complete the model by adding action language and the full code for the model can be generated. The SPARK Examiner can then be used on the fully generated code. Further detail on this approach, and on the general strategy for code generation can be found at [11].

3   Use of SPARK Annotations with the SPARK Code Generator

This section gives a brief explanation of the various annotations utilised in the SPARK code generator, for further details see [8].

The annotations currently being supported by the SPARK code generator are "global", which specifies access by subprograms to global variables and "derives", which specifies the information flow of data through the system between a procedure's, imported and exported parameters and global variables. Although SPARK subprograms can be either procedures or functions, functions do not have "derives" annotations. SPARK functions cannot have side effects, hence it is implied that the function return parameter is derived from all the function parameters and all imported global variables. "Global" and "derives" annotations are supported, as they enable the possibility of undertaking the proof of freedom from run-time errors.

"Global" and "derives" annotations are either written by the analyst or generated by the code generator. For an explanation of this see section 4.

"Own" variable annotations control access to global variables within packages. "Initializes" annotations indicate the initialisation of these global variables. Class attributes, relationships and signal queues are the global data within xUML models, and so the code generator automatically creates appropriate "own" variable annotations for each of these, along with suitable "initializes" annotations.

The "inherit" annotation is used to control the visibility of package names within a SPARK program. This is generated automatically by the code generator.

It is anticipated that future versions of the code generator will include further support for the remaining annotations (i.e. "pre", "post", "check" and "assert").

4   Derivation of the "Global" and "Derives" Annotations Which Appear in the Target Code

One of the fundamental principles of SPARK program design is that annotations should not be generated from the body of the code. This is because they are intended as an expression of design intent and if they are generated from the same source, then their value is lost.

The general package structure of the generated code is shown in Figure 2. There is a Main Program which is simply a loop that polls all the class signal dispatching packages in turn. When one of these packages has a signal on a queue, then the appropriate state action procedure is called in one of the state action packages. That state action may result in updates to data stored in the class data package, signals being placed on signal queues or operations being called.

Data flow analysis checks that the usage of parameters and global variables within subprograms corresponds to their modes, that variables are not read before being initialised and that all imported variables have been used. The "global" annotation is used in SPARK to indicate the intended use of global variables and their modes. In order to perform data flow analysis, with the SPARK Examiner, all subprograms must therefore have "global" annotations.

Where possible it is also desirable to use information flow analysis. The "derives" annotations are used to indicate the interdependencies between global variables and parameters. Information flow analysis checks that the "derives" annotations do not conflict with the variable modes, and that the interdependencies between parameters and global variables are correctly reflected in their usage in the body of the code. All the subprograms in packages below, and including, the state actions will have a "derives" annotation. A "derives" annotation for the subprograms in packages above this point would be extremely complex and therefore of little value to the analysis of the code. For example, the "derives" annotation of the procedure that selects the appropriate state action to call would have to take into consideration every state action within a

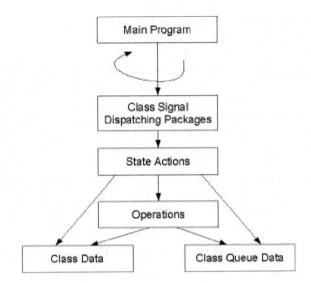

Fig. 2. Hierarchy of Procedure Calls between Code Packages

state machine. Analysis of this section of the code by the SPARK Examiner will be limited to data-flow analysis only. This is quite a common situation at the higher levels of a SPARK program and will not prevent the proof of freedom from run-time errors.

The annotations found in the generated code are derived from two sources and perform two distinct functions. These are detailed in sections 4.1 and 4.2.

4.1   Analyst Provided "Global" and "Derives" Annotations

These annotations will be provided by the analyst when creating models. They are provided in order to describe the effects of the action language on global data within the models. The elements of the UML class diagram (ie. classes, attributes, relationships etc.), along with the signal queues for the state machines, are considered to be the global data within xUML models. The logical place to incorporate these annotations in the iUML tool, are as part of the description fields in the state actions of the models state charts and the description fields of the class operations. They allow the analyst to provide a formal expression of their design intent.

The analyst will apply "global" and "derives" annotations to indicate access to class attributes and relationships between classes. The analyst will annotate to indicate the intention to place a signal on the signal queue. The "derives" annotations will have to account for any parameters belonging to the state actions and operations.

A separate annotation is also required for every class with a state machine. This is a "global" annotation, which must account for all the variables that can be changed as a result of the execution of a state action within that state machine. This annotation is used towards the top of the package hierarchy, where there is a procedure that is processing signals on signal queues and determining which state action to execute.

Format of the Analyst Provided Annotations. The format for annotations is the same as that used by SPARK as can be seen from the following extract from a description held in the iUML tool:

```
Description:
...
This operation calculates the cost of fuel delivered based on its
price per litre and the volume of fuel delivered.
...
--# global in PSC.price_per_litre;
--#        in PSC.current_volume;
--#        out PSC.cost;
--# derives PSC.cost from
--#                    PSC.current_volume,
--#                    PSC.price_per_litre;
```

"PSC" is a reference, assigned by the analyst to a class in the xUML model. This reference is known as a class key letter. "Price_per_litre", "current_volume" and "cost" are attributes of that class. The code generation process must make some small modifications to convert the class reference into its full SPARK package name and the attribute name to the name of the array in which it is stored. The following is the relevant extract from the generated package specification:

```
...
procedure calculate_cost;
--# global in PSC_DATA.price_per_litre_ARRAY;
--#        in PSC_DATA.current_volume_ARRAY;
--#        out PSC_DATA.cost_ARRAY;
--# derives PSC_DATA.cost_ARRAY from
--#                    PSC_DATA.current_volume_ARRAY,
--#                    PSC_DATA.price_per_litre_ARRAY;
...
```

As can be seen this transformation is a minor adjustment to the original annotation. It is important to note that the code generator does not check that the annotations are correct in any way; it merely searches for tokens that match class key letters in the model and makes the appropriate adjustments. (Class key letters are used as a short-form alternative to class names when referencing classes in xUML models.) Checking the correctness of the annotations is left to the SPARK Examiner.

4.2 Code Generator Generated "Global" and "Derives" Annotations

These annotations were created during the design phase of the code generator, when generic templates of the code packages were created to guide the code generation process. They represent the intentions of the designers and are used to provide a check on the code generator mechanism. They increase confidence in the design and implementation of the code generator and the automatically generated code, by reducing systematic errors.

Since there will be an infinite number of potential source models, and therefore an infinite number of sets of generated code, these annotations must still be examined by the SPARK Examiner for every new model. This will assist with the identification of potential flaws in the code generator design.

These code generator embedded annotations have already proved useful during the design and construction phases of the prototype code generator, as they have provided early identification of bugs. Some of these would have otherwise been difficult to trace in a code generator.

The use of SPARK abstract "own" variables in the generated annotations means that the analyst does not need to know the full detail of the generated implementation. This can best be illustrated by considering an example:

Consider a simple xUML class model as shown in Figure 3. This model has two classes: "Student" and "Teacher" which are linked by a relationship "R1". R1 is a one-to-many relationship. ie. one Teacher can teach many Students. Conversely, in this model, a student can only be taught by one teacher.

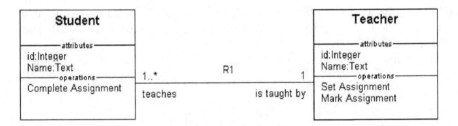

Fig. 3. A Simple xUML Class Model

In order to establish the teacher which belongs to a set of students, the analyst might write using ASL:

```
the_teacher = a_student -> R1
```

which means navigate from the instance "a_student" (an instance of the class student) along the relationship "R1" and return the instance of Teacher which is linked to "a_student".

When this is translated into SPARK code, it becomes a procedure call:

```
...
NAVIGATE_ONE_R1(a_student, LINK_EXISTS, the_teacher);
...
```

and the analyst would provide a suitable annotation to indicate that the R1 relationship global data would be accessed by this segment of ASL, in the manner described in section 4.1. For example:

```
--# global in R1;
--# .....;
--# derives ........ from ...., R1;
```

The analyst will be expected to annotate the operation or state action, in which this relationship navigation has taken place, in order to indicate access to the R1 relationship. However, they are not expected to be aware of the detail of the implementation of that navigation. This can be achieved using SPARK abstract own variables. The specification of the "Navigate_One_R1" procedure in the generated code becomes:

```
procedure NAVIGATE_ONE_R1(FROM_INSTANCE : in Student_IH_TYPE;
LINK_EXISTS : out Boolean;
TO_INSTANCE : out Teacher_IH_TYPE);
--# global in R1_RELATIONSHIP;
--# derives LINK_EXISTS, TO_INSTANCE from R1_RELATIONSHIP,
--#                                       FROM_INSTANCE;
```

but, since "R1_RELATIONSHIP" is abstract, the body of the procedure will have a concrete implementation:

```
procedure NAVIGATE_ONE_R1(FROM_INSTANCE : in Student_IH_TYPE;
LINK_EXISTS : out Boolean;
TO_INSTANCE : out Teacher_IH_TYPE)
--# global in R1_EXISTS_ARRAY;
--#        in R1_INSTANCES_ARRAY;
--# derives LINK_EXISTS from R1_EXISTS_ARRAY, FROM_INSTANCE &
--#         TO_INSTANCE from R1_INSTANCES_ARRAY, FROM_INSTANCE;
is
begin
...
end NAVIGATE_ONE_R1;
```

The implementation of the "R1_RELATIONSHIP" abstract own variable is two arrays: the "R1_EXISTS_ARRAY" and the "R1_INSTANCES_ARRAY". In the implementation produced by this code generator, the "R1_EXISTS_ARRAY" is an array of booleans, which indicate that there exists a link for this instance of Student to an instance of Teacher. The "R1_INSTANCES_ARRAY" is an array of integers representing the instance handle of Teacher to which the Student is linked.

This is a relatively simple example, but it can still be seen that the use of abstract own variables means that the analyst does not require detailed knowledge of the code generator implementation in order to make sensible annotations to the models.

The specification and body of this procedure along with the associated annotations are entirely generated by the code generator. The analyst only has to annotate for the ASL code which they have written, and the consistency of all the annotations is checked using the SPARK Examiner on the generated code.

5   Analysis of Multi-domain Builds

The work completed so far has concentrated on generating the code for a single domain build. However, it is desirable that a complete code generator should have the ability to generate code for both single and multi-domain builds.

There is a problem with simply extending the same approach to other domains and this has an impact on the way the model is annotated. The problem is that whilst the domains are constructed to be as independent as possible, they do communicate via bridge operations. This means that for complete static analysis on a multi-domain model, the annotations in one domain would have to include any effects in other domains caused by the bridge. As the domains can be mutually dependent, it becomes difficult to avoid mutual dependency of generated code packages.

It is also desirable in xUML for domains not to have knowledge of other domains. This maintains the xUML idea of domain partitioning to support the separation of concerns, as well as domain reuse and replaceability.

At present it is considered that the most appropriate solution is to partition the static analysis along domain boundaries. Although this will weaken the analysis to an extent, it should not be too severe, as the bridges between domains are normally kept to a minimum. The consequence for the annotations is that they will only refer to data in other domains as SPARK external own variables.

6   Current Results

An annotation strategy has been developed, which combines the benefits of both xUML and SPARK. A prototype code generator has been constructed using the Kennedy Carter Configurable Code Generator and iUML tool. This prototype code generator has been used to demonstrate that SPARK code and annotations can be generated from executable UML models. The generated code has been analysed using the SPARK Examiner and so it has been demonstrated that it is possible to include support for SPARK annotations within the Kennedy Carter iUML tool.

7   Future Work

It is planned to extend the prototype code generator such that it is fully capable of generating code for single-domain and later multi-domain xUML models. A single domain model of a typical subsystem will be constructed and the resulting code statically analysed. This will enable a more complete understanding of the implications of the selected architecture on static analysis capabilities.

The remaining SPARK annotations will be investigated, in order to see how they can be utilised within the models.

Above all, it is the intention to conclude whether the approach taken is suitable for development processes involving high integrity systems.

8   Conclusions

The work presented in this paper demonstrates that it is possible to incorporate SPARK annotations in xUML models. Those annotations can be used to perform static analysis upon the code generated from these models. The strategy for supporting the SPARK annotations has been implemented with a prototype code generator. An approach has been adopted which can be extended to full code generation from multi-domain xUML models.

Acknowledgements

The work described within this paper was also carried out by Colin Marsh of AWE plc and by Ian Wilkie and Mike Finn of Kennedy Carter Ltd. An important contribution was also made by Janet Barnes of Praxis High Integrity Systems, who provided advice on the SPARK language and toolset. The author also wishes to acknowledge the contributions of Alun Lewis and Wilson Ifill of AWE plc and Jeff Terrell of Kennedy Carter Ltd.

References

1. Ministry of Defence: Requirements for Safety Related Software in Defence Equipment, Defence Standard 00-55, August 1997
2. Ministry of Defence: Safety Management Requirements for Defence Systems, Interim Defence Standard 00-56, Issue 3, December 2004
3. Model Driven Architecture with Executable UML, Chris Raistrick et al, Cambridge University Press 2004
4. See www.kc.com
5. See www.sparkada.com
6. Executable Systems Design with UML 2.0, Scott Niemann, I-Logix Inc
7. The Action Specification Language Reference Manual, Ian Wilkie et al, Kennedy Carter Ltd, 2003
8. High Integrity Software: The SPARK Approach to Safety and Security, John Barnes, Addison-Wesley, 2003
9. SPARK 95 - The SPADE Ada 95 Kernel - Edition 4.3, Gavin Finnie et al, Praxis High Integrity Systems, 2005
10. The INFORMED Design Method for SPARK, Peter Amey, Praxis High Integrity Systems, 1999, 2001
11. Executable UML and SPARK Ada: The Best of Both Worlds, Ian Wilkie, Zuverlässigkeit in einegebetten Systemen, Ada Deutschlang Tagung 2005, Shaker Verlag, 2005

Runtime Verification of Java Programs for Scenario-Based Specifications*

Li Xuandong, Wang Linzhang, Qiu Xiaokang, Lei Bin, Yuan Jiesong, Zhao Jianhua, and Zheng Guoliang

State Key Laboratory of Novel Software Technology
Department of Computer Science and Technology
Nanjing University, Nanjing, Jiangsu, P.R. China 210093
lxd@nju.edu.cn

Abstract. In this paper, we use UML sequence diagrams as scenario-based specifications, and give the solution to runtime verification of Java programs for the safety consistency and the mandatory consistency. The safety consistency requires that any forbidden scenario described by a given sequence diagram never happens during the execution of a program, and the mandatory consistency requires that if a reference scenario described by the given sequence diagrams occurs during the execution of a program, it must immediately adhere to a scenario described by the other given sequence diagram. In the solution, we first instrument the program under verification so as to gather the program execution traces related to a given scenario-based specification; then we drive the instrumented program by random test cases so as to generate the program execution traces; last we check if the collected program execution traces satisfy the given specification. Our work leads to a testing tool which may proceed in a fully automatic and push-button fashion.

1   Introduction

Scenario-based specifications such as message sequence charts [1] and UML sequence diagrams [2,3] offer an intuitive and visual way of describing system requirements. They are playing an increasingly important role in specification and design of systems. Such specifications focus on message exchanges among communicating entities in real-time and distributed systems.

In this paper, we use UML sequence diagrams as scenario-based specifications, and consider runtime verification of Java programs. We concern the following four kinds of specifications which are depicted in Figure 1:

- *Safety consistency specifications* require that any forbidden scenario described by a given sequence diagram D never happens during the execution of a program;

---

* Supported by the National Natural Science Foundation of China (No.60425204, No.60233020), the National Grand Fundamental Research 973 Program of China (No.2002CB312001), and by the Jiangsu Province Research Foundation (No.BK2004080).

L.M. Pinho and M. González Harbour (Eds.): Ada-Europe 2006, LNCS 4006, pp. 94–105, 2006.

- *Forward mandatory consistency specifications* require that if a reference scenario described by a given sequence diagram D_1 occurs during the execution of a program, then a scenario described by the other given sequence diagram D_2 must follow immediately;
- *Backward mandatory consistency specifications* require that if a reference scenario described by a given sequence diagram D_1 occurs during the execution of a program, then it must follow immediately from a scenario described by the other given sequence diagram D_2; and
- *Bidirectional mandatory consistency specifications* require that if a reference scenario described by a given sequence diagram D_1 occurs during the execution of a program and a reference scenario described by another given sequence diagram D_2 follows, then in between these two scenarios, a scenario described by the third given sequence diagram D_3 must occur exactly.

For runtime verification, we first instrument the program under verification so as to gather the program execution traces related to a given scenario-based specification. Then we drive the instrumented program by random test cases so as to generate the program execution traces. Last we check if the collected program execution traces satisfy the given specification. The verification process is depicted in Figure 2. Our work can be used to detect not only the program

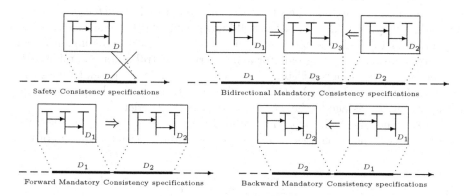

Fig. 1. Scenario-based specifications

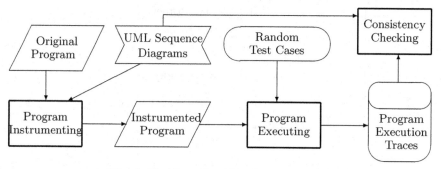

Fig. 2. The Run-Time Verification Process

bugs resulting from the wrong temporal orders of message flow, but also the incomplete UML interaction models constructed in reverse engineering for the legacy systems, and leads to a testing tool which may proceed in a fully automatic and push-button fashion.

The paper is organized as follows. In next section, we introduce UML sequence diagrams, and give their formal definition for verification. The detailed solution is given in Section 3 to the runtime verification of Java programs for the scenario-based specifications. The related works and some conclusions are given in the last section.

2   UML Sequence Diagrams

We represent the scenario-based specifications by UML sequence diagrams. A UML sequence diagram describes an interaction, which is a set of messages exchanged among objects within a collaboration to effect a desired operation or result. Its focus is on the temporal order of the message flow. A sequence diagram has two dimensions: the vertical dimension represents time, and the horizontal dimension represents different objects. Each object is assigned a column, the messages are shown as horizontal, labelled arrows [2,3]. Here we just consider simple sequence diagrams which describe exactly one scenario without any alternative and loop. For example, a simple sequence diagram is depicted in Figure 3, which describes a scenario about the well-known example of the railroad crossing system in [14,15]. This system operates a barrier at a railroad crossing, in which there are a railroad crossing monitor and a barrier controller for controlling the barrier. When the monitor detects that a train is arriving, it send a message to the controller to lower the barrier. After the train leaves the crossing, the monitor send a message to the controller to raise the barrier.

In a sequence diagram, by events we mean the message sending or the message receiving. The semantics of a sequence diagram essentially consists of the

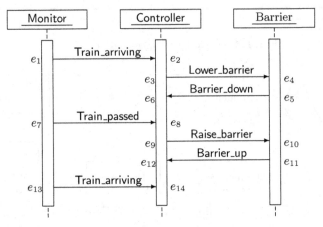

Fig. 3. A simple UML sequence diagram describing the railroad crossing system

sequences (traces) of the message sending and receiving events. The order of events (i.e. message sending or receiving) in a trace is deduced from the visual partial order determined by the flow of control within each object in the sequence diagram along with a causal dependency between the events of sending and receiving a message [1-4]. In accordance with [4], without losing generality, we assume that each sequence diagram corresponds to a visual order for a pair of events e and e' such that e precedes e' in the following cases:

- **Causality:** A sending event e and its corresponding receiving event e'.
- **Controllability:** The event e appears above the event e' on the same object column, and e' is a sending event. This order reflects the fact that a sending event can wait for other events to occur. On the other hand, we sometimes have less control on the order in which the receiving events occur.
- **Fifo order:** The receiving event e appears above the receiving event e' on the same object column, and the corresponding sending events e_1 and e'_1 appear on a mutual object column where e_1 is above e'_1.

For verifying the scenario-based specifications, we formalize sequence diagrams as follows.

Definition 1. A sequence diagram is a tuple $D = (O, E, M, L, V)$ where

- O is a finite set of objects. For each object $o \in O$, we use $\zeta(o)$ to denote the class which o belongs to.
- E is a finite set of events corresponding to sending or receiving a message.
- M is a finite set of messages. Each message in M is of the form (e, g, e') where $e, e' \in E$ corresponds to sending and receiving the message respectively, and g is the message name which is a character string.
- $L : E \to O$ is a labelling function which maps each event $e \in E$ to an object $L(e) \in O$ which is the sender (receiver) while e corresponds to sending (receiving) a message.
- V is a finite set whose elements are a pair (e, e') where $e, e' \in E$ and e precedes e', which is corresponding to a visual order. □

We use *event sequences* to represent the *traces* of sequence diagrams, which describes the temporal order of the message flow. An event sequence is of the form $e_0 \hat{\ } e_1 \hat{\ } \ldots \hat{\ } e_m$, which represents that e_{i+1} takes place after e_i for any i ($0 \le i \le m - 1$).

Definition 2. For any sequence diagram $D = (O, E, M, L, V)$, an event sequence $e_0 \hat{\ } e_1 \hat{\ } \ldots \hat{\ } e_m$ is a *trace* of D if and only if the following condition holds:

- all events in E occur in the sequence, and each event occurs only once, i.e. $\{e_0, e_1, \ldots, e_m\} = E$ and $e_i \neq e_j$ for any i, j ($0 \le i < j \le m$); and
- $e_0, e_1, \ldots, e_m$ satisfy the visual order defined by V, i.e. for any e_i ($0 \le i \le m$) and e_j ($0 \le j \le m$), if $(e_i, e_j) \in V$, then $0 \le i < j \le m$. □

3   Runtime Verification for Scenario-Based Specifications

Now we consider runtime verification of Java programs for the scenario-based specifications expressed by UML sequence diagrams. The verification process consists of three main steps: program instrumenting, program executing driven by random test cases, and consistency checking, which is depicted in Figure 2.

For a program under verification, we gather its execution traces by running its instrumented version. The test cases used to drive the programs are generated randomly. The first reason for selecting random method is its inexpensive charge. Secondly, it is automatic and can be applied in almost any systems, just like what we want. Usually, there is an important problem in random testing, which is how many random test cases are sufficient? But this problem is not so concerned with us. That is because our work aims to develop an automatic testing support tool, which may help us to find the program bugs with a low cost. Due to the inexpensive charge, the tool can run as long as possible, and we think the test cases sufficient when the tool has been running for a duration long enough, or when an apparent and believable result can be concluded, i.e. an inconsistent case is detected.

3.1   Program Instrumenting

For a Java program under verification, we need to insert some statements into its source code for gathering the program execution traces. Since the scenario-based specifications we consider in this paper are represented by the sequence diagrams, the program execution traces we gather are a sequence of events corresponding to sending and receiving messages.

In a Java program, a method call is corresponding to a message sending event, while the first statement execution in a method is corresponding to a message receiving event. Thus we insert the statements for gathering the information around each related method call and in the beginning of each related method definition. Let $D = (O, E, M, L, V)$ be a sequence diagram in a given scenario-based specification. When a sending or receiving event for a message in M happens, the information we need to log include the message, its sender or receiver, and the class which the sender or receiver belongs to. In addition, since an object may send or receive the same message many times, we need to pair a sending event and its corresponding receiving event for the same message. These pairs can be matched if there is an unique number for each pair of events. So for each method corresponding a message in M, we extend its parameter list by adding a long integer formal parameter. When such a method is called , the added parameter is given the current coordinated universal time in milliseconds and is sent to the receiver so as to establish the pair.

The instrumentation algorithm depicted in Figure 4 runs as follows. First we scan the program for parsing the source code into a file of tokens. Then we check each token for recognizing the related method call and method definitions. If a definition of method m corresponding to a message in M is found out, then we revise the formal parameter list by adding a formal parameter

```
scan the program for parsing the source code into a file of tokens;
open the file of tokens;
read an token from the token file and assign it to current_token;
while current_token ≠ eof of the file do
   begin
      if a definition of method m corresponding to a message in M is found out
      then begin
                  revise the formal parameter list by adding a formal parameter mid;
                  insert the code segment Log_Receiving_Event before the first statement
                  in the method definition;
            end
      else if a call for method m corresponding to a message in M is found out
            then begin
                  revise the actual parameter list by adding the current coordinated
                  universal time corresponding to the formal parameter mid;
                  insert the code segment Log_Sending_Event before the method call;
                  end;
      read an element from the token file and assign it to current_token;
   end;
return true.
```

Algorithm for Instrumenting Programs

```
try{ synchronized(this)
            java.io.RandomAccessFile receiveLog = new java.io.RandomAccessFile(log,"rw");
            receiveLog.seek(receiveLog.length());
            receiveLog.writeBytes(mid + "meth_exec" + (Object)this.toString()
                                              + (Object)this.getClassName() + m);
            receiveLog.close(); }}
catch(Exception e){}
```

Code Segment Log_Receivinging_Event

```
try{ synchronized(this)
            { java.io.RandomAccessFile sendLog = new java.io.RandomAccessFile(log,"rw");
            sendLog.seek(sendLog.length());
            mid = System.currentTimeMillis();
            sendLog.writeBytes(mid + "meth_call" + (Object)this.toString()
                                              + (Object)this.getClassName() + m);
            receiveLog.close(); }}
catch(Exception e){}
```

Code Segment Log_Sending_Event

Fig. 4. Instrumentation algorithm and inserted code segments

mid and insert the code segment Log_Receiving_Event depicted in Figure 4 before the first statement in the method definition for gathering the information about the receiver and the class it belongs to. If a call for method m corresponding to a message in M is found out, then we revise the actual parameter list by adding the current coordinated universal time corresponding to the formal parameter mid and insert the code segment Log_Sending_Event before the method call for gathering the information about the sender and the class it belongs to.

A message sender or receiver in a program execution trace we log is represented by the character string consisting of its class name and a hash code, which is provided by Java API class method (Object)toString. The toString method defined by class Object does return distinct hash codes for distinct objects, but since this is implemented by converting the internal address of the object into a hash code, it is still possible for different objects that exist in different time to return the same hash code. To determine the life cycles of these dynamic objects, we need to instrument the finalizer of the concerned classes. Whenever one object is finalized, its hash code is logged so that we know what a hash code exactly refers to at different time.

3.2 Consistency Checking

According to the algorithm for instrumenting programs given in Section 3.1, for an event corresponding to sending (receiving) a message, we can obtain its sender (receiver) and the class the sender (receiver) belongs to. We also can pair a sending event and its corresponding receiving event for the same message. For simplicity, from now on we represent any program execution trace we gather by a sequence which is of the form $v_0 \char`^ v_1 \char`^ \ldots \char`^ v_n$ where each v_i $(0 \leq i \leq n)$ is an event corresponding to sending (receiving) a message, and the class which the sender (receiver) of v_i belongs to is denoted by $\tau(v_i)$. In the following, we give the solutions to checking the program execution traces for the safety consistency specifications and for the mandatory consistency specifications.

For matching the program execution traces and the traces of a given sequence diagram, we define the *trails* of the sequence diagram as follows. Given a sequence diagram $D = (O, E, M, L, V)$, a program execution trace $v_0 \char`^ v_1 \char`^ \ldots \char`^ v_n$ is a *trail* of $D$ if it can be mapped into a trace of $D$, i.e., there is a corresponding trace of $D$ of the form $e_0 \char`^ e_1 \char`^ \ldots \char`^ e_n$ such that

- for each i $(0 \leq i \leq n)$, the class which the sender or receiver of v_i belongs to is the same as the one which the sender or receiver of e_i belongs to, i.e, $\tau(v_i) = \zeta(L(e_i))$;
- for each i $(0 \leq i \leq n)$; if e_i is a message sending (receiving) event, then v_i corresponds the same message sending (receiving) event;
- if (e_i, g, e_j) is in M $(0 \leq i < j \leq n)$, then v_i and v_j is a pair of the sending and receiving for the same message; and
- for any v_i and v_j $(0 \leq i < j \leq n)$, if $\tau(v_i) = \tau(v_j)$ then v_i and v_j have the same sender (receiver).

Since the different objects with the same class may occur in a program execution trace, for a given sequence diagram $D = (O, E, M, L, V)$ there may be multiple object compositions corresponding to O in the program execution trace, and when consistency checking we should consider the scenarios generated by those object compositions respectively. Let $D = (O, E, M, L, V)$ be a sequence diagram, and B be a set of objects in a program execution trace. If there is a bijection function which maps each object in O to an object in B such that their classes are the same, we say that B is an *agent* of O in the program execution trace, and the bijection function is denoted by $\theta_B : O \to B$.

Let $D = (O, E, M, L, V)$ be a sequence diagram, $\sigma = v_0 \char`^ v_1 \char`^ \ldots \char`^ v_n$ be a program execution trace, and $B$ be an agent of $O$. For a subsequence $\sigma_1$ in $\sigma$ of the form $v_i \char`^ v_{i+1} \char`^ \ldots \char`^ v_j$ $(0 \leq i < j \leq n)$, by removing any v_k $(i \leq k \leq j)$ from σ_1 such that the sender (receiver) of v_k is not in B, we get an event sequence $\sigma_1' = v_0' \char`^ v_1' \char`^ \ldots \char`^ v_m'$. If σ_1' is a trail of D, then we say that σ_1 is an *image* of D on B. Furthermore, if σ_1 is an image of D on B and $v_i = v_1' \wedge v_j = v_m'$, then we say that σ_1 is an *exact image* of D on B.

Safety Consistency Checking. A safety consistency specification consists of one sequence diagram D, denoted by $\mathcal{S}_S(D)$, and require that any forbidden scenario described by D never happens during the execution of a program. For example, there are two sequence diagrams depicted in Figure 5 which are about the railway crossing system. The left one describes a normal scenario for the preparation for the train crossing, which should occur during the program execution. The right one is an exceptional scenario in which the message Barrier_secured is sent to the monitor before the barrier is put down, which is forbidden to occur during the program execution, and forms a safety consistency specification.

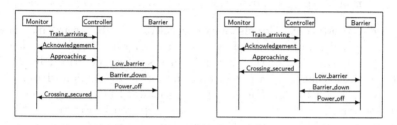

Fig. 5. Saftey consistency specifications for the railway crossing system

Let $D = (O, E, M, L, V)$. For a program execution trace σ of the form $v_0 \,\hat{}\, v_1 \,\hat{}\, \ldots \,\hat{}\, v_n$, if there are an agent B of D and a subsequence σ_1 of σ of the form $v_i \,\hat{}\, v_{i+1} \,\hat{}\, \ldots \,\hat{}\, v_j \,(0 \le i < j \le n)$ which is an image of D on B, than we say that a scenario described by D *occurs* in σ. Thus, we define that a program execution trace satisfies a safety consistency specification $\mathcal{S}_S(D)$ where $D = (O, E, M, L, V)$ if for any agent B of O, there is no image of D on B in the program execution trace.

Forward Mandatory Consistency Checking. A forward mandatory consistency specification consists of two sequence diagrams D_1 and D_2, denoted by $\mathcal{S}_F(D_1, D_2)$, and require that if a reference scenario described by D_1 occurs during the execution of a program, then a scenario described by D_2 must follow immediately. For example, a forward mandatory consistency specification for the railway crossing system is depicted in Figure 6, which requires that from the scenario for the preparation for the train crossing, the scenario for raising the barrier after the train passes must follows immediately.

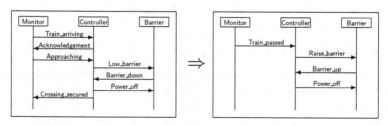

Fig. 6. Forward mandatory consistency specification for the railway crossing system

Let $D_1 = (O_1, E_1, M_1, L_1, V_1)$, $D_2 = (O_2, E_2, M_2, L_2, V_2)$, and σ be a program execution trace of the form $v_0 \char`^ v_1 \char`^ \ldots \char`^ v_n$. If for any agent $B_1$ of $O_1$, for any subsequence $\sigma_1$ of $\sigma$ of the form $v_i \char`^ v_{i+1} \char`^ \ldots \char`^ v_j$ $(0 \leq i < j \leq n)$ which is an exact image of D_1 on B_1, the following *forward mandatory condition* is satisfied:

- there is an agent B_2 of O_2 such that $\theta_{B_1}(o) = \theta_{B_2}(o)$ for any $o \in O_1 \cap O_2$, and
- there is a subsequence σ_2 of σ of the form $v_{j+1} \char`^ v_{j+2} \char`^ \ldots \char`^ v_k$ $(j < k \leq n)$ which is an image of D_2 on B_2,

then we say that the program execution trace σ *satisfies* $\mathcal{S}_F(D_1, D_2)$.

Backward Mandatory Consistency Checking. A backward mandatory consistency specification consists of two sequence diagrams D_1 and D_2, denoted by $\mathcal{S}_B(D_1, D_2)$, and require that if a reference scenario described by D_1 occurs during the execution of a program, then it must follow immediately from a scenario described by D_2. For example, a backward mandatory consistency specification for the railway crossing system is depicted in Figure 7, which requires that the scenario for raising the barrier after the train passes must follows immediately from the scenario for the preparation for the train crossing.

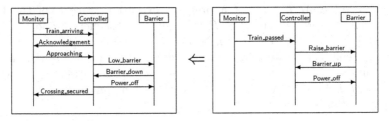

Fig. 7. Backward mandatory consistency specification for the railway crossing system

Let $D_1 = (O_1, E_1, M_1, L_1, V_1)$, $D_2 = (O_2, E_2, M_2, L_2, V_2)$, and σ be a program execution trace of the form $v_0 \char`^ v_1 \char`^ \ldots \char`^ v_n$. If for any agent $B_1$ of $O_1$, for any subsequence $\sigma_1$ of $\sigma$ of the form $v_i \char`^ v_{i+1} \char`^ \ldots \char`^ v_j$ $(0 \leq i < j \leq n)$ which is an exact image of D_1 on B_1, the following *backward mandatory condition* is satisfied:

- there is an agent B_2 of O_2 such that $\theta_{B_1}(o) = \theta_{B_2}(o)$ for any $o \in O_1 \cap O_2$, and
- there is a subsequence σ_2 of σ of the form $v_k \char`^ v_{k+1} \char`^ \ldots \char`^ v_{i-1}$ $(0 \leq k < i)$ which is an image of D_2 on B_2,

then we say that the program execution trace σ *satisfies* $\mathcal{S}_B(D_1, D_2)$.

Bidirectional Mandatory Consistency Checking. A bidirectional mandatory consistency specification consists of three sequence diagrams D_1, D_2, and D_3, denoted by $\mathcal{S}_D(D_1, D_2, D_3)$, and require that if a reference scenario described by D_1 occurs during the execution of a program and a reference scenario described by D_2 follows, then in between these two scenarios, a scenario described by D_3 must occur exactly. For example, a bidirectional mandatory consistency specification for the railway crossing system is depicted in Figure 8, which requires that between the scenarios for confirming the train arriving and for permitting the train crossing, the scenario for lowering the barrier must exist exactly.

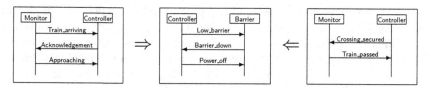

Fig. 8. Bidirectional mandatory consistency specification for RCS

Let σ be a program execution trace of the form $\sigma = e_0 \,\hat{}\, e_1 \,\hat{}\, \ldots \,\hat{}\, e_n$, and

$$D_1 = (O_1, E_1, M_1, L_1, V_1), D_2 = (O_2, E_2, M_2, L_2, V_2), D_3 = (O_3, E_3, M_3, L_3, V_3).$$

If for any agent B_1 of O_1 and any agent B_2 of O_2 such that $\theta_{B_1}(o) = \theta_{B_2}(o)$ for any $o \in O_1 \cap O_2$, for any subsequence σ_1 of σ of the form

$$\sigma_1 = e_i \,\hat{}\, e_{i+1} \,\hat{}\, \ldots \,\hat{}\, e_j \,\hat{}\, e_{j+1} \,\hat{}\, e_{j+2} \,\hat{}\, \ldots \,\hat{}\, e_{k-1} \,\hat{}\, e_k \,\hat{}\, e_{k+1} \,\hat{}\, \ldots \,\hat{}\, e_m$$

where

- $0 \le i < j < k < m \le n$,
- the subsequence $e_i \,\hat{}\, e_{i+1} \,\hat{}\, \ldots \,\hat{}\, e_j$ is an exact image of D_1 on B_1,
- the subsequence $e_k \,\hat{}\, e_{k+1} \,\hat{}\, \ldots \,\hat{}\, e_m$ is an exact image of D_2, and
- any subsequence of the form $e_a \,\hat{}\, e_{a+1} \,\hat{}\, \ldots \,\hat{}\, e_b$ $(j < a < b < k)$ is not any image of D_1 or D_2,

the following *bidirectional mandatory condition* is satisfied:

- there is an agent B_3 of O_3 such that $\theta_{B_1}(o) = \theta_{B_3}(o)$ for any $o \in O_1 \cap O_3$ and that $\theta_{B_2}(o) = \theta_{B_3}(o)$ for any $o \in O_2 \cap O_3$, and
- the subsequence $e_{j+1} \,\hat{}\, e_{j+2} \,\hat{}\, \ldots \,\hat{}\, e_{k-1}$ is an image of D_3 on B_3,

then we say that the program execution trace σ *satisfies* $S_D(D_1, D_2, D_3)$.

3.3   Support Tool and Case Study

With the work presented in this paper, we aim to develop an automatic support tool for testing, which may help us to reduce the testing cost. This tool can help us to detect the inconsistency between the behavior implemented by the program and the expected behavior specified by the scenario-based specifications. The tool may proceed in a fully automatic fashion, and we can drive this tool after we leave our office in the evening, and see the results in the next morning.

Based on our work in this paper, we have implement a prototype of this kind of tool. The tool accepts a Java program under verification, instruments the program according to the given scenario-based specifications, drives the instrumented program to execute on a set of random test cases, and reports the errors which result from the inconsistency with the specification.

By the tool, we have conducted several case studies for evaluating the potential and usability of the solution presented in this paper. One case study is an automated teller machine simulation system, which is a complete example from [5] of object-oriented analysis, design, and programming applied to a moderate size problem. The other case studies also include an microwave oven simulation system which is implemented in Java with 17 classes and 113 methods totally, and an official retirement insurance system which is a real project in the industry, and which is implemented in Java with 17 classes and 241 methods totally. In these case studies, in addition to the bugs embedded manually, by the tool we did find out several inconsistent cases resulting from the program bugs or the incomplete sequence diagrams we use as the specification. Since the algorithms for program instrumenting and consistency checking are simple and efficient, we think there is no particular obstacle to scale our approach to larger systems.

4   Conclusion

To our knowledge, there has been few literature on runtime verification of Java programs for the scenario-based specifications expressed by UML sequence diagrams. The runtime verification techniques have been used for Java programs and the other programs [6-9]. In those works, several specification languages based on temporal logics are designed to describe the relations between events, but do not support to describe the mandatory consistency specifications considered in this paper. Even for the temporal logics themselves, it is difficult and not a natural way to be used to describe the scenario-based specifications considered in this paper in some cases such that an event is allowed to occur many times in a specification and that the scenarios are required to adhere immediately with each other in a mandatory consistency specification. Compared to those specification languages, UML sequence diagrams are much more popular and the specifications expressed by UML sequence diagrams can come directly from the artifacts generated in software development processes. Furthermore, we know that it is not easy to use formal verification techniques directly in industry because the specification languages in the verification tools are too formal and theoretical to master easily. In industry, it is much more acceptable to adopt UML sequence diagrams as a specification language instead of the temporal logic based languages in formal verification tools. In addition, since the specifications are described by UML sequence diagrams, our work can also be used to detect the incomplete UML interaction models constructed in reverse engineering for the legacy systems, which is another advantage. A scenario-based testing approach is presented in [12] based on a simple subset of live sequence charts (LSCs) [13] which can not be used to describe the backward and bidirectional mandatory consistency specifications considered in this paper. There are also several works [10,11] on verifying Java programs based on model checking techniques whose capacity is restricted by the huge program state spaces.

In this paper, our work focuses on the runtime verification of Java programs, but the underlying approach and ideas are more general and can also possibly be applied to the runtime verification of the other object-oriented programs.

References

1. ITU-T. Recommendation Z.120. ITU - Telecommunication Standardization Sector, Geneva, Switzerland, May 1996.
2. J. Rumbaugh and I. Jacobson and G. Booch. *The Unified Modeling Language Reference Manual*, Addison-Wesley, 1999.
3. OMG. *UML2.0 Superstructure Specification*, availabe at http://www.uml.org, Oct. 2005.
4. Doron A. Peled. *Software Reliability Methods*. Springer, 2001.
5. Russell C. Bjork. *The Simulation of an Automated Teller Machine*. http://www.math-cs.gordon.edu/local/courses/cs211/ATMExample/Links.html.
6. Detlef Bartetzko, Clemens Fischer, Michael Moller, and Heike Wehrheim. Jass - Java with Assertions. In *Electronic Notes in Theoretical Computer Science*, Vol.55, Issure 2, Elsevier, 2001.
7. Klaus Havelund and Grigore Rou. Monitoring Java Programs with Java PathExplorer. In *Electronic Notes in Theoretical Computer Science*, Vol.55, Issure 2, Elsevier, 2001.
8. M. Kim, S. Kannan, I. Lee, O. Sokolsky and M. Viswanathan. Java-MaC: A Run-time Assurance Tool for Java Programs. In *Electronic Notes in Theoretical Computer Science*, Vol.55, Issure 2, Elsevier, 2001.
9. Mark Brorkens, Michael Moller. Dynamic Event Generation for Runtime Checking using the JDI. In *Electronic Notes in Theoretical Computer Science*, Vol.70, Issure 4, Elsevier, 2002.
10. David Y.W. Park, Ulrich Stern, Jens U. Skakebak, and David L. Dill. Java Model Checking. In *Proceedings of the First International Workshop on Automated Program Analysis, Testing, and Verification*, 2000.
11. Klaus Havelund and Thomas Pressburger. Model checking JAVA programs using JAVA PathFinder. In *International Journal on Software Tools for Technology Transfer*, (2000) 2: 366-381.
12. M. Lettrai and J. Klose. Scenario-based monitoring and testing of real-time UML models. In Proceedings of 4th International Conference on Unified Modeling Language (UML2001), LNCS 2185, Springer, 2001.
13. Werner Damm and David Harel. LSCs: Breathing life into message sequence charts. In *Formal Methods in System Design*, 19(1):45-80, 2001.
14. Olaf Kluge. Modelling a Railway Crossing with Message Sequence Chatrs and Petri Nets. In H.Ehrig et al.(Eds.): *Petri Technology for Communication-Based Systems - Advance in Petri Nets*, LNCS 2472, Springer, 2003, pp.197-218.
15. Constance L. Heitmeyer, Ralph D. Jeffords, and Bruce G. Labaw. Comparing Different Approaches for Specifying and Verifying Real-Time Systems. In *Proc.* 10th *IEEE Workshop on Real-Time Operating Syatems abd Software*. New York, 1993. pp.122-129.

Secure Execution of Computations
in Untrusted Hosts

S.H.K. Narayanan[1], M.T. Kandemir[1], R.R. Brooks[2], and I. Kolcu[3]

[1] Department of Computer Science and Engineering
The Pennsylvania State University, University Park, PA 16802, USA {snarayan,
kandemir}@cse.psu.edu
[2] Department of Electrical and Computer Engineering
Clemson University, Clemson, SC 29634, USA
rrb@acm.org
[3] Computation Department, UMIST, Manchester, M60 1QD, UK
ikolcu@umist.ac.uk

Abstract. Proliferation of distributed computing platforms, in both
small and large scales, and mobile applications makes it important to
protect remote hosts (servers) from mobile applications and mobile applications from remote hosts. This paper proposes and evaluates a solution
to the latter problem for applications based on linear computations that
involve scalar as well as array arithmetic. We demonstrate that, for certain classes of applications, it is possible to use an optimizing compiler
to automatically transform code structure and data layout so that an
application can safely be executed on an untrusted remote host without
being reverse engineered.

1 Introduction

Mobile code technology allows programs to move from node to node on a network. Java is probably the best-known mobile code implementation. Applets can
be downloaded and executed locally. Remote Method Invocation (RMI) allows
applets registered with a service to be executed on a remote node. The use of
a standardized language allows virtual machines running on different processors
to execute the same intermediate code.

The software update and patch systems for both Microsoft and the Linux community are built on mobile code infrastructures. In current security research, the
goal is to secure individual workstations and restrict program execution to a set
of trusted programs.This paper looks at the largely ignored problem of protecting programs running on remote untrusted systems, and proposes automated
compiler help to ensure secure execution of programs. Several important applications exist for this technology. A driving force for computer interoperability
and sharing of software is business-to-business e-commerce. There are real needs
to retrieve information from remote suppliers or clients. On the other hand, there

This work is supported in part by NSF Career Award 0093082 and a grant from the
GSRC.

L.M. Pinho and M. González Harbour (Eds.): Ada-Europe 2006, LNCS 4006, pp. 106–118, 2006.

are also real needs to guard corporate intellectual property. The approaches we present are an initial step towards allowing interoperability without risking reverse engineering and the loss of intellectual capital. Legal and accounting applications of the approach for auditing and monitoring systems is also foreseeable. Finally, remote sensor-based processing is another potential application domain because in many cases data remains with the sensors that collect them or our application needs data that is available only in a particular region covered by (untrusted) sensor nodes. Consequently, we need to be able to execute our application remotely and we do not know whether the sensor nodes are reliable. In all these scenarios, remote secure execution in an untrusted environment is a critical issue, and this paper proposes and evaluates a compiler-driven approach to this problem and presents experimental evidence demonstrating its applicability.

Mobile code security is not a new topic. Generally, the research in this area can be broken down into three parts. Protecting the host from malicious code, protecting the code from malicious hosts and finally, preventing man-in-the-middle type attacks which result in mobile code or generated results being leaked. In the mobile code protection domain, which is what this paper targets, prior works involve sending the original code and somehow ensuring that the right results are brought back, i.e. they concentrate on the results generated by mobile code. For example, [3] deals with spoofing and [14] addresses the problem of a malicious remote host not generating the right results. Further, [9] gives a technique to prevent one host from changing the results generated by another host.

However, the prior works assume that the original code can be shared with all hosts, irrespective of whether they are trustworthy. Our approach allows the owner of the mobile code, to protect the code itself from being revealed and hence helps to preserve intellectual capital. The proposed mechanism allows the owner to send a code that is different from the original code and still get back the results that he/she wants. Hence, this approach ensures that if the owner does not want to share the code, the confidentiality of the original code is never lost. The proposed mechanism cannot individually solve all the issues involved in mobile code security (such as spoofing, correct code execution, obtaining untampered results), but when used in conjunction with existing techniques it ensures that the code as well as the generated results are secure.

This rest of this paper is organized as follows. Section 2 discusses related work. Section 3 presents a high-level view of the proposed approach, and its mathematical details are presented in Section 4. Section 5 explains how computation matrices are formed and how our approach handles affine computations. Section 6 discusses the selection of transformation matrices for correct secure execution. Section 7 discusses how our approach is extended when we have multiple servers. Section 8 provides an example and Section 9 discusses our experimental results. Section 10 concludes the paper.

2   Related Work

The work presented in this paper is related to many efforts in distributed computing, agent-based computing, remote procedure invocation, code security/safety, and code obfuscation domains. In this section, we only focus on the secure execution of functions on untrusted hosts. This has been studied as a more general problem of confidentiality of execution in efforts such as [1, 4, 12, 13]. Most of these efforts focus on the circuit computation model which is not very well suited for general, large-scale mobile code. Sander and Tschudin [8, 10] defined a function hiding scheme, and focused on non-interactive protocols. In their framework, the privacy of a function is assured by an encrypting transformation on that function. Integrity of evaluation is the ability of the circuit owner to verify the correctness of the execution of his/her circuit. This problem has been widely studied in the view of reliability but not from the view of a malicious server. The proof-based techniques [14] suggested that the untrusted host has to forward a proof of correctness of execution together with the result.

Perhaps the most relevant prior work to the one presented in this paper is [6, 7] in which a function is encrypted using error coding and sent to the untrusted host which provides the clear-text input. The enciphered output generated by the host is then sent back to the original host, where it is decrypted and the result is verified. The authors advocate the employment of the tamper proof hardware (TPH) as a necessary mechanism to store and provide the control flow between the numerous functions that make up a program. Control flow is located on the TPH and is supplied to the untrusted host. The main difference between these studies and the work presented in this paper is that we target general scalar and array based computations not circuit-specific expressions. Consequently, the code and data transformations used by our approach are different from those employed in prior studies such as [6, 7], and are directed by an optimizing compiler. Further, our approach deals with the case with multiple untrusted hosts as well.

3   High-Level View

This section presents an overview of the proposed mechanism. First, the mechanism used for scalar codes is presented. Following this, array based codes are discussed. In both the cases, we use the term "client" to refer to the owner of the application code to be executed, and the term "server" to denote the remote untrusted host (node) that will execute this application.

3.1   Scalar Codes

The high-level view of our approach for linear scalar computations is illustrated in Figure 1(a). On the client side, we have a computation represented, in a compact form, by computation matrix C. We want to execute this computation using input data represented by vector I, and generate an output, represented by vector O. That is, the original computation that we want to perform (as the client) can be expressed in mathematical terms as:

$$O = CI. \tag{1}$$

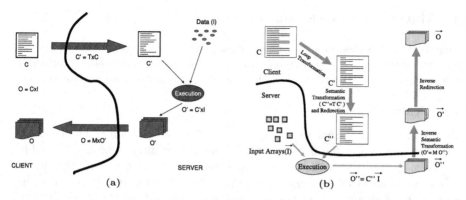

Fig. 1. High-level view of secure code execution in an untrusted server for (a) Scalar codes and (b)Array based codes. The thick curve represents the boundary between the client and the server. Both cases calculate $O = CI$.

The problem is that the client does not have input I and this input data cannot be transmitted to the client.[1] Consequently, the computation must be performed at the server side. The client transforms C to C', and sends this transformed code to the server. The server in turn executes this transformed code represented by matrix C' using input I, computes an output (O'), and sends it to the client (note that $O' \neq O$). Since only the client knows the relationship between C and C', it also knows how to obtain the originally required output O from O', and it uses an appropriate data transformation for this purpose.

3.2   Array-Based Codes

The high-level view of our approach for array based computations is illustrated in Figure 1(b). C is transformed by a loop transformation into a code C', in which the order, by which the elements of an array are accessed, within the loop is changed. In the next step, C' undergoes a semantic transformation to form a new code in which the meaning of the code itself is changed. In order to prevent the untrusted host from gleaning the locations of the arrays to which computed values are written (on the left-hand-side of the expressions), the left-hand-side arrays are replaced by different array expressions. This step is referred to as redirection or data remapping. C'' is applied to the input I by the server to generate the output O''. This output is sent back to the client, which obtains O' from it by applying the inverse of the semantic transformation used earlier. Following this, we use the inverse of the array redirection used earlier, which eventually gives us O, the desired output (i.e., $O = CI$) .

---

[1] This can be due to two potential reasons: either the data is not physically movable as in the case in a remote sensor processing environment, or the server is not willing to share data, due to security concerns.

4   Mathematical Details

This section provides the mathematical details of our proposed method. For the purpose of clarity, the determination of computation and code/data transformation matrices is dealt with separately in Section 5 and Section 6, respectively.

4.1   Scalar Codes

The main restriction that we have regarding the computation to be performed is that it should be a *linear function* of I, and as a result, can be represented by a matrix (C), as is well-known from the linear algebra theory. Note that in the execution scenario summarized above, the client performs two transformations:
• Code Transformation: This is performed to obtain C' from C. As both C' and C are linear and expressed using matrices, we can use a linear transformation matrix T to denote the transformation performed. Consequently :

$$C' = TC. \tag{2}$$

• Data Transformation: This is performed to obtaining O from O', and can also be represented using a matrix (M):

$$O = MO'. \tag{3}$$

4.2   Array-Based Codes

The client performs the following series of transformations on the computation matrix C:
• Loop Transformation: In optimizing compiler theory, loop transformations are used to reorder the points in loop iteration spaces [11]. Here it is used to obtain C' from C. Each execution of a loop body is represented by an iteration vector i. An array reference accessed in a nest is represented as:

$$Li + o, \tag{4}$$

where L is referred to as the *access matrix* and o is referred to as the *offset vector*. A linear loop transformation can be represented using a transformation matrix T_L. Upon application of this transformation, the iteration vector i is mapped to $i' = T_L i$. As a consequence, the new subscript function is given by the following expression:

$$LT_L^{-1} i' + o. \tag{5}$$

This means that the new (transformed) access matrix is $L' = LT_L^{-1}$. The loop transformation does not affect the offset vector o. The loop bounds are, however, affected by this transformation. The loop bounds of the transformed iteration space can be computed – in the most general case – using techniques such as Fourier-Motzkin elimination [11].
• Semantic Transformation: This is performed to obtain C'' from C'. Since both C'' and C' are linear and expressed using matrices, a transformation matrix T is used to denote the transformation being applied.

$$C'' = TC'. \tag{6}$$

It needs to be emphasized that T is entirely *different* from T_L. While it is true that both of them are applied to the loop nest, T_L re-orders loop iterations, whereas T modifies the loop body. Another important difference is that while T_L is a semantic-preserving transformation, T changes the meaning of the computation performed within the loop body.

• Redirection: This is a data space transformation performed to hide the memory locations in the client to which the results of computation are being stored. This also makes manipulating the results of the computation easier as the dimensions of the result matrices will be the same. Let $Li + o$ be an array reference after the loop and semantic code transformations have been applied. Our goal is to apply a data (memory layout) transformation such that the access matrix and the offset vector are mapped to desired forms. While any data transformation that changes L and o is acceptable, the one adopted in this work transforms the access matrix to the identity matrix and the offset vector to the zero vector if it is possible to do so (if not, we use an arbitrary but legal transformation). We represent a data transformation using a pair (S, s). In this pair, S is termed as the data transformation matrix and is $m \times m$ for an m-dimensional array. s is called the shift vector and has m entries. Redirection transforms, the reference $Li + o$ to:

$$SLi + So + s.$$

We want SL to be the identity matrix (I_D) and $So + s$ to be the zero vector. We solve this system of equations as follows. First, from $SL = I_D$ we solve for S. After that, we substitute this S in the second equation $(So + s = 0)$, and determine s.

• Inverse Semantic Transformation: This is performed to obtain O' from O'', and can also be represented using a matrix (M).

$$O' = MO''. \tag{7}$$

Note that, at this point, we apply the inverse of the redirection used earlier, and do not apply the inverse of the loop transformation used earlier. This is because, C and C' are semantically equivalent and the outputs generated by them are equivalent (in the context of this paper).

• Inverse Redirection: The purpose of this transformation is to obtain the original memory locations of the output elements computed. Recall that the redirection transforms reference $Li + o$ to $SLi + So + s$. To obtain the original reference from this, we use the data transformation (Y, y). This gives us:

$$Y\{SLi + So + s\} + y,$$

which expands to

$$YSLi + YSo + Ys + y.$$

Since we want $YSL = L$ and $YSo + Ys + y = o$, we determine Y and y as:

$$Y = S^{-1} \quad \text{and} \quad y = -S^{-1}s.$$

5   Determining Computation Matrix and Handling Affine Programs

An important problem is to determine matrix C, given a code fragment. Recall that this matrix captures the relationship between I and O. Let us assume for now that the program variables in I and O are disjoint; that is, the two vectors have no common variables. In this case, it is easy to convert a linear code fragment to C. As an example, consider the code fragment below:

```
a := d+e+f;
b := g-2e;
c := 3f+4d;
```

For this fragment, the input variables are e, d, f and g, and the output variables are a, b and c. Consequently, we can express I, O, and C as:

$$I = \begin{pmatrix} d \\ e \\ f \\ g \end{pmatrix}; \quad O = \begin{pmatrix} a \\ b \\ c \end{pmatrix}; \quad \text{and} \quad C = \begin{pmatrix} 1 & 1 & 1 & 0 \\ 0 & -2 & 0 & 1 \\ 4 & 0 & 3 & 0 \end{pmatrix}.$$

However, the problem becomes more difficult if there are dependencies in the code. Our solution to this problem is to use multiple C "sub-fragments". As an example, let us consider the following code fragment:

```
a := d-5c+2g;
b := e+f;
c := g+4d;
h := 3e-4d;
```

Since variable c is used both on the right-hand-side of the first statement and on the left-hand-side of the third statement, we cannot directly apply the method used in the previous case. However, we can (logically) divide the statements into two groups. The first group contains the first two statements, whereas the second group contains the remaining two statements. Note that, the only data dependence in the code (an anti-dependence in this case) goes from the first group to the second group; that is, the original code fragment is divided over the data dependence. After this division, we can assign a separate C matrix to each sub-fragment. In this example, we have:

$$I_1 = \begin{pmatrix} c \\ d \\ e \\ f \\ g \end{pmatrix}; O_1 = \begin{pmatrix} a \\ b \end{pmatrix}; C_1 = \begin{pmatrix} -5 & 1 & 0 & 0 & 2 \\ 0 & 0 & 1 & 1 & 0 \end{pmatrix} \text{ and } I_2 = \begin{pmatrix} d \\ e \\ g \end{pmatrix}; O_2 = \begin{pmatrix} c \\ h \end{pmatrix}; C_2 = \begin{pmatrix} 4 & 0 & 1 \\ -4 & 3 & 0 \end{pmatrix}.$$

The C_1 and C_2 matrices are then used to represent the computation performed by the two sub-fragments.

So far, our formulation has focused on handling linear computations. We now discuss how our approach can be extended to affine computations. These computations are different from linear computations in that the relationship between I and O is expressed as:

$$O = CI + c, \tag{8}$$

as opposed to $O = CI$, used in the linear case. Here, c is a constant vector, i.e., it contains the constant terms used in the assignment statements that form the computation. Let us define our loop transformation in this case as follows:

$$C' = TC + t, \tag{9}$$

where t is a constant vector, whose entries are to be determined (along with those of T). In this case, the server computes $O' = TCI + Tc + t$. After receiving O' from the remote (untrusted) server, the client calculates:

$$O = MO' + m, \tag{10}$$

where m is a constant vector. Hence, for correct execution, we need to have:

$$CI + c = MTCI + MTc + Mt + m \tag{11}$$

This means that the following two equalities have to be satisfied:

$$C = MTC \tag{12}$$
$$c = MTc + Mt + m \tag{13}$$

The details of the solution are omitted due to space concerns.

6   Selection of T and M

In this section, we study the required relationship between T and M to ensure correctness. First, we focus on scalar codes, and then array based codes.

6.1   Scalar Codes

We start with Equation (3), and proceed as follows:

$$O = MO'$$
$$O = MC'I$$
$$O = MTCI$$
$$CI = MTCI$$

Since $I \neq 0$ (zero vector), from this last equality, we can obtain:

$$C = MTC. \tag{14}$$

In other words, M must be left inverse of T. Let us now discuss the dimensionalities of matrices T and M. Assuming that I has n entries and O has m entries, C is $m \times n$. Therefore, the only dimensionality requirement regarding T is that it needs to have m columns, and similarly M needs to have m rows. Thus, matrices T and M are $k \times m$ and $m \times k$, respectively. That is, we have a flexibility is selecting k. There is also an alternate way of generating C' from C. More specifically, we can have $C' = CT$. In this case, we can proceed as follows:

$$O = MO'$$
$$O = MC'I$$
$$O = MCTI$$
$$CI = MCTI$$

Since $I \neq 0$ (zero vector), from this last equality, we can obtain:

$$C = MCT. \tag{15}$$

However, it should be noticed that with this formulation, we do not have a flexibility in selecting the dimensions of transformation matrices T and M. Specifically, T should be an $n \times n$ matrix, and M should be an $m \times m$ matrix; i.e., we need to work with square matrices. In this case, given a T matrix, we can determine M by solving the resulting linear system of equations. Alternately, we can adopt the following strategy. Let us select an M matrix first, and define a new matrix Q as $Q = MC$. Using this, we can proceed as follows:

$$C = MCT$$
$$C = QT$$
$$Q^T C = Q^T QT$$
$$(Q^T Q)^{-1} Q^T C = T$$

Notice that the last equality gives us the T matrix. It must be noted, however, that in order to use this strategy, we need to select a suitable M such that $Q^T Q$ is invertible, i.e., it is non-singular.

6.2   Array Based Codes

Selection of the matrices T and M for array based codes is similar to their selection for scalar codes. Starting with Equation (7), we proceed as follows:

$$O' = MO''$$
$$O' = MC''I$$
$$O' = MTC'I$$
$$C'I = MTC'I$$

Note that the last equality is obtained from the penultimate one because loop transformation changes only the order by which the elements are accessed during execution but not the result of the execution itself. So, it is correct to equate O' and $C'I$; and since $I \neq 0$ (zero vector), from this last equality, one can obtain:

$$C' = MTC'. \tag{16}$$

In other words, M must be left inverse of T. Note that similar to the case with scalar codes, there is also an alternate way of generating C'' from C'. More specifically, we can set C'' to $C'T$. The details are omitted due to space concerns.

7   Multiple Server Case

In this section, we discuss how the proposed approach can be extended to the case with multiple servers. Due to space concerns, we focus only on scalar computations. The execution scenario in this case, which is depicted in Figure 2, can be summarized as follows. The client divides the computation (C) to i sub-computations, where the ith sub-computation is represented by matrix C_i, where $1 \leq i \leq p$. In mathematical terms, this can be expressed as follows:

$$O = CI \tag{17}$$

$$\begin{pmatrix} O_1 \\ O_2 \\ \vdots \\ O_p \end{pmatrix} = \begin{pmatrix} C_1 & 0 & 0 & 0 \\ 0 & C_2 & 0 & 0 \\ \vdots & \vdots & \ddots & \vdots \\ 0 & 0 & 0 & C_p \end{pmatrix} \begin{pmatrix} I_1 \\ I_2 \\ \vdots \\ I_p \end{pmatrix}. \tag{18}$$

Note that C_i operates on input I_i and generates output O_i. The client then determines a T_i matrix and computes $C_i' = T_i C_i$. Then, C_i' is sent to the server i, which in turn computes $O_i' = C_i' I_i$, and sends it back. After having received O_i' from server i, the client calculates $O_i = M_i O_i'$, where M_i is the data transformation matrix used in conjunction with T_i. Note that, for correctness, we should have $M_i = T_i^{-1}$. After collecting O_1', O_2', ..., O_p' and obtaining O_1, O_2, ..., O_p, the client merges these outputs into the desired out vector O. A similar analysis could be conducted by using the alternate formulation as well (see Section 6).

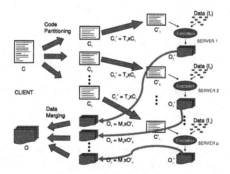

Fig. 2. High-level view of secure code execution in multiple untrusted servers. Note that the original computation, C, is divided into p sub-computations, and each sub-computation is set to get executed on a different server.

8   Example

In this section an example on our approach is presented. Due to space restrictions only an example based on scalar codes is presented.

Consider the following linear code fragment taken from [5]:

$$
\begin{aligned}
dx0 &= x0 - x1 - x12 \\
dy0 &= y0 - y1 - y12 \\
dx1 &= x12 - x2 + x3 \\
dy1 &= y12 - y2 + y3
\end{aligned}
$$

The computation matrix for this computation is:

$$
C = \begin{pmatrix}
1 & -1 & 0 & 0 & -1 & 0 & 0 & 0 & 0 & 0 \\
0 & 0 & 0 & 0 & 0 & 1 & -1 & 0 & 0 & -1 \\
0 & 0 & -1 & 1 & 1 & 0 & 0 & 0 & 0 & 0 \\
0 & 0 & 0 & 0 & 0 & 0 & 0 & -1 & 1 & 1
\end{pmatrix}.
$$

Given the input represented by

$$
I = (x0\ x1\ x2\ x3\ x12\ y0\ y1\ y2\ y3\ y12)^T = (10\ 10\ 10\ 10\ 10\ 10\ 10\ 10\ 10\ 10)^T,
$$

the original output can be computed as:

$$
O = (dx0\quad dy0\quad dx1\quad dy1)^T = CI =
$$

$$
\begin{pmatrix}
1 & -1 & 0 & 0 & -1 & 0 & 0 & 0 & 0 & 0 \\
0 & 0 & 0 & 0 & 0 & 1 & -1 & 0 & 0 & -1 \\
0 & 0 & -1 & 1 & 1 & 0 & 0 & 0 & 0 & 0 \\
0 & 0 & 0 & 0 & 0 & 0 & 0 & -1 & 1 & 1
\end{pmatrix}
(10\ \ 10\ \ 10\ \ 10\ \ 10\ \ 10\ \ 10\ \ 10\ \ 10\ \ 10)^T =
\begin{pmatrix} -10 \\ -10 \\ 10 \\ 10 \end{pmatrix}.
$$

We now discuss how the same computation is carried out in an untrusted remote server environment. Let us assume the following loop transformation matrix:

$$
T = \begin{pmatrix}
1 & 1 & 0 & -1 \\
0 & 1 & 0 & 0 \\
-1 & 0 & 1 & 0 \\
0 & -1 & 0 & 1
\end{pmatrix}.
$$

In this case, the transformed computation matrix $(C' = TC)$ is:

$$
C' = \begin{pmatrix}
1 & -1 & 0 & 0 & -1 & 1 & -1 & 1 & -1 & -2 \\
0 & 0 & 0 & 0 & 0 & 1 & -1 & 0 & 0 & -1 \\
-1 & 1 & -1 & 1 & 2 & 0 & 0 & 0 & 0 & 0 \\
0 & 0 & 0 & 0 & 0 & -1 & 1 & -1 & 1 & 2
\end{pmatrix}.
$$

Consequently, the computation performed by the remote server is:

$$
O' = C'I = (-30\quad -10\quad 20\quad 20)^T.
$$

After receiving the output generated by the server, the client needs to multiply it by $M = T^{-1}$. In this case, M can be found as:

$$
M = \begin{pmatrix}
1 & 0 & 0 & 1 \\
0 & 1 & 0 & 0 \\
1 & 0 & 1 & 1 \\
0 & 1 & 0 & 1
\end{pmatrix}.
$$

Therefore, the resulting output is:

$$
MO' = \begin{pmatrix}
1 & 0 & 0 & 1 \\
0 & 1 & 0 & 0 \\
1 & 0 & 1 & 1 \\
0 & 1 & 0 & 1
\end{pmatrix}
\begin{pmatrix} -30 \\ -10 \\ 20 \\ 20 \end{pmatrix} =
\begin{pmatrix} -10 \\ -10 \\ 10 \\ 10 \end{pmatrix},
$$

which is the same as the intended output that would be computed from $O = CI$.

9 Experiments

In this section, we explain how the overheads of the proposed mechanisms are calculated. To test the proposed approach, we implemented it within an optimizing compiler (built upon SUIF [2]) and performed experiments with three applications that model execution in a sensor-based image processing environment. The first of these applications, TRACK_SEL 2.0, implements a vehicle tracking algorithm which is used to support missile systems by maintaining surveillance against incoming targets and providing the data required for targeting, launch, and midcourse guidance. The second application, SMART_PLANNER, is an emergency exit planner. The application determines the best exit route in case of an emergency which is detected, in the current implementation, using heat sensors. Our third application is named CLUSTER and implements a dynamic cluster forming algorithm. It's main application area is energy-efficient data collection in a wireless sensor environment. All these three applications are written in C++, and their sizes range from 1,072 to 3,582 C++ lines (excluding comment lines). For each application in our experimental suite, we compared two different execution schemes. In the first scheme, which is not security oriented, the application is shifted from one workstation to another and executed there using local data. The second execution implements the proposed approach. Specifically, the application is first transformed and then sent to the remote machine and, when the results are received, they are transformed as explained in the paper. We measured the additional performance overhead incurred by our approach over the first execution scheme. More specifically, we computed the ratio

$$\frac{(\text{loop restructuring time} + \text{data transformation time})}{(\text{total execution time})},$$

where "total execution time" includes the time spent in computation in the remote machine and the time spent during communication. We found that the value of this ratio was 0.0421, 0.0388, and 0.0393 for the benchmarks TRACK_SEL 2.0, SMART_PLANNER, and CLUSTER, respectively. That is, the extra code/data transformations required by our approach do not bring significant performance overheads, which means that we pay a small price to hide the semantics of the application from the remote machine.

10 Concluding Remarks

This paper presents a novel, automated solution to the problem of protecting mobile applications from untrusted remote hosts. These applications based on scalar and array based codes, are automatically transformed with the help of an optimizing compiler to prevent reverse engineering.

Future work involves extending the proposed approach to cater to general purpose programs that cannot be readily expressed as a linear function of the inputs. In order to so, a method to represent the non-linear code in an array format is required. One possible way is to simply treat a variable, such as a, and a non-linear sub-expression that it appears in, such as a^2, to be different variables. That is, we can assume $a^2 = x$ and use x in our formulation. This technique however does not solve the problem of an expression like a^b where b is itself a variable. Further, the problem of recognizing dependencies between an assignment to a and the use of x is complicated. Once the representation mechanism exists, it can be used with the transformation techniques to hide the semantics of the original code as shown in this paper.

References

1. M. Abadi and J. Feigenbaum. Secure circuit evaluation. *Journal of Cryptology,* 2(1):112, 1990.
2. S. P. Amarasinghe, J. M. Anderson, C. S. Wilson, S.-W. Liao, B. R. Murphy, R. S. French, M. S. Lam, and M. W. Hall. Multiprocessors from a Software Perspective *IEEE Micro,* June 1996, pages 52-61.
3. A. Bremler-Barr, H. Levy. Spoofing prevention method. In *Proc. of INFOCOM 2005, Volume 1,* pages 536 - 547, 2005.
4. O. Goldreich, S. Micali, and A. Wigderson. How to play any mental game or a completeness theorem for protocols with honest majority. In *Proc. of the 19th Annual ACM Symposium on Theory of Computing,* pages 218–229, May 1987.
5. C. Li, M. Potkonjak, and W. H. Mangione-Smith. MediaBench: a tool for evaluating and synthesizing multimedia and communication systems. In *Proc. of the International Symposium on Microarchitecture,* 1997.
6. S. Loureiro, L. Bussard, and Y. Roudier. Extending tamper-proof hardware security to untrusted execution environments. In *Proc. of CARDIS,* 2002.
7. S. Loureiro and R. Molva. Function hiding based on error correcting codes. In *Proc. of the International Workshop on Cryptographic Techniques and Electronic Commerce,* pages 92–98, 1999.
8. T. Sander and C. F. Tschudin. Towards mobile cryptography. In *Proc. of the 1998 IEEE Symposium on Security and Privacy,* pp. 215–224, 1998.
9. A.Tripathi, N. Karnik. A Security Architecture for Mobile Agents in Ajanta. In *Proc. of the International Conference on Distributed Computing Systems,* 2000.
10. T. Sander and C. Tschudin. On software protection via function hiding. In *Proc. of the Second Workshop on Information Hiding,* 1998.
11. M. Wolfe. *High Performance Compilers for Parallel Computing,* Addison-Wesley Publishing Company, 1996.
12. A. C. Yao. Protocols for secure computations. In *Proc. of the IEEE Symposium on Foundations of Computer Science,* pages 160–164, 1982.
13. A. C. Yao. How to generate and exchange secrets. In *Proc. of the IEEE Symposium on Foundations of Computer Science,* pages 162–167, 1986.
14. B. Yee. A sanctuary for mobile agents. *Technical Report CS97-537,* Department of Computer Science and Engineering, April 1997.

A Systematic Approach to Developing Safe Tele-operated Robots*

Diego Alonso, Pedro Sánchez, Bárbara Álvarez, and Juan A. Pastor

Universidad Politécnica de Cartagena, Division of Systems and Electronic Engineering (DSIE) Campus Muralla del Mar, s/n. Cartagena, E-30202, Spain
diego.alonso@upct.es

Abstract. Tele–operated service robots are used for extending human capabilities in hazardous and/or inaccessible environments. Their use is undergoing an exponential increase in our society, reason why it is of vital importance that their design, installation and operation follow the strictest possible process, so that the risk of accident could be minimised. However, there is no such process or methodology that guides the full process from identification, evaluation, proposal of solutions and reuse of safety requirements, although a hard work is being done, specially by the standardisation committees. It's also very difficult to even find in the literature examples of safety requirements identification and use. This paper presents the engineering process we have followed to obtain the safety requirements in one of the robots of the EFTCoR[1] project and the way this requirements have affected the architecture of the system, with a practical example: a crane robot for ship hull blasting.

1 Introduction

Human operators use tele–operated service robots for performing more or less hazardous operations (manipulation of heavy and/or dangerous products) in more or less hostile environments (nuclear reactors, space missions, warehouses, etc). Anyway, independently of the operation, the robot has to interact with both the environment it's working on and with human operators. So, it is essential that the design (which include both software and hardware) of the robot involves no (or an acceptable level of) risk, neither for the operators, nor for the environment nor for the robot itself.

Nevertheless, it's not always possible to make a system free of failures in its design or operation. Apart from the risk inherent to the use of the mechanisms themselves, these systems work in hazardous environments, where the probability of the risk is higher than normal. Should a failure happen, the consequences

---

* This work has been partially supported by the Spanish Government programs CICYT, ANCLA (TIC2003-07804-C05-02), part of DYNAMICA (DYNamic and Aspect-Oriented Modeling for Integrated Component-based Architectures).
[1] Project EFTCoR: Environmentally Friendly and Cost-Effective Technology for Coating Removal. Fifth framework programme of the European Community for research, key action Competitive and Sustainable Growth (GRD2-2001-50004).

L.M. Pinho and M. González Harbour (Eds.): Ada-Europe 2006, LNCS 4006, pp. 119–130, 2006.
© Springer-Verlag Berlin Heidelberg 2006

of it can even involve the loss of human lives. [1] documents many cases of computer–related failures, such as the Therac–25 (a radiation–therapy device), the missiles shield in Saudi Arabia, etc.

But safety aspects are seldom included in the design process of the system from the beginning, even though they are a critic aspect. Generally, safety has to conform and adapt to the already designed system and not vice versa, when it's known that safety involves not only the design of the software but also the hardware. In fact, there are many situations in which a simple hardware solution can eliminate a hazard or simplify the design of the safety software.

However, the identification of safety requirements is not different from the identification of the rest of requirements of the system. It only requires a more thorough study, due to their importance (don't forget, human lives and equipment integrity may depend on it!). On the other hand, safety has a big repercussion in the design phase, specially when the time to define the architecture of the system arrives. Its impact is even bigger by the need to avoid *common failure modes*, that can propagate failures within different units of the system.

The objectives of this paper are to stress the importance of the capture of the safety requirements early in the design process and to present a practical experience on how to capture these safety requirements and how they can alter the design of the system. The example presents a thorough study of the safety requirements that a crane robot (a member of the EFTCoR [2, 3] project) must conform to in order to work in such a hazardous environment as shipyards are. The EFTCoR project is about to end after three years of intense work. Altough the robot fulfils the basic safety requirements, we are now thinking about making a commercial version of it, so a deeper study of safety is needed.

This paper is structured in five sections. Section 2 presents a brief description of the EFTCoR project and the safety characteristics that make it a perfect example. In section 3 the process followed to obtain the safety requirements is commented, while section 4 presents the process of identification of safety requirements for the EFTCoR crane robot. Finally, section 5 summarises the contents of the paper and outlines future lines of work.

2   EFTCoR: the Danger of Cleaning Ship Hulls in Shipyards

The EFTCoR family of robots offers a global solution to the problems related to the most dangerous hull maintenance operations, such as cleaning, blasting and painting (see Fig. 1-a). The solution is provided by means of two families of robots: tele–operated cranes and climbing vehicles, depending on the working area. All these robots consist of a primary positioning system, capable of covering large hull areas, and a secondary positioning system, mounted on the primary system, that can position a tool over a relatively small area (4 to 16 m^2). The robots have been developed to achieve the objective of performing the current hull cleaning operations in a way that avoids the emissions of residues to the environment and enhances the working conditions of the shipyard operators

a) Before EFTCoR   b) With EFTCoR crane

Fig. 1. Blasting operation

without worsening the current costs and operation times. Figure 1-b shows the crane robot in action.

The design of such a complex system as EFTCoR involves the necessity of early detection and identification of failures so that correcting measures can be adopted early in the design of the robot. The fundamental characteristics of the EFTCoR that makes it necessary to take into account the need of a safe approach when designing the robots are summarised by the following points:

▷ The operator uses a heavy mechatronic device whose range of movement can cause serious damage (see Fig. 1-b).
▷ The system has to be used outdoors, so it has to be able to deal with atmospheric agents that can alter its normal operation (rain, water on the ground, dust, noise, wind, etc).
▷ The working environment of the robots (shipyards) is very dynamic: there are many cranes, load and unload of heavy equipments, lots of operators moving around (either working on the robot or conscious or not of its presence), etc.
▷ Some maintenance operations include the blasting of the hull with high–pressure abrasive particles. The energy of the jet makes it very dangerous for human operators and for the rest of the equipment, so it's absolutely necessary to train operators in the use of the tool, to maintain the equipment in perfect conditions and to install all the security components needed. Also, as a result of the impact of the jet with the hull, a lot of dust is produced, worsening the condition of the working place.

3   A Safety Process

The purpose of this section is to present a brief summary of the steps we have followed for discovering the safety requirements for the EFTCoR and the consequences they imply on the architecture of the system. To work this out we have based our work on the ANSI standard for robotics [4] (see next point), completing it with the contribution of other authors, such as Douglass [5], that complete the proposal.

Before going on, we introduce the meaning of some words that are used in the paper. According to Douglass, a *risk* is an event or condition that can occur but is undesirable; *safety* is the characteristic of a system that does not incur too much risk to persons or equipment and an *accident* is damage to property o harm to persons, the happening of a risk. A *safety system* is, according to the definition of ANSI/RIA, a system that has been tested, evaluated and proven to operate in a reliable and acceptable manner when applied in a function critical to health and welfare of personnel. Leveson [6] defines a *hazard* as a state or set of conditions of a system (or object) that, together with other conditions in the environment of the system (or object) will inevitably lead to an accident (loss event).

3.1 Survey of Safety Standards and Techniques

There are several approaches to manage safety in literature. Many deal with the problem of designing a standard that guides the whole process (from identification to solution) while others are simple tools or techniques. Among the standards we want to stress the European Standard EN 61508:2001 [7] and the American ANSI/RIA R15.06-1999 [4]. Among the techniques for safety designs we highlight fault trees [8] and ROPES [5] (*Rapid Object-oriented Process for Embedded Systems*).

EN 61508:2001. This European standard sets up a generic approximation for dealing with all the activities related to the life–cycle of the systems that use electric and/or electronic and/or programmable devices for safety functions. The other main purpose of this standard is to serve as basis for the development of specific standards for each application sector, that would take into account techniques and solutions typical of the sector.

ANSI/RIA R15.06-1999. The objective of this standard is to enhance the safety of personnel using industrial robot systems by establishing requirements for the manufacture (including remanufacture and overhaul), installation, safeguarding methods, maintenance and repair of manipulating industrial robots. It is the intention of this standard that the manufacturer (including remanufacturer and rebuilder), the installer and the end–user have specific responsabilities.

Fault Trees. It's one of the most popular approaches to identify, evaluate and manage safety requirements. These trees provide a graphical notation and a formal support that makes it easy to make the analysis from the perspective of the system failures and their origins. However, they do not offer a global framework for requirement specification as a discipline.

ROPES. ROPES is, in words of Douglass, "a development process that emphasises rapid turnaround, early proofs of correctness and low risk". It's an iterative process that makes the design in small, incremental steps. Douglass proposes an eight–steps methodology for dealing with the safety aspects of any system.

3.2   Process of Elicitation of Requirements

As last section shown, until a new standard derived from EN 61508 and targeted to robotics appear, only the ANSI standard offers an specific guide to this kind of systems. But ANSI encourages the use of hardware solutions (such as barriers, light beams, buttons, etc), and does not provide any guide on the use of more complex, software based, solutions.

To complete this lack of detail, the proposal "eight steps to safety" from Douglass has been adopted. In it, Douglass proposes some design patterns oriented to the achievement of a particular safety objective, such as *multi–channel voting pattern, watchdog pattern, safety executive pattern,* etc. By using these patterns we can design software solutions that conform to the needs imposed by the ANSI standard, according to the level of risk of a particular hazard.

Finally, the technique of *fault trees* can be used to obtain the possible causes of the failures that are analysed in the second step of the methodology we propose. Fault trees is a very used and mature technique, but it doesn't help in neither measuring nor classifying nor solving failures. We haven't use this technique for obtaining the causes of the failures, although we think it would have been a good idea to do so.

The four–steps methodology we present proposes the fusion of the standards and techniques presented in subsection 3.1. It encourages the tracking of safety throughout the life–cycle of the robot (as EN 61508 proposes) and uses the ANSI standard as a guide to classify hazards and to propose solutions. By completing ANSI with the contributions of Douglass, it is possible to deal with the design of software–based solution that are more complex than a simple barrier.

Step 1 ▶ Identify hazards. It is desirable that a system should normally work without imminent hazards. So, the first step is to identify all the tasks that involve the use of the system and that have potential hazards. After that, for each task an analysis of the hazards is performed. Some possible sources for the identification of hazards, that can serve as a starting point in their identification, are the following ones (extracted from [4]):

- The movement of mechanical components, especially those which can cause trapping or crushing.
- Stored energy in moving parts, electrical or fluid components.
- Power sources: electrical, hydraulic, pneumatic.
- Hazardous atmospheres, material or conditions: explosive or combustible, radioactive, high temperature and/or pressure, etc.
- Acoustic noise, vibrations, EMI, etc.
- Human failures in design, construction, installation, and operation, whether deliberate or not.

This analysis of hazards also include the identification of the possible causes of the failure (hardware, software or human), the task in which it can happen, the reaction to the happening of the hazard, and some temporal data (adopted from Douglass) relative to how long can the hazard be tolerated before it results in an accident (tolerance time), the maximum amount of time to detect the happening (detection time) and the maximum time to react to it (reaction time).

Step 2 ▶ Identify risks. The objective of this second step is to identify the possible risks of the system and classify them, according to the impact they have on the environment and linking them to the hazards identified on the the first step. The ANSI standard says that, for each risk, three characteristics have to be evaluated. They are the level of severity, the level of exposure and the level of avoidance, each with two different values (for a total of eight possible combinations). Depending on the different values of these characteristics, a Risk Reduction Category (RRC) is obtained. Based on the RRC, ANSI requires a certain level of performance of the safeguard and circuit that are to be design to reduce the risk (simple, single channel, single channel with monitoring and control reliable). Moreover, ANSI also recommend the adoption of safety policies to help human operators avoid some risks (training, presence detectors, security barriers, etc).

After applying the safeguards designed for the specific RRC of the risk, a new analysis is performed to calculate the residual risk, just to be sure that the risk is kept at a tolerable level for both the system and the environment. This process does not end here but has to be repeated during the life–cycle of the robot to ensure that no new risk appears and that the risk already identified are kept under control.

Step 3 ▶ Specify safety requirements. The purpose of this third step is to extract the safety requirements for the system from the results of the previous steps. This is quite difficult to do, because neither ANSI nor Douglass offer a methodology to deduce the requirements from the previous results, so this extraction has been handmade. At this point, it's necessary to have an appropriate process for the harvest of requirements, a way to catalogue them so that they can be reused in other systems of the domain of application (tele–operated robots in our case), as well as tools for tracking the use of the requirements throughout the development process and, in particular, until the architecture of the system. This is the kind of work the Universidad de Murcia is doing inside DYNAMICA.

Step 4 ▶ Make safe designs. The design of the architecture of the system must consider the safety measures and avoid that the failure in a part spread through the rest of the system. A safe design must start off with the previous requirements of security (third step) to adopt a concrete architectural pattern that could be periodically reviewed when new hazards are identified. To be able to do it, to be able to be adaptable, a rigorous architectural approach that allows the evolution of the architectural model due to new requirements or by evolution of the conditions of work is necessary.

4   Safety in the EFTCoR Project

In this section we present an example of the application of the process to obtain the safety requirements for the crane robot of the EFTCoR project. The crane robot uses a commercial crane as the primary positioning system (see Fig. 2-a) and a XYZ table as the secondary positioning system (see Fig. 2-b). The crane has its own control (provided by the manufacturer), a height of twelve meters and a weight of twenty tons, which make unavoidable the movement of the robot with the consideration of safety requirements. It also has, in its central zone, an articulated arm of two tons for holding the XYZ table (which includes a cleaning tool). The control system of the XYZ table has been designed to follow the cleaning instructions from a human operator or from a computer vision system, which finds the areas of the hull to be blasted.

a) Crane   b) XYZ table

Fig. 2. Crane robot for cleaning vertical surfaces in EFTCoR

Due to the extension of the work, only the results of the safety analysis for the primary position system (tasks, hazards and risks) will be presented (see subsection 4.1). Subsection 4.2 presents the solution adopted for the hazard *"The arm of the primary system does not stop"* (see table 2, H13).

4.1 Identification of Hazards and Risks for the Primary System

Using the functional requirements of the EFTCoR system as a starting point, a total of 30 different tasks with a potential hazard have been identified (excerpt in Table 1). These tasks are performed not only by the operator of the robot but also by the maintenance and cleaning staff, can have been planned or not,

Table 1. Excerpt of tasks related to the primary system

#	Type	Description
T1	Operator	Move the primary (rail)
T2	Operator	Move the primary (vertical axis)
T8	Operator	Execute a sequence
T20	Maintenance	Calibrate one of the axes of the primary
T23	Maintenance	Repair an axis (primary or secondary)

Table 2. Excerpt of hazards related to the primary system

Hazard	Risk	Origin	Prob.	Reaction
H3.Person in the rail	Very severe	There's a person standing on the rail	Med.	Raise alarm. Stop the primary. Emergency stop
H4.Obstacle in the rail	Severe	There's an obstacle on the rail	Med.	Raise alarm. Stop the primary. Emergency stop
H5.Obstacle in the vertical axis	Very severe	There's an obstacle on the trajectory	High	Raise alarm. Stop the primary. Emergency stop
H7.The limit switch of the vertical axis is passed	Very severe	Sensor or software error. Comm failure	Low	Raise alarm. Emergency stop
H8.The limit switch of the rail is passed	Very sever	Sensor or software error. Comm failure	Low	Raise alarm. Stop power source
H13.The arm of the primary system does not stop	Very severe	Joint control error. Comm or power failure	Low	Raise alarm. Stop power source. Emergency stop
H15.The sequence of the primary does not end	Very severe	Sequence control error. Comm failure	Low	Raise alarm. Stop primary

Table 3. Excerpt of solutions for the primary system hazards

#	Risk	RRC	Solution	RRC
H3	Run over a person	R2A	Add presence sensors to the rail. Add an acoustic signal when the robot moves	R3B
H4	Damage obstacle and primary	R2A	Add presence sensors to the rail. Add an acoustic signal when the robot moves	R3B
H5	Damage obstacle and primary	R1	Add presence sensors to the vertical axis.	R3B
H7	Damage to equipment or primary or persons	R2B	Add mechanic limits	R4
H8	Damage to equipment or primary or persons	R2B	Add mechanic limits	R4
H13	Damage to equipment or primary or persons	R2B	Add an emergency stop mechanism. Add sensors external to the control loop	R4
H15	The robot can even knock over	R2B	Add an emergency stop mechanism. Add sensors external to the control loop	R4

and their frequency can be daily, weekly, monthly, annually, etc. Table 2 shows an excerpt of the 31 hazards related to the tasks to be performed by the robot (only the hazards related to the primary are shown). These two tables comprise the first step.

Finally, Table 3 shows the results of the step identify risks, but just for the hazards related to the primary positioning system (with the consequences of an accident, the RRC required according to ANSI, the safeguard adopted and the residual RRC).

4.2 Analysis of a Hazard: "The Arm of the Primary System Does Not Stop"

An analysis with detail of this hazard takes us to associate the following possible sources of error: (1) any sensor integrated with the motors that move the arm fails; (2) the electric power is off and (3) the control unit does not run correctly (a hardware fail or a software error). The hazard H13 may imply the breaking of mechanical parts, the precipitation of components to the floor or damages to the human operator. See table 2 and table 3 for the characterisation of this hazard.

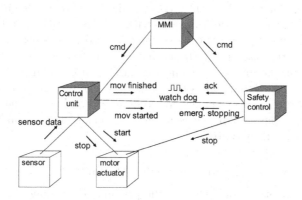

Fig. 3. Deployment diagram for H13

Following the ANSI standard, the levels of the severity of the injury, the frequency of the exposure and the probability of avoidance are evaluated. This evaluations results in a RRC of R2B. Figure 3 shows the deployment partitioning of the system (using an extension of the standard UML notation) that accomplishes the R2B to R4 risk reduction for the hazard H13. This particular solution uses the *watchdog pattern* from Douglass [5]. The limitation of space in this paper does not allow us to give all the details related to the real implementation of the safeguard for this hazard, although table 4 shows the connection between the entities shown in the deployment diagram and their implementation in Ada. Anyway, the full description of the solution follows:

1. When a movement command is received, the Man Machine Interface (MMI) node forwards it simultaneously to the Control Unit node (that will execute it) and to the redundant node, which is in charge of detecting possible hazards (Safety Control node).

Table 4. Relation between deployment diagram and Ada objects

Element from Fig. 3	Ada implementation	Note
Node	Task	Does its main function (control, monitor and MMI).
Watchdog	Task	Synchronous rendezvous with time-out.
Access to hardware	Protected object	Periodically updated by a task.
Real time issues	—	Both node and watchdog are periodic tasks. Watchdog has higher priority.

2. The Control node reads periodically the current position of the joint from a sensor and controls the actuator. The Safety node is in charge of stopping the motor when it detects that the motor is not working properly.
3. Just before the execution of any command, the Control node sends a message to the Safety node, authorising the start of the movement. From here, the Control Unit sends to the Safety node the current value just read from the sensor. The Safety node answers with an acknowledgement that includes as parameter the estimated value of the motor position. Both nodes compute the curve of the discrete positions that must be reached by the robot arm, depending on the initial value and the movement command. Any difference between the calculated values (or no data at all) implies an anomaly in the function of the robot movement (or communication link), which triggers the stop of the robot and the generation of an emergency signal (both nodes have access to the actuator).

4.3   Safety Conclusions for the Crane Robot

Although only the study of safety for the primary positioning system has been presented, in this last subsection we want to present a summary of the conclusion that can be extracted of the whole study. To do so, the 31 identified hazards have been classified in six groups, depending on the type of safeguard adopted. The following conclusions can be extracted from this study:

- 45% of the safety requirements do not affect neither the design of the architecture nor its possible evolution.
- 55% of the safety requirements do affect architecture:
  - 40% imply the addition or extension of some components so that the values of the actuators can be double–checked.
  - 6.66% imply the design and adoption of redundant nodes as the one described in subsection 4.2.
  - 8.66% imply the addition of new sensors to the robot to monitor the system (generally, safety–related sensors).

These extensions or additions to the basic architecture (based only on the functional requirements) due to the safety requirements, mean the need of making cross verifications in practically every level of the architecture, which makes the process of designing the architecture harder and more complicated.

5   Conclusions and Future Works

It is always desirable to make the analysis of the possible hazards for any system to improve its design and safety. When the system interacts with the environment and/or with humans (as project EFTCoR does), the analysis becomes indispensable. But the analysis of hazards is a complex process that needs the support of a methodology. The more domain–specific the methodology, the more accurate the results will be. We have used the ANSI/RIA standard as the basis for the identification and classification of the hazards, risks and the safeguards to be adopted to reduce the risks to acceptable levels. This standard can be complemented by the safety patterns extracted from Douglass when designing a more complex solution and the use of fault trees to identify the possible causes of failure. In this sense, we hope that soon an European standard, derived from EN 61508 and specifically targeted to robotics systems, soon appears to fulfil the lack of a methodology for safety requirements specification and solutions in the EU.

Although it may seem that this work is the result of applying together ("glued" even) several standars, the contribution of this work goes further on because:

1. It gathers the methodologic experience of diverse authors, since this experience is usually absent in most of the standards.
2. The range of application of the proposal is wider than that of one of a single standard or technique seen in subsection 3.1, because this work covers from requirements specification to the implementation patterns applied in architectural design.
3. Lastly, a case study of a real application has been presented, where the safety requirements were naturally present from the beginning of the proyect, not added later.

From the work on safety requirements for the crane robot two important conclusions can be extracted: (1) only half of the safety requirements really affect the software architecture of the system and (2) only a few fraction of them require the use of external redundant control that must conform to the strictest level of safety. Nevertheless, since security requirements are, conceptually, independent of the functional ones, it would be more than desirable to have an architectural approach that allows this conceptual separation of concerns could be used by the designer. This is the line of work we are currently working on in the context of the research project DYNAMICA with the Universidad Politécnica de Valencia (Spain) and its ADL, PRISMA. It's also necessary to have a proper methodology to extract the safety requirements from the tables of risks and hazards and to have tools to catalogue them and to track their use and ease their reuse in another products of the same family, which is the aim of that project also shared with the University of Murcia in Spain.

References

1. P. Neumann. *Computer-Related Risks*. Addison-Wesley Professional, October 1994. ISBN: 0-201-55805-X.
2. C. Fernández, A. Iborra, B. Álvarez, J.A. Pastor, P. Sánchez, J.M. Fernández, and N. Ortega. Co-operative Robots for Hull Blasting in European Shiprepair Industry. November 2004. ISSN: 1070-9932.
3. EFTCoR Official Site. http://www.eftcor.com/.
4. ANSI/RIA R15.06: american national standard for industrial robots and robot systems safety requirements. Robotic Industries Association, 1999.
5. Bruce Powel Douglass. *Doing hard time: developing real-time systems with UML, objects, frameworks and patterns*. Object Technology. Addison-Wesley Longman Publishing Co., Inc., 1999. ISBN: 0-201-49837-5.
6. Nancy Leveson. *Safeware: system safety and computers*. ACM Press, New York, NY, USA, 1995. ISBN: 0-201-11972-2.
7. EN 61508: functional safety of electrical/electronic/programmable electronic safety-related systems. European Committee for Electrotechnical Standardization, 2003.
8. K. Hansen, A. Ravn, and V. Stavridou. From safety analysis to software requirements. 24(7):573–584, July 1998.

Towards Developing Multi-agent Systems in Ada⋆

G. Aranda, J. Palanca, A. Espinosa, A. Terrasa, and A. García-Fornes

Information Systems and Computation Dept.
Technical University of Valencia, Spain
{garanda, jpalanca, aespinos, aterrasa, agarcia}@dsic.upv.es

Abstract. Agent-oriented technology is a rising paradigm for developing quality software in complex domains. Currently, no Ada interface or middleware
exist for the development of agent-based applications. In this paper, an Ada binding for developing agent and multi-agent-based applications in Ada is proposed.
This binding is compatible with an existing open-source agent platform named
SPADE.

1 Introduction

Agent-based systems are one of the most active areas of research and development in
information technology. Many researchers believe that agents represent the most important new paradigm for software development since object orientation. The concept
of agent introduces a high level of abstraction, which is appropriate to the development
of complex computational systems, especially in open and dynamic environments.

As shown in [1], software agents are generally presented as computational entities
with a human behavior. They run on regular computers (i.e. PCs, PDAs, mobile phones,
etc.) and in network nodes. They are autonomous and are able to take decisions for
themselves, to reason, to learn, to communicate with other agents, to organize themselves, and to move from one node to another. They use their capacities to solve problems in an intelligent, pro-active and helpful way for the user. An agent can do this in a
collaborative way (cooperating with other agents) or by itself.

In this context, one of the most important topics to be considered is the development
of technologies that provide infrastructures and supporting tools for agent systems, such
as agent programming languages and software engineering methodologies. As stated
in [2], "any infrastructure deployed to support the execution of agent applications must
be long-lived and robust. More generally, middleware, or platforms for agent interoperability, as well as standards, will be crucial for the medium-term development of agent
systems".

Over the last few years, several initiatives have appeared for the definition and standardization of agent technologies, such as KQML [3], OMG [4] or, more recently, the
Agentcities Project [5]. Among these, one of the best known is FIPA (Foundation for
Intelligent Physical Agents) [6] . This foundation has proposed some important aspects
for agent communication, like platform interoperability or message transport protocols.

⋆ This work is partially supported by the TIC2003-07369-C02-01 and TIN2005-03395 projects
of the spanish government.

L.M. Pinho and M. González Harbour (Eds.): Ada-Europe 2006, LNCS 4006, pp. 131–142, 2006.

However, there is still a lack of maturity both in methodologies and programming tools. Current tools work well in straightforward situations with few agents; but, in general, they do not address the development of large-scale, efficient agent systems. These tools do not offer facilities for monitoring or tuning the behavior of such complex systems. In addition, languages for high-level programming of multi-agent systems are also needed. These languages should be expressive, easy-to-use, and efficient, in order to coordinate large, open, scalable, dynamic and heterogeneous systems.

Agent technology displays very interesting features and new approaches to solve problems. But in practice, the agent community has limited itself to the use of very few computer technologies. Nearly all the relevant agent-based products and developments are done in the Java programming language. Moreover, these products generally operate in a way that only agents programmed in Java are compatible with them.

In order to contribute to cover part of this gap, we have developed SPADE [7]. SPADE (Smart Python multi-Agent Development Environment) is a fully FIPA compliant agent platform. Its main objective is to provide good performance while retaining strong scalability options and to provide an open design that allows the implementation of platform components and agents in several high-level programming languages.

The work presented in this paper is to provide the means to allow the development of SPADE agents with Ada, and to propose the necessary middleware to do so. This middleware allows the Ada and agent technologies to be integrated with each other, effectively combining the advantages of both. On the one hand, the development of agents can benefit from the use of Ada in cases when safety, reliability or real-time features are needed. On the other hand, Ada engineers can benefit from the higher level of abstraction of the agent-based technology. For example, in cases when high-level communication protocols enabling complex interactions are useful; or when abstractions more complex than the inheritance are needed; or when developing heterogeneous systems which require the integration of different technologies (such as databases, web applications, software components, etc.).

The rest of the paper is structured as follows. In Section 2, a review of the SPADE agent platform is done. Later, in Section 3, a programming interface to develop agents for the SPADE agent platform with the Ada programming language is introduced. Finally, conclusions and future work lines are presented.

2 SPADE

SPADE is a multi-agent platform which provides a new framework to build agents using a communication model different from other platforms. This platform provides a simple interface for the agent development using the above-mentioned communication model. Thanks to this interface, agents can be built in any programming language with total independence of the SPADE platform.

As every component inside the SPADE platform has been developed as an agent, this communication model is also used to communicate the internal elements of the platform.

In addition, SPADE has a special agent to provide a user-friendly view of the platform. This GUI agent provides a mechanism to load and unload agents in the platform.

It allows the user to search for agents and services and to send messages to any agent. This feature can be used as a *dummy* agent to send simple messages to other agents and to show their answers.

The basic SPADE components have been developed using the Python programming language. It is a versatile interpreted language that runs on several architectures and operating systems, although it has a poorer performance than compiled languages like Ada or C. In particular, being implemented in Python allows the platform to be executed in systems such as Windows, Linux, MacOS, Windows Mobile, PalmOS, SymbianOS (for mobile phones), etc.

The core of the communication layer of the platform is a standard, well-known protocol called Jabber[8], which provides virtual channels to put in contact conversational entities, like agents.

The most popular application of the Jabber protocol is a social communication network with similar functionalities to the ones present in legacy systems like AIM, ICQ, MSN or Yahoo Messenger. These networks allow for the interconnection of known users by means of trust networks, and are tested and used by thousands of users simultaneously every day.

The Jabber protocol uses a distributed client-server topology. The servers that route the Jabber messages are designed to support a very large number of users and messages. This feature helps to improve the SPADE performance and scalability.

The interface between the SPADE platform and its agents is purely Jabber-based (in fact, TCP/IP-based at its lowest level). Therefore, SPADE agents can be implemented with any framework that supports Jabber communications and with any programming language capable of dealing with Jabber and/or TCP/IP communications. To ease the development of SPADE agents, we provide the necessary code-base to develop agents in the Ada and Python programming languages. Besides using the Jabber protocol, SPADE also supports the HTTP protocol, which is used in other agent platforms. The following sections introduce the different models that compose SPADE.

2.1 The Platform Model

The SPADE platform is modeled according to the FIPA standard proposal for a multi-agent platform [6]. It features the standard basic FIPA services (such as an Agent Management System and a Directory Facilitator), which have been designed as Jabber server components (or add-ins).

Although the core communication system relies on the Jabber technology, other legacy message transport protocols, such as the *HTTP* protocol, are also supported.

Platform Elements. In this section, the elements that make up the SPADE platform are described.

- The **XML Router** is the main platform element, the one that the rest of the platform components and agents are connected to. It is a standard XMPP server[8] that routes all the messages from its sender to the specified receiver without having the user to intervene. This XML Router acts as the Message Transport System (MTS) and it is the only external component of the platform that has been reused. It has been chosen for its flexibility: this component can be replaced with no re-writing of any other component, so the developer is free to replace it with any other XML Router of choice.

– One of the components connected to the router is the **SPADE Agent Communication Channel** (ACC). It manages all the communication within the platform and receives the FIPA-ACL[1][9] messages that arrive to the platform. After arrival, it redirects the messages to the correct destination element. This destination can be either an agent or another component. Should the receiver element is an agent, the MTS would relay the message to the agent and it would be held in the agent's message queue for later processing.

– A default **Message Transport Protocol** (MTP) is built within the platform. In addition to internally connecting the platform elements, the XML Router is the element that connects the platform to outside entities (like other platforms or even human-agent communications).

– The **Agent Management System** is the component that implements the basic management services for the agents. The AMS agent complies with the entire *'fipa-agent-management'* ontology.

– The **Directory Facilitator** is a component that provides a *service* directory to register and query services offered by the agents that are registered at the platform. The DF agent also complies with the fully *'fipa-agent-management'* ontology.

A brief schematic view of the SPADE Platform can be seen in Figure 1.

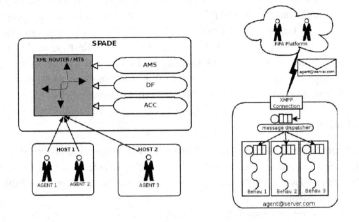

Fig. 1. SPADE Platform and Agent Models

There is a graphical block that represents the MTS (using the Jabber protocol) which handles all the received messages and redirects them to their actual receivers. A receiver can be an agent, a platform component, or even a human user. Moreover, control information (*iq* queries) and routing information are managed by the MTS. The ACC, AMS and DF elements are plugged into to the platform as modular components. Besides, all of them are built as agents, so they have the full functionality provided by a standard

---

[1] FIPA Agent Communication Language.

SPADE agent. As it can be seen in the figure, agents are also connected to the MTS, which virtually connects them with the SPADE Platform.

2.2   The Agent Model

As mentioned above, every component inside a SPADE platform is built as an agent. SPADE agents are elements connected to the MTS that can send messages to each other and to other platforms (or even to human users).

The Agent Model of SPADE is basically composed of a connection module to the platform, a message dispatcher, and a group of different behaviors that the dispatcher gives the messages to (–see Figure 1). Every SPADE agent needs an identifier called *Jabber ID* (JID) and a correct password to make a connection with the platform. Should the default platform registration process be disabled, the platform administrator would have to define alternate registration policies.

The *JID* is composed by a **username**, an '@', and a **server domain**. It will be the internal name that identifies an agent in the platform. The agent virtual address (which is another important field on the Agent Identifier) would be the JID of the platform's ACC (i.e: xmpp://acc.gti-ia.dsic.upv.es). The prefix xmpp:// has been defined for the XMPP addresses.

A **behavior** is a task that an agent can execute using scheduling patterns. A SPADE agent can run several behaviors simultaneously. SPADE provides some predefined behavior types: Cyclic, One-Shot, Periodic, Time-Out, and Finite State Machine Behavior. These behavior types help the implementation of the different tasks that a SPADE agent can perform:

A behavior has a message template associated to it. The message dispatcher uses this template to know which types of messages a behavior must receive: it compares every arriving message with the templates of the behaviors.

Every SPADE agent can have as many behaviors as wanted. When a message arrives to a SPADE agent, the message dispatcher forwards it to the message queues of the adequate behaviors (–see Figure 1).

3   Ada Application Programming Interface

As stated above, SPADE agents can be developed by default using Python (like the core platform components). Now, we introduce the possibility of developing SPADE agents in Ada. In this section, the programming API for creating a SPADE agent with Ada is presented.

The structure of the application interface is shown in Figure 2. There are 8 packages included in a main package called Spade.

3.1   Package Spade

Spade is the main package that contains the rest of the application interface packages. It also includes some basic Ada types to help in common operations (like String lists).

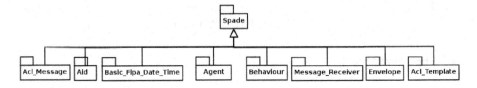

Fig. 2. SPADE Package Structure

3.2 Package `Spade.Aids`

This package provides the interface to build Agent Identifiers (called *AID*). An Agent Identifier is a record composed by the name of the agent, its addresses (an agent can have more than one address). The interface provides an Ada type called Aid and some Set_ and Get_ procedures to manipulate Agent Identifiers.

```
package Spade.Aids is

type Aid is private;

function   Get_Name      ( From: Aid ) return Aid_Name;
function   Get_Addresses ( From: Aid ) return List_Addresses;
function   Get_Resolvers ( From: Aid ) return List_Resolvers;
procedure Set_Name       ( To   : in out Aid; Name:      in Aid_Name );
procedure Add_Address    ( To   : in out Aid; Address:   in Address  );
procedure Add_Resolver   ( To   : in out Aid; Resolver: in Resolver );    10
...

end Spade.Aids;
```

3.3 Package `Spade.Basic_Fipa_Date_Times`

This package provides a help class to manage dates and times in the FIPA standard format. This format is a string composed by the year, the month, the day, a separator, the hour, minutes, seconds and milliseconds with 3 digits (e.g. 20051103T234521343). An example of the API is as follows.

```
package Spade.Basic_Fipa_Date_Times is

type Basic_Fipa_Date_Time is tagged private;

function Get_Day            ( From: Basic_Fipa_Date_Time ) return Day;
function Get_Milliseconds   ( From: Basic_Fipa_Date_Time ) return Milliseconds;
procedure Set_Day           ( To: in out Basic_Fipa_Date_Time; Day: in Day );
procedure Set_Milliseconds ( To: in out Basic_Fipa_Date_Time; Milli: in Milliseconds );
procedure From_String       ( To: in out Basic_Fipa_Date_Time; String_Date : in String );
function To_String          (From: Basic_Fipa_Date_Time ) return String;    10
...

end Spade.Basic_Fipa_Date_Times;
```

3.4   Package Spade.Envelopes

A FIPA Message is a structure that contains a *Payload* and an *Envelope*. The payload has the content of the message and some meta-information. This payload can be in some different languages (like ACL). The envelope contains the routing information for the message like the receiver, the sender, the encoding, the date, etc.

A brief example of some of the interface methods is now shown:

```
package Spade.Envelopes is

     type Envelope is tagged private;

     function   Get_To        ( From: Envelope ) return List_Aid;
     function   Get_From       ( From: Envelope ) return Aid;
     function   Get_Comments ( From: Envelope ) return String;
     procedure Set_Payload_Length        ( To: in out Envelope; Len : in Length );
     ...
end Spade.Envelopes;                                                    10
```

3.5   Package Spade.Acl_Messages

The package Acl_Messages contains the Ada type `Acl_Message`, used to build the payload of a FIPA Message. This payload has the content of the message and some meta-information like the language and ontology of the content, or the *performative*.

```
package Spade.Acl_Messages is

     type Acl_Message is tagged private;

     function   Get_Conversation_Id ( From: Acl_Message ) return Id;
     procedure Set_Language ( To: in out Acl_Message; Lang: in Language );
     procedure Set_Ontology ( To: in out Acl_Message; Onto: in Ontology );
     -- Creates a reply of the message
     function   Create_Reply ( From: Acl_Message ) return Acl_Message;
     ...                                                                10
end Spade.Acl_Messages;
```

Once Envelopes and Acl_Messages packages are viewed, it is possible to build a FIPA Message, which is the basic communicative structure used by agents. Sending messages of this kind between FIPA compliant agents (like SPADE agents) ensures the success of a communicative act.

3.6   Package `Spade.Message_Receivers`

This package provides the Message_Receiver type. Objects of this type are entities capable of sending and receiving messages. This tagged type is extended by other packages (like agent or behavior) that will be introduced later.

---

package Spade.Message_Receivers **is**

    type Message_Receiver **is tagged private**;

    function Is_Alive (Who   : Message_Receiver Class) **return** Boolean;
    function Receive   (From : Message_Receiver Class) **return** Acl_Message;
    function Blocking_Receive (From : Message_Receiver Class;
                             Time_Out: Time) **return** Acl_Message;

    . . .

end Spade.Message_Receivers;   10

The *Receive* and *Blocking_Receive* functions return an Acl_Message when a message arrives to a Message_Receiver. If there is no message in the *inbox*, it returns an empty Acl_Message. The function *Blocking_Receive* also accepts a Time_Out parameter. This parameter indicates the time (in seconds) that the function will wait for a message (it can also be *forever*).

3.7   Package `Spade.Behaviors`

Agents are entities composed of SPADE's *'behaviors'*. These behaviors are supposed to provide the intelligence to the agent. Programmers must implement these behaviors and add them to the agent to compose the *brain* that controls the agent.

The package `Spade.Behaviors` contains the five behaviors currently supported by SPADE:

- **Behavior:** This is the Cyclic Behavior type. Its code is executed continuously.
- **Periodic_Behavior:** The Periodic Behavior type runs every user-defined 'period'.
- **One_Shot_Behavior:** One Shot Behavior type. Runs only one time.
- **Time_Out_Behavior:** The Time Out Behavior type is a Periodic Behavior with a 'timeout'. It is executed every period with a time lag (the timeout).
- **FSM_Behavior:** Finite State Machine (FSM) Behavior type. It runs different behaviors according to a defined FSM. The nodes of the FSM are behavior types (which can be any kind of behavior: cyclic, one shot or even another FSM). The transitions between nodes are called events. Each of these events has a value which is the exit codes of a behavior node.

Figure 3 shows the Types Hierarchy. Some of the presented classes are simply support classes with access methods to manage FIPA information structures. However, more interesting Ada types (such as the hierarchy of 'Behavior' types) provide a full interface to create software agents with a simple middleware. The next block is an example of the behavior interface.

```ada
package Spade.Behaviors is

        type Behavior is new Message_Receiver with private;
        function Exit_Code ( From: Behavior Class ) return Integer;
        --Executed when the behavior finishes
        procedure On_End ( From: in out Behavior Class );
        --Executed when the behavior starts
        procedure On_Start ( From: in out Behavior Class );
        --Executed when the behavior is running
        procedure Process ( From: in out Behavior Class );               10

        type Periodic_Behavior is new Behavior with private;
        function   Get_Period ( From: Periodic_Behavior ) return Time;
        procedure Set_Period ( To: in out Periodic_Behavior; Period: in Time );
        procedure On_Tick ( From: in out Periodic_Behavior );

        type Time_Out_Behavior is new Periodic_Behavior with private;
        function   Get_Time_Out ( From: Time_Out_Behavior) return Time;
        procedure Set_Time_Out ( To: in out Time_Out_Behavior; Time_Out: in Time);
                                                                          20
        type One_Shot_Behavior is new Behavior with private;

        type FSM_Behavior is new Behavior with private;
        procedure Register_First_State (From: in out FSM_Behavior;
                                        State: in Behavior Class;
                                        Name: in String);
        procedure Register_Last_State   (From: in out FSM_Behavior;
                                        State: in Behavior Class;
                                        Name: in String);
        procedure Register_State        (From: in out FSM_Behavior;      30
                                        State: in Behavior Class;
                                        Name: in String);
        procedure Register_Transition   (From: in out FSM_Behavior;
                                        From_Node: in String;
                                        To_Node: in String;
                                        Event: in Integer);
        . . .
end Spade.Behaviors;
```

Examples of use of such behavior interface range from simple to really complex agents. For instance, agents mostly reactive that perform quick responses to environment changes can be developed using a reduced number of behaviors executed in a cyclical scheme with a short period. On the contrary, agents displaying a sophisticated and deliberative (intelligent) functionality can be implemented by using a higher number of behaviors of more complex types, like finite state machines.

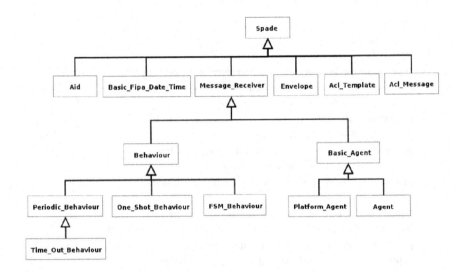

Fig. 3. SPADE Class Hierarchy

A behavior executes the code defined in the procedure `Process`. In addition, procedures `On_Start` and `On_End` are run when a behavior is created and finishes (or it is killed), respectively.

3.8   Package `Spade.Acl_Templates`

A behavior can be configured to receive only the messages that match with a defined template. When a message arrives to an agent, the message dispatcher of the agent puts the received message in the *inbox* of the behaviors which template matches. If there is no match, the message is sent to a default behavior (defined with the `Behaviors.Set_Default_Behavior` procedure).

The interface is very similar to the `Acl_Messages` package.

---

package Spade.Acl_Templates **is**

      type Acl_Template **is tagged private**;
      function Get_Sender(From: Acl_Template) **return** Aid;
      function Get_Conversation_Id(From: Acl_Template) **return** Id;
      procedure Set_Performative(To: **in out** Acl_Template; Perf: **in** Performative);

      . . .
end Spade.Acl_Templates;

The procedure `Behavior.Add_Template` is used to add a template to a behavior.

3.9   Package `Spade.Agents`

Finally, the agent interface is now introduced. There is a basic type called Basic_Agent from which the two agent types are inherited. There is a Platform_Agent type for internal purposes (like component agents: AMS, DF, etc.) and a simple Agent type, used to develop user agents. This hierarchy can also be viewed in Figure 3. The interface is now shown:

```
package Spade.Agents is
        type Basic_Agent is new Message_Receiver with private;

        function Get_Aid(From: Basic_Agent Class) return Aid;
        procedure Start (What: in out Basic_Agent Class);
        procedure Take_Down (What: in out Basic_Agent Class);
        procedure Setup (What: in out Basic_Agent Class);
        procedure Kill (What: in out Basic_Agent Class);
        procedure Add_Behavior (To: in out Basic_Agent Class;
                                Behav: in Behavior Class;                    10
                                Template: in Acl_Template);

        function Search_Agent (From: Basic_Agent Class;
                               Template: Ams_Agent_Description)
                               return List_Ams_Agent_Description;
        procedure Register_Service (From: in Basic_Agent Class;
                                    Service: in Df_Agent_Description);
        procedure Send_Message (From: in out Basic_Agent Class;
                                Env: in Envelope;
                                Message: in Acl_Message);                     20

        type Agent is new Basic_Agent with private;
        type Platform_Agent is new Basic_Agent with private;
        ...
end Spade.Agents;
```

Finally, the following code contains an example of use of this interface. The example creates an agent and two behaviors that are included into the agent Then it is started.

```
An_Agent: Agent;
Behavior_One: Periodic_Behavior;
Behavior_Two: One_Shot_Behavior;
A_Template: Acl_Template;

Set_Default_Behavior (To => An_Agent, Behav => Behavior_One);
Add_Template (To => Behavior_Two, Template => A_Template);
Add_Behavior (To => An_Agent, Behav => Behavior_Two);

Start (What => An_Agent);                                                     10
```

4   Conclusions and Future Work

A middleware that allows the development of intelligent agents using Ada has been developed. This middleware focuses on creating Ada agents that are compatible with the

SPADE agent platform. The middleware's API is object-oriented, which is a paradigm fully supported under Ada.

This middleware opens the possibility of creating agents in Ada, which is a very interesting topic since it allows bringing the advantages of Ada to the agent realm and vice-versa. Robust and stable agents can be created due to Ada's proved robustness. In scenarios where performance is a key element, Ada can show its celerity against interpreted languages (like Python) or Virtual Machine-based ones (like Java). Moreover, due to Ada's fitting in the real-time domain, the possibility of developing real-time SPADE agents with Ada is now opened.

In the future, we intend to study the behavior of this software solution, from both the efficiency and the scalability points of view. Our intention is to perform tests to compare the performance of agents built using this middleware against SPADE agents implemented in other programming languages, and also against agents developed in different agent platforms.

References

1. Mas, A.: Agentes software y sistemas multiagente. Pearson Educacion (2005)
2. Luck, M., McBurney, P., Shehory, O., Willmott, S.: Agent Technology Roadmap. A Roadmap for Agent Based Computing. AgentLink III (2005)
3. Finin, T., Fritzson, R., McKay, D., McEntire, R.: KQML as an Agent Communication Language. In Adam, N., Bhargava, B., Yesha, Y., eds.: Proceedings of the 3rd International Conference on Information and Knowledge Management (CIKM'94), Gaithersburg, MD, USA, ACM Press (1994) 456–463
4. Object Management Group: OMG: Object Services - Request for Information. RfI 91.11.6 (1991)
5. AgentCities Homepage. http://www.agentcities.org/ (2005)
6. FIPA Abstract architecture specification. Technical Report SC00001L (2002)
7. Smart python multi-agent development environment. http://magentix.gti-ia-dsic.upv.es (2005)
8. Jabber Software Foundation: Extensible Messaging and Presence Protocol (XMPP): Core. Technical report, http://www.ietf.org/rfc/rfc3920.txt (2004)
9. FIPA: Agent ACL message structure specification. Technical Report XC00061E (2001)

A Software Reliability Model Based on a Geometric Sequence of Failure Rates*

Stefan Wagner[1] and Helmut Fischer[2]

[1] Institut für Informatik
Technische Universität München
Boltzmannstr. 3, 85748 Garching b. München, Germany
[2] Siemens AG
COM E QPP PSO
Hofmannstr. 51, 81379 München, Germany

Abstract. Software reliability models are an important tool in quality management and release planning. There is a large number of different models that often exhibit strengths in different areas. This paper proposes a model that is based on a geometric sequence (or progression) of the failure rates of faults. This property of the failure process was observed in practice at Siemens among others and led to the development of the proposed model. It is described in detail and evaluated using standard criteria. Most importantly, the model performs constantly well over several projects in terms of its predictive validity.

1   Introduction

Software reliability engineering is an established area of software engineering research and practice that is concerned with the improvement and measurement of reliability. For the analysis typically stochastic software reliability models are used. They model the failure process of the software and use other software metrics or failure data as a basis for parameter estimation. The models are able (1) to estimate the current reliability and (2) to predict future failure behaviour.

There are already several established models. The most important ones has been classified by Miller as exponential order statistic (EOS) models in [5]. He divided the models on the highest level into deterministic and doubly stochastic EOS models arguing that the failure rates either have a deterministic relationship or are again randomly distributed. For the deterministic models, Miller presented several interesting special cases. The well-known Jelinski-Moranda model [3], for example, has *constant rates*. He also stated that *geometric rates* are possible as documented by Nagel [9, 8].

This geometric sequence (or progression) between failure rates of faults was also observed in projects of the communication networks department of the Siemens AG. In several older projects which were analysed, this relationship fitted well to the data. Therefore, a software reliability model based on a geometric sequence of failure rates is proposed.

---

* This research was partially supported by the DFG in the project *InTime*.

L.M. Pinho and M. González Harbour (Eds.): Ada-Europe 2006, LNCS 4006, pp. 143–154, 2006.

Problem. The problem which software reliability engineering still faces is the need for accurate models for different environments and projects. Detailed models with a geometric sequence of failure rates have to our knowledge not been proposed so far.

Contribution. We describe a detailed and practical software reliability model that was motivated out of practical experience and contains a geometric sequence of failure rates which was also suggested by theoretical results. A detailed comparison shows that this model has a constantly good performance over several projects, although other models perform better in specific projects. Hence, we validated the general assumption that a geometric sequence of failure rates is a reasonable model for software.

Outline. We first describe important aspects of the model in Sec. 2. In Sec. 3 the model is evaluated using several defined criteria, most importantly its predictive validity in comparison with established models. We offer final conclusions in Sec. 4. Related work is cited where appropriate.

2   Model Description

The core of the proposed model is a geometric sequence for the failure rates of the faults. This section describes this and other assumptions in more detail, introduces the main equations and the time component of the model and gives an example of how the parameters of the model can be estimated.

2.1   Assumptions

The main theory behind this model is the ordering of the faults that are present in the software based on their failure rates. The term failure rate describes in this context the probability that an existing fault will result in an erroneous behaviour of the system during a defined time slot or while executing an average operation. In essence, we assign each fault a time-dependent probability of failure and combine those probabilities to the total failure intensity. The ordering implies that the fault with the highest probability of triggering a failure comes first, then the fault with the second highest probability and so on. The probabilities are then arranged on a logarithmic scale to attain an uniform distribution of the points on the x-axis. The underlying assumption being that there are numerous faults with low failure rates and only a small number of faults with high failure rates. In principle, we assume an infinite number of faults because of imperfect debugging and updates.

As mentioned above, the logarithmic scale distributes the data points in approximately the same distance from each other. Therefore, this distance is approximated by a constant factor between the probabilities. Then we can use the following geometric sequence (or progression) for the calculation of the failure rates:

$$p_n = p_1 \cdot d^{(n-1)}, \tag{1}$$

where p_n is the failure rate of the n-th fault, p_1 the failure rate of the first fault, and d is a project-specific parameter. It is assumed that d is an indicator for the complexity of a system that may be related to the number of different branches in a program. In past projects of Siemens d was calculated to be between 0.92 and 0.96. The parameter d is multiplied and not added because the distance is only constant on a logarithmic scale.

The failure occurrence of a fault is assumed to be geometrically distributed. Therefore, the probability that a specific fault occurred by time t is the following:

$$P(T_a \leq t) = F_a(t) = 1 - (1 - p_a)^t. \tag{2}$$

We denote with T_a the random variable of the failure time of the fault a.

In summary, the model can be described as the sum of an infinite number of geometrically distributed random variables with different parameters which in turn are described by a geometric sequence.

2.2 Equations

The two equations that are typically used to describe a software reliability model are the mean number of failures $\mu(t)$ and the failure intensity $\lambda(t)$. The mean value function needs to consider the expected value over the indicator functions of the faults:

$$\begin{aligned}
\mu(t) &= E(N(t)) \\
&= E\left(\sum_{i=a}^{\infty} I_{[0,t]}(X_a)\right) \\
&= \sum_{a=1}^{\infty} E(I_{[0,t]}(X_a)) \\
&= \sum_{a=1}^{\infty} P(X_a \leq t) \\
&= \sum_{a=1}^{\infty} 1 - (1 - p_a)^t.
\end{aligned} \tag{3}$$

This gives us a typical distribution as depicted in Fig. 1. Note that the distribution is actually discrete which is not explicitly shown because of the high values used on the x-axis.

We cannot differentiate the mean value equation directly to get the failure intensity. However, we can use the probability density function (pdf) of the geometric distribution to derive this equation. The pdf of a single fault is

$$f(t) = p_a(1 - p_a)^{t-1}. \tag{4}$$

Therefore, to get the number of failures that occur at a certain point in time t, we have to sum up the pdf's of all the faults:

$$\lambda(t) = \sum_{a=1}^{\infty} p_a(1 - p_a)^{t-1}. \tag{5}$$

An interesting quantity is typically the time that is needed to reach a certain reliability level. Based on the failure intensity objective that is anticipated for the release, this can be derived using the equation for the failure intensity. Rearranging Eq. 4 gives:

$$t = \frac{\ln \lambda}{\sum_{a=1}^{\infty} p_a - p_a^2} + 1. \tag{6}$$

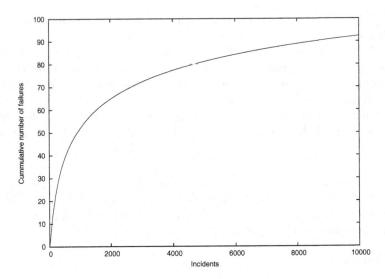

Fig. 1. A typical distribution of the model

What we need, however, is the further required time Δt to determine the necessary length of the test or field trial. We denote the failure intensity objective λ_F and use the following equation to determine Δt:

$$\Delta t = t_F - t = \frac{\ln \lambda_F - \ln \lambda}{\sum_{a=1}^{\infty} p_a - p_a^2} \tag{7}$$

Finally, the result needs to be converted into calendar time to be able to give a date for the end of the test or field trial.

2.3 Time Component

In the proposed model time is measured in incidents, each representing a usage task of the system. To convert these incidents into calendar time it is necessary to introduce an explicit time component. This contains explicit means to convert from one time format into another.

There are several possibilities to handle time in reliability models. The preferable is to use execution time directly. This, however, is often not possible. Subsequently, a suitable substitute must be found. With respect to testing this could be the number of test cases, for the field use the number of clients and so forth. Fig. 2 shows the relationships between different possible time types.

The first possibility is to use in-service time as a substitute. This requires knowledge of the number of users and the average usage time per user. Then the question arises how this relates to the test cases in system testing. A first approximation is the average duration of a test case. The number of incidents is, opposed to the in-service time, a more task-oriented way to measure time. The main advantage of using incidents, apart from the fact that they are already in use at Siemens, is that in this way, we can obtain very intuitive metrics,

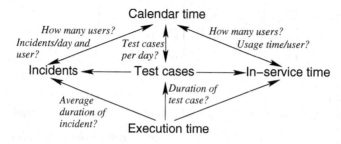

Fig. 2. The possible relationships between different types of time

e.g., the average number of failures per incident. There are usually some estimations of the number of incidents per client and data about the number of sold client licenses.

However, the question of the relation to test cases is also open. A first cut would be to assume a test case is equal to an incident. A test case, however, has more "time value" than one incident because it is generally directed testing, i.e., cases with a high probability of failure are preferred. In addition, a test case is usually unique in function or parameter set while the normal use of a product often consists of similar actions. When we do not follow the operational profile this should be accounted for. A possible extension of the model is proposed in [12] but needs further investigation.

2.4 Parameter Estimation

There are two techniques for parameter determination currently in use. The first is prediction based on data from similar projects. This is useful for planing purposes before failure data is available.

However, estimations should also be made during test, field trial, and operation based on the sample data available so far. This is the approach most reliability models use and it is also statistically most advisable since the sample data comes from the population we actually want to analyse. Techniques such as Maximum Likelihood estimation or Least Squares estimation are used to fit the model to the actual data.

Maximum Likelihood. The Maximum Likelihood method essentially uses a likelihood function that describes the probability of a certain number of failures occurring up to a certain time. This function is filled with sample data and then optimised to find the parameters with the maximum likelihood.

The problem with this is that the likelihood function of this model gets extremely complicated. Essentially, we have an infinite number of random variables that are geometrically distributed, but all with different parameter p. Even if we constrain ourselves to a high number N of variables under consideration it still results in a sum of $\binom{N}{x}$ different products. This requires to sum up every possible permutation in which x failures have occurred up to time t. The number of possibilities is $\binom{N}{x}$. Each summand is a product of a permutation in which different faults resulted in failures.

$$L(p_1, d) = \prod_{i=1}^{x} 1 - (1 - p_i)^t \cdot \prod_{i=x+1}^{N} (1 - p_i)^t +$$
$$\prod_{i=2}^{x+1} 1 - (1 - p_i)^t \cdot \prod_{i=x+2}^{N} (1 - p_i)^t \cdot (1 - p_1)^t +$$
$$\prod_{i=3}^{x+2} 1 - (1 - p_i)^t \cdot \prod_{i=x+3}^{N} (1 - p_i)^t \cdot \prod_{i=1}^{2} (1 - p_1)^t + \tag{8}$$
$$\dots ,$$

where $p_i = p_1 d^{i-1}$.

An efficient method to maximise this function has not been found.

Least Squares. For the Least Squares method an estimate of the failure intensity is used and the relative error to the estimated failure intensity from the model is minimised. We use the estimate of the mean number of failures for this because it is the original part of the model. Therefore, the square function to be minimised in our case can be written as follows:

$$S(p_1, d) = \sum_{j=1}^{m} [\ln r_j - \ln \mu(t_j; p_1, d)]^2, \tag{9}$$

where m is the number of measurement points, r_j is the measured value for the cumulated failures, and t_j is the time at measurement j.

This function is minimised using the simplex variant of Nelder and Mead [10]. We found this method to be usable for our purpose.

3   Evaluation

We describe several criteria that are used to assess the proposed model.

3.1   Criteria

The criteria that we use for the evaluation of the Fischer-Wagner model are derived from Musa et al. [6]. We assess according to five criteria, four of which can mainly be applied theoretically, whereas one criterion is based on practical applications of the models on real data. The first criterion is the *capability* of the model. It describes whether the model is able to yield important quantities. The criterion *quality of assumptions* is used to assess the plausibility of the assumptions behind the model. The cases in which the model can be used are evaluated with the criterion *applicability*. Furthermore, *simplicity* is an important aspect for the understandability of the model. Finally, the *predictive validity* is assessed by applying the model to real failure data and comparing the deviation.

3.2   Capability

The main purpose of a reliability model is to aid managers and engineers in planning and managing software projects by estimating useful quantities about the software reliability and the reliability growth. Following [6] such quantities, in approximate order of importance, are

1. current reliability,
2. expected date of reaching a specified reliability,
3. human and computer resource and cost requirements related to the achievement of the objective.

Furthermore, it is a valuable part of a reliability model if it can predict quantities early in the development based on software metrics and/or historical project data.

The model yields the current reliability as current failure intensity and mean number of failures. It is also able to give predictions based on parameters from historical data. Furthermore, the expected date of reaching a specified reliability can be calculated. Human and computer resources are not explicitly incorporated. There is an explicit concept of time but, it is not as sophisticated as, for example, in the Musa-Okumoto model [7].

3.3   Quality of Assumptions

As far as possible, each assumption should be tested by real data. At least it should be possible to argue for the plausibility of the assumption based on theoretical knowledge and experience. Also the clarity and explicitness of the assumptions are important.

The main assumption in the proposed model is that the failure rates of the faults follow a geometric sequence. The intuition is that there are many faults with low failure rates and only a small number of faults with high failure rates. This is in accordance with software engineering experience and supported by [1]. Moreover, the geometric sequence as relationship between different faults has been documented in a NASA study [9, 8].

Furthermore, an assumption is that the occurrence of a failure is geometrically distributed. The geometric distribution fits because it can describe independent events. We do not consider continuous time but discrete incidents.

Finally, the infinite number of faults makes sense when considering imperfect debugging, i.e., fault removal can introduce new faults or the old faults are not completely removed.

3.4   Applicability

It is important for a general reliability model to be applicable to software products in different domains and of different size. Also varying project environments or life cycle phases should be feasible. There are four special situations identified in [6] that should be possible to handle.

1. Software evolution
2. Classification of severity of failures into different categories
3. Ability to handle incomplete failure data with measurement uncertainties
4. Operation of the same program on computers of different performance

All real applications of the proposed model have been in the telecommunications area. However, it was used for software of various sizes and complexities. Moreover, during the evaluation of the predictive validity we applied it also to other domains (see Sec. 3.6). In principle, the model can be used before and during the field trial. Software evolution is hence not explicitly incorporated. A classification of failures is possible but has not been used so far. Moreover, the performance of computers is not a strong issue in this domain.

3.5 Simplicity

A model should be simple enough to be usable in real project environments: it has to be simple to collect the necessary data, easy to understand the concepts and assumptions, and the model should be implementable in a tool.

While the concepts themselves are not difficult to understand, the model in total is rather complicated because it not only involves failures but also faults. Furthermore, for all these faults the failure is geometrically distributed but each with a different probability.

A main criticism is also that the assumed infinite number of faults make the model difficult to handle. In practical applications of the model and when building a tool, an upper bound of the number of faults must be introduced to be able to calculate model values. This actually introduces a third model parameter in some sense.

The two parameters, however, can be interpreted as direct measures of the software. The parameter p_1 is the failure probability of the most probable fault and d can be seen as a measure of system complexity.

3.6 Predictive Validity

The most important and "hardest" criterion for the evaluation of a reliability model is its predictive validity. A model has to be a faithful abstraction of the real failure process of the software and give valid estimations and predictions of the reliability. For this we follow again [6] and use the *number of failures approach*.

Approach. We assume that there have been q failures observed at the end of test time (or field trial time) t_q. We use the failure data up to $t_e(\leq t_q)$ to estimate the parameters of the mean number of failures $\mu(t)$. The substitution of the estimates of the parameters yields the estimate of the number of failures $\hat{\mu}(t_q)$. The estimate is compared with the actual number at q. This procedure is repeated with several t_es.

For a comparison we can plot the relative error $(\hat{\mu}(t_q) - q)/q$ against the normalised test time t_e/t_q. The error will approach 0 as t_e approaches t_q. If the points are positive, the model tends to overestimate and accordingly underestimate if the points are negative. Numbers closer to 0 imply a more accurate prediction and, hence, a better model.

Models for Comparison. As comparison models we apply four well-known models: Musa basic, Musa-Okumoto, Littlewood-Verall, and NHPP. All these models are implemented in the tool SMERFS [2] that was used to calculate the necessary predictions. We describe each model in more detail in the following.

Musa Basic. The Musa basic execution time model assumes that all faults are equally likely to occur, are independent of each other and are actually observed. The execution times between failures are modelled as piecewise exponentially distributed. The intensity function is proportional to the number of faults remaining in the program and the fault correction rate is proportional to the failure occurrence rate.

Musa-Okumoto. The Musa-Okumoto model, also called logarithmic Poisson execution time model, was first described in [7]. It also assumes that all faults are equally likely to occur and are independent of each other. The expected number of faults is a logarithmic function of time in this model, and the failure intensity decreases exponentially with the expected failures experienced. Finally, the software will experience an infinite number of failures in infinite time.

Littlewood-Verall Bayesian. This model was proposed for the first time in [4]. The assumptions of the Littlewood-Verall Bayesian model are that successive times between failures are independent random variables each having an exponential distribution. The distribution for the i-th failure has a mean of $1/\lambda(i)$. The $\lambda(i)$s form a sequence of independent variables, each having a gamma distribution with the parameters α and $\phi(i)$. $\phi(i)$ has either the form: $\beta(0) + \beta(1) \cdot i$ (linear) or $\beta(0) + \beta(1) \cdot i^2$ (quadratic). We used the quadratic version of the model.

NHPP. Various models based on a non-homogeneous Poisson process are described in [11]. The particular model used also assumes that all faults are equally likely to occur and are independent of each other. The cumulative number of faults detected at any time follows a Poisson distribution with mean $m(t)$. That mean is such that the expected number of faults in any small time interval about t is proportional to the number of undetected faults at time t. The mean is assumed to be a bounded non-decreasing function with $m(t)$ approaching the expected total number of faults to be detected as the length of testing goes to infinity. It is possible to use NHPP on time-between-failure data as well as failure counts. We used the time-between-failure version in our evaluation.

Data Sets. We apply the reliability models to several different sets of data to compare the predictive validity. The detailed results for all of these projects can be found in [12]. We describe only the combined results in the following. The used data sets come (1) from the *The Data & Analysis Center for Software (DACS)* of the US-American Department of Defence and (2) from the telecommunication department of Siemens. The DACS data has already been used in several evaluations of software reliability models. Hence, this ensures the comparability of our results. In particular, we used the projects 1, 6, and 40 and their failure data from system tests measured in execution time.

The Siemens data gives additional insights and analysis of the applicability of the model to these kind of projects. We mainly analyse two data sets containing the failure data from the field trial of telecommunication software and a web application. The Siemens data contains no execution time but calendar time can be used as approximation because of constant usage during field trial. All these projects come from different domains with various sizes and requirements to ensure a representative evaluation.

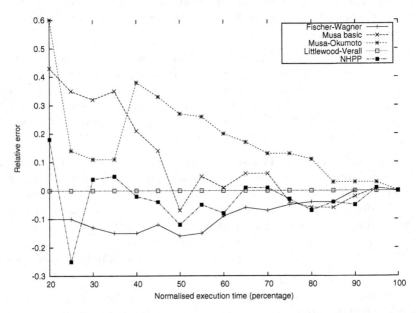

Fig. 3. Median relative errors for the different models based on all analysed data sets

Analysis and Interpretation. The usage of the number of failures approach for each project resulted in different curves for the predictive validity over time. For a better general comparison we combined the data into one plot which can be found in Fig. 3. This combination is straight-forward as we only considered relative time and relative errors. To avoid that strongly positive and strongly negative values combined give very small errors we use medians instead of average values. The plot shows that with regard to the analysed projects the Littlewood-Verall model gives very accurate predictions, also the NHPP and the proposed model are strong from early on.

However, for an accurate interpretation we have to note that the data of the Littlewood-Verall model for one of the Siemens projects was not incorporated into this comparison because its predictions were far off with a relative error of about 6. Therefore, the model has an extremely good predictive validity if it gives reasonable results but unacceptable predictions for some projects. A similar argument can be made for the NHPP model which made the weakest predictions for one of the DACS projects. The proposed model cannot reach the validity of these models for particular projects, but has a more constant performance over all projects. This is important because it is difficult to determine which of the models gives accurate predictions in the early stages of application since there is only a small amount of data. Using the Littlewood-Verall or NHPP model could lead to extremely bad predictions in some cases.

4   Conclusions

We conclude with a summary of our investigations and give some directions for future work.

Summary. We propose a software reliability model that is based on a geometric series of the failure rates of faults. This basis is suggested from the theory by Miller in [5] as well as from practice in Nagel et al. in [9, 8] and Siemens projects.

The model has a state-of-the-art parameter determination approach and a corresponding prototype implementation of it. Several data sets from DACS and Siemens are used to evaluate the predictive validity of the model in comparison to well-established models. We find that the proposed model often has a similar predictive validity as the comparison models and outperforms most of them. However, there is always one of the models that performs better than ours. Nevertheless, we are able to validate the assumption that a geometric sequence of failure rates of faults is a reasonable model for software reliability.

Future Work. The early estimation of the model parameters is always a problem in reliability modelling. Therefore, we plan to evaluate the correlation with other system parameters. For example the parameter d of the model is supposed to represent the complexity of the system. Therefore, one or more complexity metrics of the software code could be used for early prediction. This needs extensive empirical analysis but could improve the estimation in the early phases significantly.

Furthermore, a time component that also takes uncertainty into account would be most accurate. The Musa basic and Musa-Okumoto models were given such components (see [6]). They model the usage as a random process and give estimates about the corresponding calendar time to an execution time.

Further applications with other data sets and comparison with other types of prediction techniques, such as neural networks, are necessary to evaluate the general applicability and predictive validity of the proposed model.

Finally, we plan to use the model in an economics models for software quality [13] and work further on a possibility to estimate the test efficiency using the proposed model. Some early ideas are presented in [12].

Acknowledgements

We are grateful to Christine Dietrich and Lothar Quoll for their help in gathering the necessary data and to Sebastian Winter for useful comments on the paper.

References

1. Edward N. Adams. Optimizing Preventive Service of Software Products. *IBM Journal of Research and Development*, 28(1):2–14, 1984.
2. William H. Farr and Oliver D. Smith. Statistical Modeling and Estimation of Reliability Functions for Software (SMERFS) Users Guide. Technical Report NAVSWC TR-84-373, Naval Surface Weapons Center, 1993.
3. Z. Jelinski and Paul B. Moranda. Software Reliability Research. In W. Freiberger, editor, *Statistical Computer Performance Evaluation*. Academic Press, 1972.
4. Bev Littlewood and J.L. Verall. A Bayesian Reliability Growth Model for Computer Software. *Applied Statistics*, 22(3):332–346, 1973.
5. Douglas R. Miller. Exponential Order Statistic Models of Software Reliability. *IEEE Transactions on Software Engineering*, 12(1):332–346, 1986.
6. John D. Musa, Anthony Iannino, and Kazuhira Okumoto. *Software Reliability: Measurement, Prediction, Application*. McGraw-Hill, 1987.
7. John D. Musa and Kazuhira Okumoto. A Logarithmic Poisson Execution Time Model for Software Reliability Measurement. In *Proc. Seventh International Conference on Software Engineering (ICSE'84)*, pages 230–238, 1984.
8. P.M. Nagel, F.W. Scholz, and J.A. Skrivan. Software Reliability: Additional Investigations into Modeling with Replicated Experiments. NASA Contractor Rep. 172378, NASA Langley Res. Center, Jun. 1984.
9. P.M. Nagel and J.A. Skrivan. Software Reliability: Repetitive Run Experimentation and Modeling. NASA Contractor Rep. 165836, NASA Langley Res. Center, Feb. 1982.
10. John A. Nelder and Roger Mead. A Simplex Method for Function Minimization. *The Computer Journal*, 7(4):308–313, 1965.
11. Hoang Pham. *Software Reliability*. Springer, 2000.
12. Stefan Wagner and Helmut Fischer. A Software Reliability Model Based on a Geometric Sequence of Failure Rates. Technical Report TUMI-0520, Institut für Informatik, Technische Universität München, 2005.
13. Stefan Wagner and Tilman Seifert. Software Quality Economics for Defect-Detection Techniques Using Failure Prediction. In *Proc. 3rd Workshop on Software Quality (3-WoSQ)*. ACM Press, 2005.

Adaptive Random Testing Through Iterative Partitioning

T.Y. Chen[1], De Hao Huang[1,*], and Zhi Quan Zhou[2]

[1] Faculty of Information & Communication Technologies,
Swinburne University of Technology, Hawthorn, 3122, Australia
{tchen, dhuang}@ict.swin.edu.au
[2] School of IT & Computer Science, University of Wollongong,
Wollongong, 2522, Australia
zhiquan@uow.edu.au

Abstract. Random testing (RT) is a fundamental and important software testing technique. Based on the observation that failure-causing inputs tend to be clustered together in the input domain, the approach of Adaptive Random Testing (ART) has been proposed to improve the fault-detection capability of RT. ART employs the location information of previously executed test cases to enforce an even spread of random test cases over the entire input domain. There have been several implementations (algorithms) of ART based on different intuitions and principles. Due to the nature of the principles adopted, these implementations have their own advantages and disadvantages. The majority of them require intensive computations to ensure the generation of evenly spread test cases, and hence incur high overhead. In this paper, we propose the notion of iterative partitioning to reduce the amount of the computation while retaining a high fault-detection capability. As a result, the cost effectiveness of ART has been improved.

1 Introduction

There has been an increasing demand for high quality software products. The quality of software depends on the quality of the development process, in which testing always plays a critical role [12]. Among the various testing methods, *random testing* (RT) is a fundamental and straightforward approach [13, 14]. It simply selects test cases from the entire input domain randomly and independently. It avoids the overhead of specification-based or program-based partitioning of the input domain, which can be very expensive in many situations. Moreover, when the formal specification or the program code is not available, RT can often be a practical solution to generate a large number of inputs to cover cases that are possible to occur in real life but may often be overlooked by human testers [9, 21]. As a result, RT has been widely used in many real-life applications [7, 9, 10, 17-22]. In 1990, for example, Miller developed the fuzzy system that generated random data streams to test programs in several versions of the UNIX system [17]. It has been reported that 24% to 33% of the programs tested failed on valid inputs that are randomly generated. Apart from academia, RT

---

* Corresponding author.

L.M. Pinho and M. González Harbour (Eds.): Ada-Europe 2006, LNCS 4006, pp. 155–166, 2006.

techniques have been adopted by large software corporations and implemented in their software testing tools (e.g., [1]).

Recently, the approach of *Adaptive Random Testing* (ART) has been proposed to further improve the performance of RT in terms of using fewer test cases to detect the first failure [5, 15]. ART is based on the observation that failure-causing inputs form different failure patterns, which can be coarsely classified into three types, namely block, strip and point patterns [6]. In the block and strip patterns, failure-causing inputs are clustered in one or a few regions. In other words, the failure-causing inputs are "denser" in some areas of the input domain. Examples of these failure patterns for a program with a 2-dimensional input domain are given in the schematic diagrams in Fig. 1, where the outer square represents the input domain and the shaded areas represent the failure-causing inputs. With respect to the types of fault that yield these types of failure patterns, interested reader many consult [3]. Intuitively, when failure-causing inputs are clustered together, selecting a test case close to previously executed test cases that have revealed no failure is less likely to reveal the failure. Hence, ART proposes to have test cases evenly spread and far apart from each other.

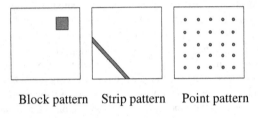

Block pattern   Strip pattern   Point pattern

Fig. 1. Examples of three types of failure patterns

It has been reported that ART improves the fault-detection capability of RT greatly. In [5], 12 programs were studied to investigate the effectiveness of ART. These programs are faulty versions of some numerical computation programs published in [8] with about 30 to 200 statements each. Typical errors were seeded into the programs. It was found that the fault-detection capability of ART (in terms of average number of test cases required to reveal the first failure) had generally achieved an improvement in the order of 30%, and occasionally up to 50%, over that of RT.

Several methods (algorithms) have been proposed to implement ART. Most of these methods require additional computations to achieve an even spread of test cases. To reduce the cost of computations, an ART method, *ART through Dynamic Partitioning* (DP-ART), has been proposed [3]. It significantly reduces the amount of computation in test case generation, but at the cost that its fault-detection capability is lower than that of the other ART methods.

In this paper we propose a new ART method to reduce the time cost of most ART methods (as DP-ART does) while retaining a high fault-detection capability. The paper is organized as follows. Section 2 reviews some existing ART methods. Section 3 introduces our proposed approach and Section 4 reports the results of our experiments. Section 5 will present some discussions and conclude the paper.

2   A Brief Review of Existing ART Method

For convenience of discussion, this paper adopts the notations in [6]. An input is called a *failure-causing input*, if it causes the program to produce an incorrect output. We use d, m and n to denote the domain size, total number of failure-causing inputs and number of test cases, respectively. The *failure rate*, θ, is defined as m/d. In this paper, *F-measure* (that is, the number of test cases needed to detect the first failure) is adopted as a metric to assess the failure-causing capability of different testing strategies. Aimed at achieving an even spread of test cases, ART exploits the location information of previously executed test cases. Several implementations of ART have been recently developed [2, 3, 15].

2.1   Distance-Based ART

Distance-based ART (D-ART) [5, 15] is the first implementation of ART. This method maintains a set of candidate test cases and a set of executed test cases. Every time a test case is required, a fixed number of test case candidates will be randomly generated from the whole input domain to form the candidate set, and then the next test case is selected according to the criterion of maximizing the minimum Cartesian distance between the test case candidate and all the previously executed test cases. This procedure is elaborated as follows.

Let $C = \{C_1, C_2, ..., C_k\}$ and $E = \{E_1, E_2, ..., E_l\}$ be the set of candidate test cases and the set of executed test cases, respectively. Let us denote the Cartesian distance in an n-dimensional input space between a test case candidate $C_i = (c_{i_1}, c_{i_2}, ..., c_{i_n})$ and an executed test case $E_j = (e_{j_1}, e_{j_2}, ..., e_{j_n})$, where $n \geq 1$, by $dist(C_i, E_j) = \sqrt{\sum_{p=1}^{n} (c_{i_p} - e_{j_p})^2}$. Let Min_i be the minimum Cartesian distance between test case candidate C_i and all the members of E, that is, $Min_i = \min\{dist(C_i, E_j) | 1 \leq j \leq l\}$. Then D-ART algorithm will select a candidate C_q, where Min_q is the largest among Min_1, Min_2, ..., Min_k, to be the next test case and discard all the other candidates.

If the test case C_q does not reveal a failure, then it will be put into the executed set E and the above procedure will be repeated until a failure is detected or the testing resources are exhausted.

2.2   Restriction Random Testing

Restriction Random Testing (RRT) [2] is another implementation of ART. In D-ART, the enforcement of even spread of test cases is based on the notion of selecting the best, whereas in RRT, the enforcement is based on the notion of selecting the first that satisfies a constraint/qualification. RRT specifies exclusion zones around each executed test case. Test case candidates are generated from the whole input domain randomly and the first one outside all exclusion zones is selected as the next test case. Similar to D-ART, the test case will be put into the set of executed test cases if it does not reveal a failure, and the process will be repeated until a failure is detected or the testing resources are exhausted.

2.3 ART Through Dynamic Partitioning

Though D-ART and RRT use different principles to ensure an even spread of test cases, in both these methods all the elements of the entire input domain have equal chances of being selected as the test case candidates. However, after the executions of several successful test cases, the input domain becomes *uneven* in that some regions have a higher density of executed test cases than other regions. Hence, in order to achieve an even spread of test cases, the next test case should be generated from the sparsely populated regions. It seems, therefore, that treating every element of the input domain equally as in D-ART and RRT is not efficient because it has not fully utilized the location information of executed test cases.

Based on the observation, another ART method, *ART through Dynamic Partitioning* (DP-ART), has been proposed [3]. Instead of generating test case candidates from the entire input domain and then conducting distance computations to decide the most appropriate one as the next test case, this method partitions the input domain first and then directly generates the next test case (rather than the "candidates") from the sparsely populated regions. This approach applies a partitioning scheme on the input domain to differentiate regions of varying densities of executed test cases.

In DP-ART [3], two dynamic partitioning schemes for the input domain have been proposed: (1) *ART by Random Partitioning*, which partitions the input domain using the executed test cases themselves (that is, dividing a region by drawing straight lines perpendicular to each other crossing at the most recently executed test case), and then chooses the subregion having the largest size to generate the next test case; (2) *ART by Bisection*, which divides the input domain into subdomains of equal size, and then randomly chooses a subdomain that does not contain any executed test case as the region to generate the next test case. If all subdomains contain executed test cases, then each subdomain will be subdivided into halves and the testing process is repeated until a failure is detected or the testing resources are exhausted.

Because DP-ART does not involve the generation of extra candidates and the selection of test cases amongst the candidates, its time cost is very low compared with that of D-ART and RRT. On the other hand, however, the experiment results [3] showed that the fault-detection capability (in terms of F-measure) of this method is not as good as that of D-ART and RRT. A major reason for this is that in this method there are chances that the new test case is still close to some previously executed ones, as illustrated in Fig. 2 and Fig. 3, where the outer square represents the input domain, the black points represent the test cases and the highlighted rectangle

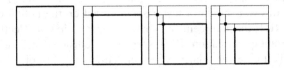

Fig. 2. An unfavorable scenario of ART by random partitioning

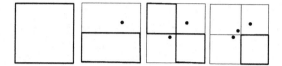

Fig. 3. An unfavorable scenario of ART by bisection

represents the region where the next test case is to be generated from. As also shown in the two figures, the follow-up partitioning scheme is always to further subdivide the previous one.

3 Adaptive Random Testing Through Iterative Partitioning (IP-ART)

To overcome the shortcomings of the previous ART methods while retaining their advantages, we have developed a new ART method, namely *ART through Iterative Partitioning* (IP-ART). Similar to DP-ART, IP-ART does not require the generation of extra candidates or the identification of the next test case among candidates. Hence, it retains the advantage of low overhead. Furthermore, by categorizing the subdomains into three different types, we can identify partitions that are close to existing test cases, and therefore avoid selecting test cases from those regions. As a result, it achieves a fault-detection capability comparable to that of D-ART and RRT but at a much lower time cost.

3.1 Overview

To illustrate the basic idea of IP-ART, let us consider Fig. 4. Fig. 4(a) shows a square input domain. Suppose we have already run three test cases, represented by the black points, but no failure has been revealed so far. According to the principle of ART, now we want to generate a new test case far apart from all the existing ones. The input domain can be partitioned, for example, using a 5×5 grid as shown in Fig. 4(b). We call the cells that contain the executed test cases *occupied cells*. Obviously, the next test case should not be generated from these cells. Furthermore, we call the cells that are surrounding neighbours of the occupied cells *adjacent cells*. These cells themselves do not contain any executed test case but share at least a common side or a common vertex with an occupied cell, as shaded in Fig. 4(b). If the next test case is generated from an adjacent cell, then it still has a chance of being close to previous test cases. Hence, adjacent cells are also not desirable for test case generation. IP-ART therefore requires that the next test case be generated from the regions that are neither occupied nor adjacent cells, known as *candidate cells*. The blank areas in Fig. 4(b) represent the 5 candidate cells. Obviously, a test case generated from a candidate cell has a higher chance of being far apart from all existing test cases.

After a new test case is generated, the lists of occupied, adjacent and candidate cells need to be updated and, sooner or later, all candidate cells will be used up. Then IP-ART will discard the current partitioning scheme (the $n{\times}n$ grid) and generate a finer $(n+1) \times (n+1)$ grid to partition the input domain all over again.

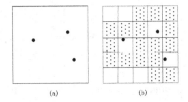

Fig. 4. Partitioning the input domain and identifying candidate cells

3.2 The Grid Coordinates Used in IP-ART

The concept of grid is widely used in many areas. For example, to make a map more manageable, it can be partitioned by a set of vertical and horizontal lines into regularly sized grid cells. The size of the cells is set according to the resolution required by the user.

In IP-ART, the whole input domain is divided into equally sized grid cells under a certain resolution, and any grid cell can be referred to using coordinates. Suppose we have a program $q(a, b)$ in a 2-dimentional input domain, where a and b are real numbers and $0 \leq a, b < M$, and suppose the input domain is partitioned by a $p \times p$ grid, where p is a positive integer. Let C be the side length of each grid cell, then $C = M/p$. Each grid cell is labeled with a pair of integers. The grid cell (i, j) refers to the cell whose lower left vertex has coordinates $(i \times C, j \times C)$. To conform to rounding conventions, a point on a vertical border belongs to the cell on its right, and a point on a horizontal border belongs to the cell above it. It is straightforward to map any point in the input domain to a grid cell. For any valid test case (x, y), it is mapped into grid cell $(\lfloor x/C \rfloor, \lfloor y/C \rfloor)$. If the input domain is partitioned by a 10×10 grid, and M is set to 100, as an example, the test case $(28.8, 12.6)$ is mapped into grid cell $(2, 1)$.

3.3 Categorization of Grid Cells

We categorize grid cells into 3 types: *occupied cells* that contain executed test cases; *adjacent cells* that do not contain any test case but are surrounding neighbours of some occupied cells; all the other remaining cells are *candidate cells*. In an n-dimensional input space, let $(o_1, o_2, ..., o_n)$ and $(a_1, a_2, ..., a_n)$ be the coordinates of an occupied cell and one of its adjacent cells, respectively, where $1 \leq n$, then $| a_i - o_i | \leq 1$, for $i = 1, 2, ..., n$.

3.4 The Algorithm

To perform IP-ART, we need to first decide the resolution of the grid for partitioning the input domain. If it is at the early stage of testing, then the number of executed test cases is small and, hence, a coarse grid is appropriate. This is because, if the grid is too fine at the beginning, then many candidate cells will not be sufficiently far away from the occupied cells. Hence, the algorithm starts with a coarse grid. If no failure is revealed and no candidate cell is available, then the current $n \times n$ partitioning scheme will be discarded and a finer partitioning scheme using an $(n+1) \times (n+1)$ grid will be applied to partition the input domain all over again.

The algorithm to be elaborated below is for a 2-dimensional square input domain with a size of $M{\times}M$. Extension to input domains of higher dimensions is straightforward. A Boolean matrix *GridCells* is used to represent the partitioning grid. Each entry of the matrix corresponds to a grid cell. If a matrix entry corresponds to an occupied or adjacent cell, then it will be assigned a value of F; otherwise it corresponds to a candidate cell and will be assigned a value of T. In the algorithm, p indicates the resolution of the grid. For example, $p = 2$ indicates a $2{\times}2$ partitioning grid.

IP-ART Algorithm

(It is assumed that the program under test is *program(parameter$_1$, parameter$_2$)*, where *parameter$_1$* and *parameter$_2$* are real numbers and $0 \le parameter_1, parameter_2 < M$.)

1. Initialize the grid by setting $p = 1$. Set the executed set, E, to be empty.
2. Construct a $p{\times}p$ Boolean matrix, *GridCells*, and assign T to all its entries. Use *CntCandidateCell* to count the number of candidate cells, and set *CntCandidateCell* $= p{\times}p$.
3. Map each executed test case e (*parameter$_1$* $= s$, *parameter$_2$* $= t$) in E into a grid cell by assigning F to the corresponding occupied cell *GridCells* ($\lfloor s{\times}p/M \rfloor$, $\lfloor t{\times}p/M \rfloor$). Update *CntCandidateCell*.
4. For each occupied cell *GridCells(x, y)*, assign F to all its adjacent cells, namely *GridCells(x-1, y-1)*, *GridCells(x-1, y)*, *GridCells(x-1, y+1)*, *GridCells(x, y-1)*, *GridCells(x, y+1)*, *GridCells(x+1, y-1)*, *GridCells(x+1, y)*, *GridCells(x+1, y+1)*, as necessary. Update *CntCandidateCell*.
5. If *CntCandidateCell* > 0 then generate a random integer r, where $0 < r \le$ *CntCandidateCell*, and search *GridCells* row by row until the rth candidate cell, R, is encountered. Otherwise go to step 8.
6. Randomly generate a test case *tc* within R.
7. If *tc* is a failure-causing input, report the failure and terminate. Otherwise add *tc* to E, assign F to R and its adjacent cells, update *CntCandidateCell*. Go to step 5.
8. Discard (release) the Boolean matrix *GridCells*. Set $p=p+1$. Go to step 2.

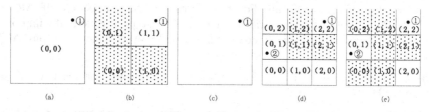

Fig. 5. An example that illustrates the IP-ART algorithm

An example that illustrates the above algorithm has been given in Fig. 5. Initially, no test case has been generated. The only candidate cell is the whole input domain. A test case ① is randomly generated and the cell becomes occupied. Suppose this is not a failure-causing input. Then, since there is no candidate cell, the input domain is partitioned by a $2{\times}2$ grid. The executed test case is mapped into the new partition and cell (1, 1) is identified as the occupied cell, and cells (0, 0), (0, 1) and (1, 0) are adjacent cells. Hence, this partitioning scheme cannot provide us with any candidate cell. As a result, this partitioning scheme is discarded as shown in Fig. 5(c). Then the input domain is partitioned again using a 3×3 grid as shown in Fig. 5(d), and the occupied and adjacent cells are accordingly identified. Now cells (0, 2), (0, 1), (0, 0), (1, 0) and (2, 0) are candidate cells and one of them, say, (0, 1), is randomly selected as the region for generating the next test case. A test case ② is randomly generated within this region. Then the adjacent cells surrounding ② are marked as shown in Fig. 5(e). Fig. 5(e) also shows that the cell (2, 0) is now the only remaining candidate cell and, therefore, the third test case will be generated from this region. This process will be repeated until a failure is detected or the testing resources are exhausted.

4 The Experiments

To compare the fault-detection capability of IP-ART with that of existing methods, a series of simulations have been conducted. For each test run, a failure-causing region with a specified failure rate θ and a specified failure pattern was randomly placed within the input domain. For the block failure pattern, it was a square; for the strip failure pattern, two points on the adjacent borders of the input domain were randomly chosen and connected to form a strip with a certain width; for the point failure pattern, 10 circular regions were randomly placed in the input domain without overlapping so that their total area yields the specified failure rate. For each combination of failure pattern and failure rate, 5000 test runs were executed. For random testing with replacement, it is easy to prove that the expected number of trials before first failure (*Expected F_{RT}*) is $1/\theta$, no matter what the failure patterns is. For ART methods, *Mean F_{ART}* records the average F-measure of 5000 test runs on each combination of failure pattern and failure rate. In order to illustrate the improvement of ART over RT, F_{ART}/F_{RT} records the ratio of F_{ART} and F_{RT}.

Table 1 presents the results of the simulations conducted in a 2-dimensional input domain with failure rates θ varied from 0.01 to 0.001 with respect to three types of failure patterns. For the block pattern, the F-measure of IP-ART is about 37~40% lower than that of random testing. For the strip pattern, the F-measure of IP-ART is about 22~23% lower than that of random testing. For the point pattern, the improvement is not significant. Table 2 compares the performance among various ART

Table 1. F-measure of IP-ART under 3 failure patterns on a 2-dimensional input domain (on average of 5000 trials)

Failure Rate θ	Expected F_{RT} (1/ θ)	Block Pattern		Strip Pattern		Point Pattern	
		Mean F_{ART}	F_{ART}/F_{RT}	Mean F_{ART}	F_{ART}/F_{RT}	Mean F_{ART}	F_{ART}/F_{RT}
0.01	100	63	63%	78	78%	96	96%
0.005	200	122	61%	156	78%	188	94%
0.002	500	301	60%	387	77%	476	95%
0.001	1000	605	61%	781	78%	925	93%

Table 2. A comparison of the performance of different ART methods (on average of 5000 trials, with $\theta = 0.001$ and a block failure pattern)

Dimensions	ART methods F_{ART} / F_{RT}				
	D-ART	RRT	ART by random partition	ART by bisection	IP-ART
2	66%	62%	77%	72%	61%
3	74%	71%	85%	79%	74%

Table 3. Recorded CPU time of different ART methods (with block failure pattern, $\theta=0.001$, for a run of 5000 trials each method)

ART Method	D-ART	RRT	ART by random partition	ART by bisection	IP-ART
CPU time (in seconds)	3645.8	1562.1	1141.1	6.4	12.0

methods with respect to 2 and 3 dimensional input domains and with θ being set to 0.001. We can see that the F-measure of IP-ART is comparable to that of D-ART and RRT, but obviously smaller than that of ART by random partitioning and ART by bisection.

We also investigated the overhead of each ART method by recording and comparing the CPU time they consumed. Simulations for all ART methods were conducted in the same hardware and software environment: an HP Compaq PC with 2.6 GHz Intel Pentium IV processor equipped with 256M RAM, running Microsoft Windows XP SP1. Table 3 lists the CPU time we recorded for running 5000 trials of each method. It shows that the time cost of IP-ART is negligible compared to D-ART, RRT and ART by random partition, and less than twice that of ART by bisection. The table shows that the overhead of ART by random partition is also quite high. This is because, although it avoids distance computations, ART by random partition has to search in the entire input domain for the subregion with the largest size to be the test case generation region, and hence incurs the overhead.

5 Discussions

Random Testing (RT) is simple in concept and easy to implement. RT has been the underlying technique of many software testing tools, such as those developed by IBM [1] and Bell Laboratories [11]. As pointed out in [11], Random Testing "can be remarkably effective at finding software bugs".

Adaptive Random Testing (ART) improves the fault-detection capability of RT in real-life situations where the failure-causing inputs are often clustered in one or a few regions. Compared with other black- or white-box testing strategies, ART retains the advantages of RT in that (1) both ART and RT do not require the knowledge of the source code of the program under test; (2) both ART and RT only need to know the input space without any further information from the specification; in contrast, all the other specification-based testing methods require intensive analysis of the specification by the human tester (such as the identification of classifications and associated classes in the well-known Classification-Tree method).

This paper has proposed a new implementation of ART, namely ART through Iterative Partitioning (IP-ART). By applying a partitioning scheme on the input domain, the favorable regions for test case generation can be easily identified. If such a favorable region cannot be identified, then the current partitioning scheme will be discarded and a refined one will be applied again. We start to partition the input domain by a coarse grid, and then iteratively refine the partitioning scheme.

To compare with DP-ART [3], IP-ART obviously achieves a higher failure-causing capability. The major extra computation is only the identification of adjacent cells. It should be noted that DP-ART also identifies a potential test case generation region by means of partitioning. However, its new partitioning scheme is always to subdivide the preceding partitioning scheme. It can be viewed as imposing the new partitioning scheme on the previous one, and hence is a multilevel partitioning process. In IP-ART, on the other hands, any new partitioning scheme is not based on the previous ones (which are in fact discarded). It is therefore an iterative partitioning process.

Compared with D-ART and RRT, IP-ART has a comparable fault-detection capability, but at a negligible computation cost. In D-ART and RRT, all elements in the input domain have an equal chance of being selected as test case candidates. To find the most suitable test case from the candidates, the computation involves the location data of *all* executed test cases. In IP-ART, on the other hand, the most favorable region is always located prior to test case generation. The expensive distance computations as well as the generation of multiple candidates are therefore avoided. In addition, in RRT, every time a new test case is generated, the exclusion zone needs to be adjusted; but this is not the case for IP-ART although it also repartitions the input domain at a certain stage.

Some methods have recently been developed to combine DP-ART with D-ART and RRT by using the concept of localization [4, 16]. These methods improved the fault-detection capability of DP-ART by applying D-ART or RRT in a selected test case generation region (rather than the entire input domain) with respect to only the test cases around that region. The classification of grid cells in our method is also based on the concept of localization.

Finally, we would like to point out some potential advantages of IP-ART that have not yet been employed:

1. Instead of coarsely classifying the cells into 3 different types, different grid cells can actually be assigned different weights according to their locations relative to the occupied cells.
2. Instead of initializing the input domain as a 1×1 grid, a finer grid can be used to partition the input domain at the very beginning if the program is anticipated to have a low failure rate.
3. Instead of refining the grid by 1 in each iteration, a greater increment may be used to accelerate the test case generation process.

It should be noted that the F-measure of our method was investigated by means of simulations. It is worthwhile to conduct more experiments using real programs. Moreover, we shall also study how to apply our method to test programs with input parameters involving advanced programming constructs such as arrays and objects.

Acknowledgements

This research project is partially supported by an Australia Research Council Discovery Grant (DP0557246) and a URC Small Grant of the University of Wollongong.

References

1. Bird, D. L. and Munoz, C. U. Automatic generation of random self-checking test cases. IBM Systems Journal, 22(3): 229-245, 1983.
2. Chan, K. P., Chen, T. Y., and Towey, D. Normalized restricted random testing. In Proceedings of 8th Ada-Europe International Conference on Reliable Software Technologies, pages 368-381, Springer-Verlag, 2003.
3. Chen, T. Y., Eddy, G., Merkel, R., and Wong, P. K. Adaptive random testing through dynamic partitioning. In Proceedings of the 4th International Conference on Quality Software (QSIC 2004), pages 79-86, IEEE Computer Society Press, 2004.
4. Chen, T. Y. and Huang, D. H. Adaptive random testing by localization. In Proceedings of the 11th Asia-Pacific Software Engineering Conference (APSEC,04), pages 292-298, IEEE Computer Society, 2004.
5. Chen, T. Y., Leung, H., and Mak, I. K. Adaptive Random Testing. In Proceedings of the 9th Asian Computing Science Conference (ASIAN 2004), Vol. 3321 of LNCS, pages 320-329, Springer-Verlag, 2004.
6. Chen, T. Y., Tse, T. H., and Yu, Y. T. Proportional sampling strategy: a compendium and some insights. The Journal of Systems and Software, 58(1): 65-81, 2001.
7. Cobb, R. and Mills, H. D. Engineering software under statistical quality control. IEEE Software, 7(6): 45-54, 1990.
8. Collected Algorithms from ACM. edition. Association for Computing Machinery, 1980.
9. Dabóczi, T., Kollár, I., Simon, G., and Megyeri, T. Automatic testing of graphical user interfaces. In Proceedings of the 20th IEEE Instrumentation and Measurement Technology Conference 2003 (IMTC '03), pages 441-445, 2003.
10. Forrester, J. E. and Miller, B. P. An empirical study of the robustness of Windows NT applications using random testing. In Proceedings of the 4th USENIX Windows Systems Symposium, pages 59-68, 2000.
11. Godefroid, P., Klarlund, N., and Sen, K. DART: directed automated random testing. In Proceedings of ACM SIGPLAN 2005 Conference on Programming Language Design and Implementation (PLDI), pages 213-223, 2005.
12. Hailpern, B. and Santhanam, P. Software debugging, testing, and verification. IBM Systems Journal, 41(1): 4-12, 2002.
13. Hamlet, R. Random testing. In J. Marciniak, editor, Encyclopedia of Software Engineering. John Wiley & Sons, second edition, 2002.
14. Loo, P. S. and Tsai, W. K. Random testing revisited. Information and Software Technology, 30(7): 402-417, 1988.

15. Mak, I. K. On the effectiveness of random testing. Master's thesis, Department of Computer Science, The University of Melbourne, 1997.
16. Mayer, J. Adaptive Random Testing by Bisection and Localization. In Proceedings of the 5th International Workshop on Formal Approaches to Testing of Software (FATES 2005), pages, 2005.
17. Miller, B. P., Fredriksen, L., and So, B. An empirical study of the reliability of UNIX utilities. Communications of the ACM, 33(12): 32-44, 1990.
18. Miller, B. P., Koski, D., Lee, C. P., Maganty, V., Murthy, R., Natarajan, A., and Steidl, J. Fuzz revisited: A re-examination of the reliability of UNIX utilities and services. Technical Report CS-TR-1995-1268, University of Wisconsin, 1995.
19. Miller, E. Website testing.
http://www.soft.com/eValid/Technology/White.Papers/website.testing.html.
20. Nyman, N. In defense of monkey testing: Random testing can find bugs, even in well engineered software. http://www.softtest.org/sigs/material/nnyman2.htm. Microsoft Corporation.
21. Slutz, D. Massive stochastic testing of SQL. In Proceedings of the 24th International Conference on Very Large Data Bases (VLDB98), pages 618-622, 1998.
22. Yoshikawa, T., Shimura, K., and Ozawa, T. Random program generator for Java JIT compiler test system. In Proceedings of the 3rd International Conference on Quality Software (QSIC 2003), pages 20-24, IEEE Computer, 2003.

Run-Time Detection of Tasking Deadlocks in Real-Time Systems with the Ada 95 Annex of Real-Time Systems

Jingde Cheng

Department of Information and Computer Sciences, Saitama University
Saitama, 338-8570, Japan
cheng@ics.saitama-u.ac.jp

Abstract. Any existing detection method or tool for Ada 95 programs cannot detect all types of tasking deadlocks in an Ada program with the Ada 95's annex of real-time systems. This paper investigates synchronization waiting relations in Ada 95 programs with the annex of real-time systems, extends the representation of Task-Wait-For Graph to deal with synchronization waiting relations defined in the annex of real-time systems, shows the necessary and sufficient conditions for tasking deadlock occurrences, and present a run-time tasking deadlock detector we implemented for real-time systems with the Ada 95's annex of real-time systems.

1 Introduction

A tasking deadlock in a concurrent Ada program is a situation where some tasks form a circular waiting relation at some synchronization points that cannot be resolved by the program itself (including the behavior of other tasks), and hence these tasks can never proceed with their computation by themselves [2, 4, 5, 6, 7]. Tasking deadlock is one of the most serious and complex problems concerning the reliability of concurrent systems with Ada 95. However, any existing detection method or tool for Ada 95 programs cannot detect all types of tasking deadlocks in an Ada program with the Ada 95's annex of real-time systems, because they take only the core Ada 95 but not the Ada 95's annex of real-time systems into account [3, 14]. Ada 95's annex of real-time systems defined a synchronization waiting relation concerning suspension objects [1, 13]. By combinations of the suspension waiting relation and those synchronization waiting relations in the core Ada 95, there may be a lot of different types of tasking deadlocks which may occur in programs with the Ada 95's annex of real-time systems [4, 18]. All tasking deadlocks concerning the suspension waiting cannot be detected by any existing detection method or tool for Ada 95 programs.

This paper investigates synchronization waiting relations in Ada 95 programs with the annex of real-time systems, extends the representation of Task-Wait-For Graph to deal with suspension waiting relations, shows the necessary and sufficient conditions for tasking deadlock occurrences, and present a run-time tasking deadlock detector we implemented for real-time systems with the Ada 95's annex of real-time systems.

L.M. Pinho and M. González Harbour (Eds.): Ada-Europe 2006, LNCS 4006, pp. 167–178, 2006.

2 Basic Notions and Terminology

First of all, we define the terminology about tasking deadlocks and livelocks in Ada programs for discussing our subject clearly and unambiguously. In this paper, we use the term 'task' to represent an execution of a task unit, and use the term 'task type' and/or 'single task' to represent the source code of a task unit.

A task in an Ada program is said to be *blocked* in an execution state of the program if it is waiting at a synchronization point in its thread of control for synchronization with one or more other tasks or even itself and this waiting state will be kept until either the synchronization has occurred or the task is aborted.

A *tasking deadlock* in an Ada program is an execution state of the program where some synchronization waiting relations among some tasks blocked at some synchronization points form a cycle that cannot be resolved by the program itself (including the behavior of other tasks), and hence these blocked tasks can never proceed with their computation by themselves. Any of the blocked tasks involved in the cycle is said to be *deadlocked*. A task calling its own entry can be regarded as a special case of tasking deadlock.

A blocked task in an execution state is said to be *deadlock-blocked* if it is waiting for synchronization with a deadlocked task but not involved in the cycle the deadlocked task is involved in. Note that a task waiting for synchronization with several tasks may be deadlocked in a tasking deadlock and at the same time be blocked by another tasking deadlock.

Obviously, from the viewpoint of deadlock resolution, to break the waiting of a task blocked by a tasking deadlock cannot change the deadlock state of any deadlocked task in the tasking deadlock, and hence has no effect on resolution of that tasking deadlock. Therefore, if a tasking deadlock detection method does not explicitly distinguish deadlocked tasks from deadlock-blocked tasks, then the detection method cannot work well for tasking deadlock resolution.

A *tasking livelock* in an Ada program is an infinite series of execution states of the program where each member of a group of tasks keeps forever rendezvousing with only tasks in the group and hence can never respond to a synchronization request from any task outside the group. Any of the tasks involved in the group is said to be *livelocked*. A task executing an infinite loop can never respond to any synchronization request from other tasks can be regarded as a special case of tasking livelock.

A blocked task in an execution state is said to be *livelock-blocked* if it is waiting for synchronization with a livelocked task. Note that a task waiting for synchronization with several tasks may be blocked by a tasking deadlock and at the same time be blocked by a tasking livelock.

The purpose of this paper is to investigate tasking deadlocks and their detection. We must introduce livelock since both livelock and deadlock may occur in the same Ada program. In this case, the detection of the tasking deadlock may depend upon the ability to detect the tasking livelock. At present, how to detect a livelock in a concurrent program is a completely open problem. The topic how to detect tasking deadlocks when tasking livelocks occur simultaneously is too large to be considered in this paper, we will deal with the issue as a subject of future work.

On the other hand, from the viewpoint of deadlock resolution, if a local tasking deadlock and a local tasking livelock exist simultaneously during an execution of an

Ada program, to break the waiting of a livelock-blocked task cannot change the dead-lock state of any deadlocked task in the tasking deadlock, and hence has no effect on resolution of that tasking deadlock. Therefore, if a tasking deadlock detection method does not explicitly distinguish deadlocked tasks from livelock-blocked tasks, then the detection method cannot work well for deadlock resolution.

Besides deadlocks and livelocks, a task may be blocked forever when it is waiting for accepting an entry call from some unspecified task or tasks even if such tasks are never existent. In an execution state of an Ada program, a blocked task waiting for accepting an entry call from other tasks is said to be *acceptance-starved* if it is nether deadlocked, nor deadlock-blocked, nor livelock-blocked, and there does not exist an entry call to one of its entries from any other task.

Similarly, in an execution state of an Ada program, a blocked task waiting for sus-pension until the value of the suspension object is true is said to be *suspension-starved* if it is neither deadlocked, nor deadlock-blocked, nor livelock-blocked, and no task has a statement to set the value of the suspension object true.

The terminology defined above can also be used for other concurrent programming languages if we replace 'task' by 'process' or 'thread.' For concurrent programs where deadlocks and livelocks may occur simultaneously, to explicitly distinguish and identify deadlocked processes, deadlock-blocked processes, livelock-blocked processes, and starved processes is the key to design and develop an effective method for deadlock discrimination and detection. Unfortunately, almost all works on dead-lock discrimination and detection did not pay careful attentions on this issue [7].

3 Synchronization Waiting Relations and Task-Wait-For Graph

In order for tasks to synchronize and communicate with each other, Ada 95 defines various types of synchronization waiting relations between tasks [1, 13]. The follow-ing synchronization waiting relations concern tasking deadlocks:

Activation waiting: A task that created some new tasks and initiated their activations in its own body, or in the body of a block statement executed by it, or in a subpro-gram, which may be unprotected or protected called by it, is blocked until all of the activations complete. The execution of an entry body that created some new tasks and initiated their activations is also blocked until all of the activations complete.

Finalization waiting: A master is the execution of a task body, a block statement, a subprogram body, an entry body, or an accept statement. Each task depends on one or more masters. The first step of finalizing a master is to wait for the termination of any tasks dependent on the master. A completed construct, i.e., a completed task, a completed block statement, a completed subprogram, or a completed entry body, executing a master is blocked until the finalization of the master has been performed.

Completion waiting: A task depends on some master and is blocked at a selective accept statement with an open terminate alternative; it must wait for completion to-gether with other dependents of the master considered that are not yet completed.

Acceptance waiting: A task executing an accept statement or a selective accept statement with some open accept alternative but no open delay alternatives and no else part is blocked until a caller of the corresponding entry is selected.

Entry-calling waiting: A task calling an entry by a simple entry call is blocked until the corresponding rendezvous has finished or the call is cancelled by a requeue with abort. Similarly, if a task is calling an entry by a timed entry call, a conditional entry call, or a simple entry call as the triggering statement of an asynchronous select and the corresponding rendezvous has started, then it is blocked until the corresponding rendezvous has finished or the call is cancelled by a requeue with abort.

Protection waiting: A task calling a protected procedure or a protected entry of a protected object is blocked until a new protected action can be started on the protected object, i.e., no another protected action on the same protected object is underway.

Protected-entry-calling waiting: A task calling a protected entry and the corresponding protected action has started is blocked until the execution of the corresponding entry body has finished. Similarly, if a task is calling a protected entry by a conditional or timed entry call, the corresponding protected action has started, and the execution of the corresponding entry body has started, then it is blocked until the execution of the corresponding entry body has finished.

Suspension waiting: A task calling the procedure Suspend_Unit_True of a suspension object is blocked until the state of the suspension object becomes true.

In the above synchronization waiting relations, the activation waiting, finalization waiting, completion waiting, acceptance waiting, entry-calling waiting, protection waiting, and protected-entry-call waiting relations were defined in the core Ada 95, while the suspension waiting relation is defined in the Ada 95's annex of real-time systems. From our investigation, we have not found other synchronization waiting relations defined in the full Ada 95's annexes.

Note that in the above synchronization waiting relations we do not consider those selective accept statements with open delay alternatives or else part and those timed entry calls, conditional entry calls, or simple entry calls as the triggering statements of asynchronous selects which have not yet been accepted because a task reaching any such selective accept or entry call can change its own waiting state. As a result, all of the above waiting relations have a common property, i.e., the waiting task in any waiting relation cannot change its own waiting state if there is not an event, including the execution of an abort statement, in the execution of its partner or partners. Therefore, a circular waiting relation formed among some tasks implies that a tasking deadlock might have occurred there.

By combinations of the suspension waiting relation and those synchronization waiting relations in the core Ada 95, there may be a lot of different types of tasking deadlocks which may occur in programs with Ada 95's annex of real-time systems. No tool that does not take Ada 95's annex of real-time systems into account can detect a tasking deadlock concerning the suspension waiting relation. We are not aware of any tool which takes this annex into account.

The following example program shows a simple Ada 95 program involved all types of synchronization waiting relations. More examples can be found in [18].

Example: An Ada 95 program involved all types of synchronization waiting relations

```
with Ada.Synchronous_Task_Control;          task T6;
use Ada.Synchronous_Task_Control;       task T7;
procedure Main is                       task body T6 is
  type ITEM is new Integer;                 begin T5.E5; end T6;
  task T1 is entry E1; end T1;              task body T7 is
  task T2 is entry E2; end T2;                Y: ITEM;
  task T3;                                    begin V.W(Y); end T7;
  S : Suspension_Object;                    begin null; end B;
  function GET return ITEM is         T1.E1;
  begin                                   end T4;
    T2.E2;                                task body T5 is
    return 0;                             task T8;
  end GET;                                task body T8 is
  protected V is                          begin
    Procedure W(X: in ITEM);                Set_False(S);
    entry R(X: out ITEM);                   Suspended_Until_True(S);
  private Var:                            end T8;
  end V;                                   begin accept E5; end T5;
  protected body V is                     begin accept E1; end T1;
    procedure W(X: in ITEM) is        task body T2 is
    begin Var := X; end W;              begin
    entry R(X: out ITEM) when TRUE is    select
    begin X := GET;                        when FALSE => accept E2;
    end R;                                 or
  end V;                                    terminate;
  task body T1 is                          end select;
    task T4;                               Set_True(S);
    task T5 is entry E5; end T5;          end T2;
    task body T4 is                     task body T3 is
    begin                                 Z: ITEM;
      B:                                  begin V.R(Z); T1.E1; end T3;
      declare                         begin null; end Main;
```

To formally investigate tasking deadlocks and their detection, we need a representation of the tasking waiting state in an execution of an Ada program. Arc-classified digraph is a good representation tool for our purpose because we can use different types of arcs to represent different types of task synchronization waiting relations. We have defined a kind of arc-classified digraph, named the Task-Wait-For Graph (TWFG for short), which explicitly represents various types of task synchronization waiting relations in an execution of a program with the core Ada 95 [5, 6]. It has been used as a formal model for run-time detection of tasking deadlocks in core Ada 95 programs. We now extend it to deal with synchronization waiting relations defined in the full Ada 95.

A *tasking object* in an execution state of an Ada program is any one of the following: a task whose activation has been initiated and whose state is not terminated; a block statement that is being executed by a task; a subprogram that is being called by a task; a protected subprogram that is being called by a task; a protected object on which a protected action is underway.

A *Task-Wait-For Graph* at time t (this time may be a physical time in an interleaved implementation of Ada 95 or a virtual time in a distributed implementation of

Ada 95) in an execution of an Ada program P, denoted by TWFG (P, t), is a tuple
(V(P, t), E(P), SO(P), Act, Fin, Com, Acc, EC, Pro, PEC, Sus) as defined below:
(V(P, t), Act, Fin, Com, Acc, EC, Pro, PEC, Sus) is an arc-classified digraph where
V(P, t)=T(P, t)∪BS(P, t)∪P(P, t)∪PS(P, t) represents the set of all tasking objects of
P at t, T(P, t) is the set of tasks, BS(P, t) is the set of blocks and subprograms, P(P, t)
is the set of protected objects, PS(P, t) is the set of protected subprograms; E(P)
represents the set of unprotected and protected entries of P; SO(P) represents the set
of suspension objects of P; Act ⊆ V(P, t) × T(P, t), Fin ⊆ V(P, t) × V(P, t), Com
⊆ T(P, t) × T(P, t), Acc ⊆V(P, t) × T(P, t) × E(P), EC ⊆ V(P, t) × T(P, t) × E(P), Pro
⊆ V(P, t) × P(P, t), PEC ⊆ V(P, t) × P(P, t) × E(P), Sus ⊆ V(P, t) × T(P, t) × SO(P),
and an element of Act, Fin, Com, Acc, EC, Pro, PEC, and Sus, called an *activation
waiting arc, finalization waiting arc, completion waiting arc, acceptance waiting
arc, entry-calling waiting arc, protection waiting arc, protected entry-calling wait-
ing arc*, and *suspension waiting arc*, respectively, corresponds to an activation wait-
ing relation, finalization waiting relation, completion waiting relation, acceptance
waiting relation, entry-calling waiting relation, protection waiting relation, protected-
entry-calling waiting relation, and suspension waiting relation between two elements
of V(P, t), respectively.

As an example, Fig. 1 shows the TWFG of the example program where some tasking deadlocks have occurred.

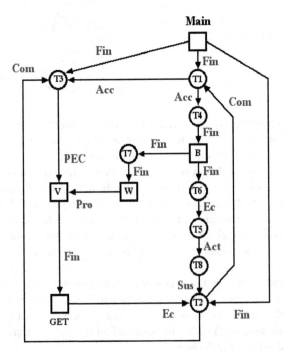

Fig. 1. The Task-Wait-For-Graph of the example program when tasking deadlocks occurred

4   Run-Time Detection of Tasking Deadlocks

Based on the above definitions, we now discuss how to detect all types of tasking deadlocks at run-time. First of all, we have the following propositions as the direct results of the above definitions and the full Ada 95 definition [13].

Proposition 1. In an execution state of an Ada program, if a task is blocked, then it must keep one and only one of the following five states: deadlocked, deadlock-blocked, livelock-blocked, acceptance-starved, or suspension-starved.

Proposition 2. For any vertex v of a TWFG (P, t), all outgoing arcs of v are type exclusive, i.e., if out-degree(v)>0 then all outgoing arcs of v must be a subset of any one of Act, Fin, Com, Acc, EC, Pro, PEC, and Sus of the TWFG (P, t).

For any TWFG (P, t), a vertex v is called an *AND-activation vertex* if all its outgoing arcs are activation-waiting arcs, and any path from an AND-activation vertex is called an *AND-activation path*.

For any TWFG (P, t), a vertex v is called an *OR-acceptance vertex* if all its outgoing arcs are acceptance-waiting arcs, and any path from an OR-acceptance vertex is called an *OR-acceptance path*. For any TWFG (P, t), a vertex v is called an *OR-suspension vertex* if all its outgoing arcs are suspension-waiting arcs, and any path from an OR-suspension vertex is called an *OR-suspension path*. An *OR-waiting vertex* is either an OR-acceptance vertex or an OR-suspension vertex. An *OR-waiting path* is either an OR-acceptance path or an OR-suspension path.

The *potential synchronization task set* of an entry or a suspension object in an Ada program, denoted by PST(e), is a set of task types and/or single tasks such that: (1) if e is an entry, then every member of the set has at least one call to e in its body or in the body of a subprogram it can call directly or indirectly; or (2) if e is a suspension object, then every member of the set has at least one call to the procedure Set_True of e in its body or in the body of a subprogram it can call directly or indirectly. For any entry or suspension object e in an Ada program, PST(e) can be obtained by a static analysis of the program. Note that PST(e) just represents a static property of an Ada program. Not all member of PST(e) must have a corresponding task at every time point in an execution of the program. Moreover, a task corresponding to a member of PST(e) just maybe call e or the procedure Set_True of e but not necessarily really does that in an execution of the program.

For any TWFG (P, t), an OR-waiting path from v_i is said to be *stable* if any task corresponding to a member of PST(e), where e is the entry or suspension object involved in the acceptance waiting or suspension waiting of v_i, is blocked, and the path satisfies any of the following conditions: (1) excluding v_i, it includes no OR-waiting vertex, and (2) excluding v_i, it includes some other OR-waiting vertices while every OR-acceptance path starting from any of the OR-waiting vertices is stable. Note that in fact the condition "any task corresponding to a member of PST(e) is blocked" is a sufficient but not necessary one to the discrimination and detection of tasking deadlocks. That is, it is too strong to the discrimination and detection of some tasking deadlocks.

Based on the above discussions, we have the following Proposition 3 that shows the necessary condition for occurrences of all types of tasking deadlocks, and

Proposition 4 that shows the sufficient condition for occurrences of all types of tasking deadlocks.

Proposition 3. For any Ada program P, if a tasking deadlock occurs at time t in an execution of P, then there exists a cycle in TWFG (P, t) such that each arc of the cycle corresponds to a synchronization waiting relation involved in the tasking deadlock.

Proposition 4. For any TWFG (P, t), if (1) there exists a cycle, and (2) for every OR-waiting path starting from every OR-waiting vertex in the cycle, either it is a part of a cycle or it is stable, then a tasking deadlock occurs in the execution of P at time t.

Note that the existence of a cycle is the sufficient condition for occurrences of some types of tasking deadlocks, i.e., those tasking deadlocks involving nether acceptance waiting relation nor suspension waiting relation, but not the sufficient condition for occurrences of all types of tasking deadlocks.

Thus, having TWFGs as a formal representation for the tasking waiting state in an execution of a program with the Ada 95's annex of real-time systems, in order to detect all types of tasking deadlocks, we just need to monitor the tasking behavior of the program, construct and update a TWFG for the program at run-time, detecting cycles in the TWFG, checking the necessary and sufficient conditions for occurrences of all types of tasking deadlocks, and reporting detected tasking deadlocks.

From the viewpoint of practice, an ideal method or tool for detecting Ada tasking deadlocks should satisfy the following three basic requirements:

Completeness: The method must be able to detect any tasking deadlock in any arbitrary Ada program.

Soundness: The method must not report any nonexistent tasking deadlock in any arbitrary Ada program.

Efficiency: The method must be able to be implemented such that it can detect tasking deadlocks in any arbitrary Ada program of an application system using a reasonable time allowed by the system.

However, the three basic requirements are difficult to satisfy. For target programs with the Ada 95's annex of real-time systems, unfortunately, as we have pointed out in Section 1, none of those tasking deadlock detection methods and tools proposed until now can deal with all tasking deadlocks, and therefore, they are far from complete. For target programs with the core Ada 95, from the viewpoints of completeness and soundness, the current best result is the run-time detection method and tool we developed that can certainly detect all types of tasking deadlocks (Note that here we just say "all types of tasking deadlocks" but not "all tasking deadlocks"), without reporting any nonexistent tasking deadlock, in programs with the core Ada 95 that are livelock-free [11, 14]. Finally, form the viewpoint of efficiency, there is no experimental result reported until now.

5   A Run-Time Tasking Deadlock Detector

To detect tasking deadlocks in a target Ada program at run-time, it is indispensable to monitor the tasking behavior of the program. There are three approaches to monitor the tasking behavior of Ada programs, i.e., the source program transformation approach, the run-time environment support approach, and the self-measurement approach. In the source program transformation approach, a target Ada program P is transformed by a preprocessor into another Ada program P', called the subject program of P, such that P' preserves the tasking behavior of P and during its execution P' will communicate with a run-time monitor when each tasking event of P occurs in P' and pass information about the tasking event to the run-time monitor [9, 10, 14]. In the run-time environment support approach, the run-time monitoring function is implemented in the run-time support environment of Ada language and information concerning tasking events in a target Ada program is provided by the run-time support environment. In the self-measurement approach, a run-time monitor is implemented as a permanent component of the target program itself and information concerning tasking events in the target program is provided by the run-time monitor [8, 15].

We have implemented a run-time tasking deadlock detector for Ada 95 programs with the Ada 95's annex of real-time systems by extending the detector we developed for programs with the core Ada 95 [9, 14]. We implemented our tasking deadlock detector in the source program transformation approach. Our detector has two separate components, i.e., a preprocessor and a run-time monitor. The preprocessor transforms a target Ada program P into its subject program P' such that some Ada codes are inserted at each point where a tasking event occurs for passing information about the tasking event to the run-time monitor. To monitor tasking behavior of P, P' is compiled, linked with the separately compiled run-time monitor, and then executed. During its execution, P' communicates with the run-time monitor when a tasking event of P occurs in P' and pass information about the tasking event to the run-time monitor. The run-time monitor records the collected information, constructs and updates the TWFG of P, detects cycles in the TWFG when it is updated, and checks and reports detected tasking deadlocks, if any, that have occurred in P.

In the implementation of the preprocessor of our detector, we use the Source Code Analysis Tool Construction (SCATC) Domain-Specific Kit (DSK) [12], which contains modified versions of the AFLEX lexical analyzer generator, AYACC parser generator and a specification file for the Ada 95 syntax [16, 17].

To correctly create and update a TWFG for a target Ada program, the run-time monitor must be able to identify any task of the program uniquely during its lifetime. Ada 95 provides a package Task_Identification in the System Programming Annex which can be used to obtain the identity of any task [1, 13]. This makes possible for a task to get its own unique identity, called task ID. Our detector can obtain a unique identifier of any instance task of the same task type, while our Ada 83 tasking deadlock detector cannot do.

The run-time monitor is provided as a package that contains a task and a protected objects, some data objects, and some other functions and procedures. The task is called Tasking Information Collector (TIC for short). When the subject program reports a tasking event, it calls an entry of the TIC. The protected object is called Task-Wait-For Graph Manager (TWFGM for short). This object manages a TWFG of the target program and some other information of the target program as protected data. Different from the TIC, this object is not visible for the subject program. The subprograms and the entries of the TWFGM are only called from the TIC.

We have tested our run-time tasking deadlock detector by the following examples.

(1) The example program given in this paper: This program has all 8 types of synchronization waiting relations during its execution. Our detector successfully detected all three tasking deadlocks in the program.

(2) An example program that has a tasking deadlock concerning only suspension waiting relation: A tasking deadlock formed by some suspension waiting relations occurs in this program and it was successfully detected by our detector.

(3) An example program that has cycles of synchronization waiting relations temporarily: This program has some cycles formed by some synchronization waiting relations but the cycles are resolved by a task that is not in the cycles. Our detector successfully detected the cycles in the program but did not report any tasking deadlock.

(4) An example program that is a slight modification of example program (3) but where a tasking deadlock occurs certainly. This program is just like example program (3) but the order of two statements is exchanged such that a tasking deadlock occurs certainly. Our detector successfully detected the tasking deadlock in the program.

(5) An example program that has both a tasking deadlock and a tasking livelock: This program occurs a tasking deadlock and a tasking livelock simultaneously during its execution. In the example program, a task issued a call on suspension statement for a suspension object is involved a cycle of synchronization waiting relations. However, other tasks not involved in the cycle are livelocked. This type of tasking deadlock cannot be detected only by checking cycles in a TWFG, because the TWFGs do not handle tasking livelocks. Our detector did not report any tasking deadlock in this program.

Our analysis and implementations have shown that our run-time tasking deadlock detector can detect all types of tasking deadlocks (again, note that here we just say "all types of tasking deadlocks" but not "all tasking deadlocks"), without reporting any nonexistent tasking deadlock, in programs with the Ada 95's annex of real-time systems that are livelock-free.

6   Concluding Remarks

Although the work and results presented in this paper are an extension of our previous work, we have made some important improvements on basic notions, terminology, formal definitions on our previous ones in order to provide a standard reference on Ada 95 tasking deadlocks for designers and developers of real-time systems with the Ada 95's annex of real-time systems.

We are developing a tasking behavior monitor with general-purpose as an Ada 95 generic package such that its instances can be used as permanent components in various target systems which need to monitor tasking behavior at run-time by themselves based on the self-measurement principle.

Future work should be focused on designing and developing complete, sound, and efficient detection methods and tools for run-time detection of all tasking deadlocks. In particular, some works should be done on the open problem how to detect tasking deadlocks when tasking livelocks occur simultaneously.

Acknowledgements

The author would like to thank Mr. Yasushi Tojo for his help in the implementation of our deadlock detector. The author would also like to thank Dr. Stephen Michell and referees for their valuable comments for improving the quality of this paper.

References

1. Barnes J. (Ed.): Ada 95 Rationale: The Language, the Standard Libraries. Lecture Notes in Computer Science, Vol. 1247. Springer-Verlag, Berlin Heidelberg New York (1997)
2. Barnes, J.: Programming in Ada 95 (2nd Edition). Addison-Wesley, (1998)
3. Blieberger, J., Burgstaller, B., Scholz, B.: Symbolic Data Flow Analysis for Detecting Deadlocks in Ada Tasking Programs. In: Keller, H.B., Ploedereder, E. (eds.): Reliable Software Technologies - Ada-Europe 2000, 5th International Conference on Reliable Software Technologies, Potsdam, Germany, June 2000, Proceedings. Lecture Notes in Computer Science, Vol. 1845. Springer-Verlag, Berlin Heidelberg New York (2000) 225-237
4. Burns, A., Wellings, A.: Concurrency in Ada (2nd Edition). Cambridge University Press, Cambridge (1998)
5. Cheng, J.: A Classification of Tasking Deadlocks. ACM Ada Letters, Vol. 10, No. 5 (1990) 110-127
6. Cheng, J.: Task-Wait-For Graphs and their Application to Handling Tasking Deadlocks. In: Proc. 3rd ACM Annual TRI-Ada Conference (1990) 376-390
7. Cheng, J.: A Survey of Tasking Deadlock Detection Methods. ACM Ada Letters, Vol. 11, No.1 (1991) 82-91
8. Cheng, J.: The Self-Measurement Principle: A Design Principle for Large-scale, Long-lived, and Highly Reliable Concurrent Systems. In: Proc. 1998 IEEE-SMC Annual International Conference on Systems, Man, and Cybernetics, Vol. 4 (1998) 4010-4015
9. Cheng, J., Kasahara, Y., Ushijima, K.: A Tasking Deadlock Detector for Ada Programs. In: Proc. 15th IEEE-CS Annual International Computer Software & Applications Conference (1991) 56-63
10. Cheng, J., Ushijima, K.: Partial Order Transparency as a Tool to Reduce Interference in Monitoring Concurrent Systems, In: Ohno, Y. (ed.): Distributed Environments. Springer-Verlag, Tokyo (1991) 156-171
11. Cheng, J., Ushijima, K.: Tasking Deadlocks in Ada 95 Programs and their Detection. In: Strohmeier, A. (ed.): Reliable Software Technologies - Ada-Europe '96, 1996 Ada-Europe International Conference on Reliable Software Technologies, Montreux, Switzerland, June 1996, Proceedings. Lecture Notes in Computer Science, Vol. 1088. Springer-Verlag, Berlin Heidelberg New York (1996) 135-146
12. Conn, R.: Software Version Description (SVD) and Software User's Manual (SUM) Source Code Analysis Tool Construction Domain-Specific Kit (SCATC DSK). Public Ada Library (1998)
13. International Organization for Standardization: Information Technology: Programming Language – Ada. ISO/IEC 8652:1995(E) (1995)
14. Nonaka, Y., Cheng, J., Ushijima, K.: A Tasking Deadlock Detector for Ada 95 Programs. Ada User Journal, Vol. 20, No. 1 (1999) 79-92

15. Nonaka, Y., Cheng, J., Ushijima, K.:   A Supporting Tool for Development of Self-measurement Ada Programs. In: Keller, H.B., Ploedereder, E. (eds.): Reliable Software Technologies - Ada-Europe 2000, 5th International Conference on Reliable Software Technologies, Potsdam, Germany, June 2000, Proceedings. Lecture Notes in Computer Science, Vol. 1845. Springer-Verlag, Berlin Heidelberg New York (2000) 69-81
16. Self, J.: Aflex - An Ada Lexical Analyzer Generator Version 1.1. UCI-90-18 (1990)
17. Taback, D., Tolani, D., Schmalz, R.J., Chen, Y.: Ayacc User's Manual Version 1.1. Arcadia Document UCI-94-01 (1994)
18. Tojo, Y., Nara, S., Goto, Y., Cheng, J.: Tasking Deadlocks in Programs with the Full Ada 95. ACM Ada Letters, Vol. 25, No. 1 (2005) 48-56

Abstract Interface Types in GNAT: Conversions, Discriminants, and C++

Javier Miranda[1] and Edmond Schonberg[2]

[1] Applied Microelectronics Research Institute
University of Las Palmas de Gran Canaria
Spain and AdaCore
jmiranda@iuma.ulpgc.es
[2] AdaCore
104 Fifth Avenue, 15th floor
New York, NY 10011
schonberg@adacore.com

Abstract. Ada 2005 Abstract Interface Types provide a limited and practical form of multiple inheritance of specifications. In this paper we cover the following aspects of their implementation in the GNAT compiler: interface type conversions, the layout of variable sized tagged objects with interface progenitors, and the use of the GNAT compiler for interfacing with C++ classes with compatible inheritance trees.

Keywords: Ada 2005, Abstract Interface Types, Tagged Types, Discriminants, GNAT.

1 Introduction

In recent years, a number of language designs [1, 2] have adopted a compromise between full multiple inheritance and strict single inheritance, which is to allow multiple inheritance of *specifications*, but only single inheritance of *implementations*. Typically this is obtained by means of *"interface"* types. An interface consists solely of a set of operation specifications: it has no data components and no operation implementations. A type may implement multiple interfaces, but can inherit code from only one parent type [4, 7]. This model has much of the power of full-blown multiple inheritance, without most of the implementation and semantic difficulties that are manifest in the object model of C++ [3].

At compile time, an interface type is conceptually a special kind of *abstract tagged type* and hence its handling does not add special complexity to the compiler front-end (in fact, most of the current compiler support for abstract tagged types has been reused in GNAT). At run-time we have chosen to give support to dynamic dispatching through abstract interfaces by means of secondary dispatch tables. This model was chosen for its time efficiency (constant-time dispatching through interfaces), and its compatibility with the run-time structures used by G++ (this is the traditional nickname of GNU C++).

L.M. Pinho and M. González Harbour (Eds.): Ada-Europe 2006, LNCS 4006, pp. 179–190, 2006.

This is the third paper in a series describing the implementation in the GNAT compiler of Ada 2005 features related to interfaces (the previous papers are [13] and [14]). We discuss the interesting implementation challenges presented by interface type conversions, and the layout of variable sized tagged objects with *progenitors*, which is the Ada 2005 term that designates the interfaces implemented by a tagged type [4, Section 3.9.4 (9/2)]. Finally, we show how our implementation makes it possible to write multi-language object-oriented programs with interface inheritance. We present a small mixed-language example that imports into Ada a C++ class hierarchy with multiple inheritance, when all but one of the *base* classes have only *pure virtual* functions [3, Chapter 9].

This paper is structured as follows: In Section 2 we give a brief overview of Ada 2005 abstract interfaces. In Section 3 we summarize the data layout adopted by GNAT (for more details read [13] and [14]). In Section 4 we describe the implementation of interface conversions. In Section 5 we discuss possible approaches to the layout of tagged objects with components constrained by discriminants, and their impact on conversion. In Section 6 we present an example of mixed-language object-oriented programming; this example extends in Ada 2005 a C++ class whose *base* classes have only *pure virtual functions* [3, Chapter 9]. We close with some conclusions and the bibliography.

2   Abstract Interfaces in Ada 2005

The characteristics of an Ada 2005 interface type are introduced by means of an interface type declaration and a set of subprogram declarations [4, Section 3.9.4]. The interface type has no data components, and its primitive operations are either abstract or null. A type that implements an interface must provide non-abstract versions of all the abstract operations of its *progenitor(s)*. For example:

```
package Interfaces_Example is
    type I1 is interface;                                  -- 1
    function P (X : I1) return Natural is abstract;

    type I2 is interface and I1;                           -- 2
    procedure Q (X : I1) is null;
    procedure R (X : I2) is abstract;

    type Root is tagged record ...                         -- 3
    ...
    type DT1 is new Root and I2 with ...                   -- 4
    --  DT1 must provide implementations for P and R
    ...
    type DT2 is new DT1 with ...                           -- 5
    --  Inherits all the primitives and interfaces of the ancestor
end Interfaces_Example;
```

The interface I1 defined at −1− has one subprogram. The interface I2 has the same operations as I1 plus two subprograms: the null subprogram *Q* and the abstract subprogram *R*. (Null procedures are described in AI-348 [10]; they behave as if their body consists solely of a *null_statement*.) At –3– we define the root of a derivation class. At –4– *DT1* extends the root type, with the added commitment of implementing (all the abstract subprograms of) interface I2. Finally, at –5– type *DT2* extends DT1, inheriting all the primitive operations and interfaces of its ancestor.

The power of multiple inheritance is realized by the ability to dispatch calls through interface subprograms, using a controlling argument of a class-wide interface type. In addition, languages that provide interfaces [1, 2] provide a run-time mechanism to determine whether a given object implements a particular interface. Accordingly Ada 2005 extends the membership operation to interfaces, and allows the programmer to write the predicate *O in I'Class*. Let us look at an example that uses the types declared in the previous fragment, and displays both of these features:

```
procedure Dispatch_Call (Obj : I1'Class) is
begin
   if Obj in I2'Class then    -- 1: membership test
      R (I2'Class (Obj));     -- 2: interface conversion plus dispatch call
   else
      ... := P (Obj);         -- 3: dispatch call
   end if;

   I1'Write (Stream, Obj);    -- 4: dispatch call to predefined op.
end Dispatch_Call;
```

The type of the formal *Obj* covers all the types that implement the interface I1. At –1– we use the membership test to check if the actual object also implements I2. At –2– we perform a conversion of the actual to the class-wide type of I2 to dispatch the call through I2'Class. (If the object does not implement the target interface and we do not protect the interface conversion with the membership test then Constraint_Error is raised at run-time.) At –3– the subprogram safely dispatches the call to the *P* primitive of I1. Finally, at –4– we see that, in addition to user-defined primitives, we can also dispatch calls to predefined operations (that is, 'Size, 'Alignment, 'Read, 'Write, 'Input, 'Output, Adjust, Finalize, and the equality operator).

Ada 2005 extends abstract interfaces for their use in concurrency: an interface can be declared to be a non-limited interface, a limited interface, a synchronized interface, a protected interface, or a task interface [9, 11]. Each one of these imposes constraints on the types that can implement such an interface: a task interface can be implemented only by a task type or a single task; a protected interface can only be implemented by a protected type or a single protected object; a synchronized interface can be implemented by either task types, single tasks, protected types or single protected objects, and a limited interface can be implemented by tasks types, single tasks, protected types, single protected objects, and limited tagged types.

The combination of the interface mechanism with concurrency means that it is possible, for example, to build a system with distinct server tasks that provide similar services through different implementations, and to create heterogeneous pools of such tasks. Using synchronized interfaces one can build a system where some coordination actions are implemented by means of active threads (tasks) while others are implemented by means of passive monitors (protected types). For details on the GNAT implementation of synchronized interfaces read [14].

3   Abstract Interfaces in GNAT

Our first design decision was to adopt as much as possible a dispatching model compatible with the one used by G++, in the hope that mixed-language programming would intermix types, classes, and operations defined in both languages. A compatible design decision was to ensure that dispatching calls through either classwide types or interface types should take constant time.

As a result of these choices, the GNAT implementation of abstract interfaces is compatible with the C++ Application Binary Interface (ABI) described in [6]. That is, the compiler generates a secondary dispatch table for each progenitor of a given tagged type. Thus, dispatching a call through an interface has the same cost as any other dispatching call. The model incurs storage costs, in the form of additional pointers to dispatch tables in each object.

Figure 1 presents an example of this layout. The dispatch table has a header containing the offset to the top and the Run-Time Type Information Pointer (RTTI). For a primary dispatch table, the first field is always set to 0 and the RTTI pointer points to the GNAT *Type Specific Data* (the contents of this record are described in the GNAT sources, file a-tags.adb). The tag of the object points to the first element of the table of pointers to primitive operations. At the bottom of the same figure we have the layout of a derived type that implements two interfaces I1 and I2. When a type implements several interfaces, its run-time data structure contains one primary dispatch table and one secondary dispatch table per interface. In the layout of the object (left side of the figure), we see that the derived object contains all the components of its parent type plus 1) the tag of all the implemented interfaces, and 2) its own user-defined components. Concerning the contents of the dispatch tables, the primary dispatch table is an extension of the primary dispatch table of its immediate ancestor, and thus contains direct pointers to all the primitive subprograms of the derived type. The *offset_to_top* component of the secondary tables holds the displacement to the top of the object from the object component containing the interface tag. (This offset provides a way to find the top of the object from any derived object that contains secondary virtual tables and is necessary in abstract interface type conversion; this will be described in Section 4.)

In the example shown in Figure 1, the offset-to-top values of interfaces I1 and I2 are m and n respectively. In addition, rather than containing direct pointers to the primitive operations associated with the interfaces, the secondary dispatch tables contain pointers to small fragments of code called *thunks*. These thunks are generated by the compiler, and used to adjust the pointer to the base of the object (see description below).

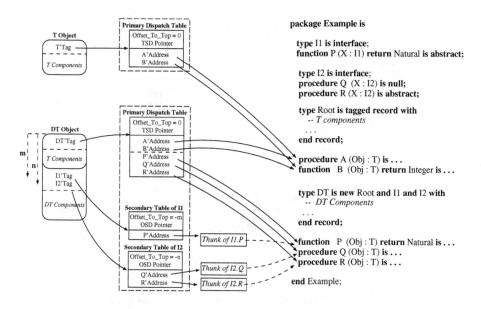

Fig. 1. Layout compatibility with C++

4 Abstract Interface Type Conversions

In order to support interface conversions and the membership test, the GNAT run-time has a table of interfaces associated with each tagged type containing the tag of all the implemented interfaces plus its corresponding offset-to-top value in the object layout. Figure 2 completes the run-time data structure described in the previous section with the *Type Specific Data* record which stores this table of interfaces.

In order to understand the actions required to perform interface conversions, let us recall briefly the use of this run-time structure for interface calls. At the point of call to a subprogram whose controlling argument is a class-wide interface, the compiler generates code that displaces the pointer to the object by m bytes, in order to reference the tag of the secondary dispatch table corresponding to the controlling interface. This adjusted address is passed as the pointer to the actual object in the call. Within the body of the called subprogram, the dispatching call to P is handled as if it were a normal dispatching call. For example, because P is the first primitive operation of the interface I1, the compiler generates code that issues a call to the subprogram identified by the first entry of the primary dispatch table associated with the actual parameter. Because the actual parameter is a displaced pointer that points to the I1'Tag component of the object, we are really issuing a call through the secondary dispatch table of the object associated with the interface I1. In addition, rather than a direct pointer to subprogram Q, the compiler also generates code that fills this entry of the secondary dispatch table with the address of a *thunk* that 1) subtracts the m bytes displacement corresponding to I1 in order to adjust the address so that

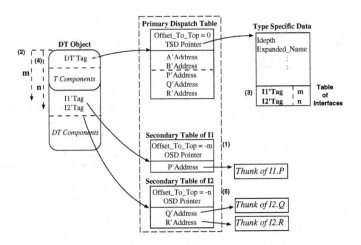

Fig. 2. Object Layout

it refers to the real base of the object, and 2) does a direct jump to the body of subprogram Q.

Now let us see the work performed by the GNAT run-time to support interface conversion. Let us assume that we are again executing the body of the subprogram with the class-wide formal, and hence that the actual parameter is a displaced pointer that points to the I1'Tag component of the object. In order to get access to the table of interfaces the first step is to read the value of the offset-to-top field available in the header of the dispatch table (see 1 in the figure). This value is used to displace upwards the actual parameter by m bytes to designate the base of the object (see 2). From here we can get access to the table of interfaces and retrieve the tag of the target interface (see 3). If found we perform a second displacement of the actual by using the offset value stored in the table of interfaces (in our example n bytes) to displace the pointer downwards from the root of the object to the component that has the I2'Tag of the object (see 4). If the tag of the target interface is not found in the table of interfaces the run-time raises Constraint_Error. As a result, an interface conversion incurs a run-time cost proportional to the number of interfaces implemented by the type. An extensive examination of the Java libraries indicates that in the great majority of cases there are no more than 4 progenitors for any given class. Thus this overhead is certainly acceptable. More sophisticated structures could be used to speed up the search for the desired interface, but we defer such optimizations until actual performance results indicate that they are needed.

5   Discriminant Complications

The use of abstract interface types in variable sized tagged objects requires some special treatment. Complications arise when a tagged type has a parent that includes some component whose size is determined by a discriminant. For example:

```
type Root (D : Positive) is tagged record
   Name : String (1 .. D);
end record;

type DT is new Root and I1 and I2 with ...
Obj : DT (N);    -- N is not necessarily static
```

In this example it is clear that the final position of the components containing the tags associated with the secondary dispatch tables of the progenitors depends on the actual value of the discriminant at the point the object Obj is elaborated. Therefore the offset-to-top values can not be placed in the header of the secondary dispatch tables, nor in the table of interfaces itself. However as we described in the previous section the offset-to-top values are required for interface conversions. The C++ ABI does not address this problem for the simple reason that C++ classes do not have non-static components.

At this point it is clear that we must provide a way to 1) displace the pointer up to the base of the object, and 2) displace the pointer down to reference the tag component associated with the target interface. Two main alternatives were considered to solve this problem (obviously the naive approach of generating a separate dispatch table for each object was declared unacceptable at once). Whatever alternative was chosen, it should not affect the data layout when discriminants are not present, so as to maintain C++ compatibility for the normal case. The two plausible alternatives are:

1. To place the interface tag components at negative (and static) offsets from the object pointer (cf. Figure 3). Although this solution solves the problem, it was rejected because the value of the *Address* attribute for variable size tagged objects would not be conformant with the Ada Reference Manual, which explicitly states that *"X'Address denotes the address of the first of the storage elements allocated for X"* [5, Annex K]. In addition, programmers generally assume that the allocation of an object can be accurately described using *'Address* and *'Size* and therefore they generally expect to be able to place the object at the start of a particular region of memory by using an offset of zero from that starting address.

2. The second option is to store the offset-to-top values immediately following each of the interface tags of the object (that is, adjacent to each of the object's secondary dispatch table pointers). In this way, this offset can be retrieved when we need to adjust a pointer to the base of the object. There are two basic cases where this value needs to be obtained: 1) The thunks associated with a secondary dispatch table for such a type must fetch this offset value and adjust the pointer to the object appropriately before dispatching a call; 2) Class-wide interface type conversions need to adjust the value of the pointer to reference the secondary dispatch table associated with the target type. In this second case this field allows us to solve the first part

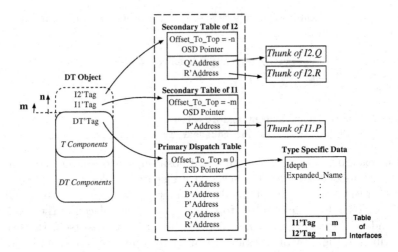

Fig. 3. Approach I: Interface tags located at negative offsets

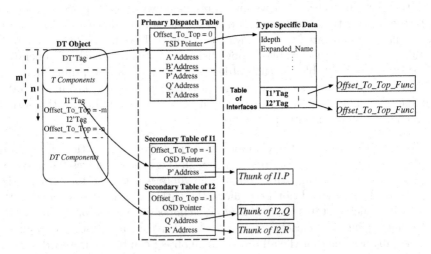

Fig. 4. Approach II: Offset value adjacent to pointer to secondary DT

of the problem, but we still need this value in the table of interfaces to be able to displace down the pointer to reference the field associated with the target interface. For this purpose the compiler must generate object specific functions which read the value of the offset-to-top hidden field. Pointers to these functions are themselves stored in the table of interfaces.

The latter approach has been selected for the GNAT compiler. Figure 4 shows the data layout of our example following this approach. Note: The value -1 in the *Offset_To_Top* of the secondary dispatch tables indicates that this field does not have a valid offset-to-top value.

6   Collaborating with C++

The C++ equivalent of an Ada 2005 abstract interface is a class with pure virtual functions and no data members. For example, the following declarations are conceptually equivalent:

```
class I1 {                              type I1 is interface;
public: virtual void p () = 0;          procedure P (X : I1) is abstract;
}
```

```
class I2 {                              type I2 is interface;
public: virtual void q () = 0;          procedure Q (X : I2) is abstract;
        virtual int  r () = 0;          function  R (X : I2) return Integer
}                                          is abstract;
```

Let us see the correspondence between classes derived from these declarations in the two languages:

```
class Root {                            type Root is tagged record with
public:                                    R_Value : Integer;
  int r_value;                          end record;
  virtual void Root_Op ();              procedure Root_Op (X : Root);
};
```

```
class A : Root, I1, I2 {                type A is new Root and I1 and I2 with
public                                     A_Value: Float;
  float a_value;                        end record;

  virtual void  p ();                   procedure P (X : A);
  virtual void  q ();                   procedure Q (X : A);
  virtual int   r ();                   function  R (X : A) return Integer;
  virtual float s ();                   function  S (X : A) return Float;
};
```

Because of the chosen compatibility between GNAT run-time structures and the C++ ABI, interfacing with these C++ classes is easy. The only requirement is that all the primitives and components must be declared exactly in the same order in the two languages. The code makes use of several GNAT-specific pragmas, introduced early in our Ada 95 implementation for the more modest goal of using single inheritance hierarchies across languages. These pragmas are CPP_Class, CPP_Virtual, CPP_Import, and CPP_Constructor.

First we must indicate to the GNAT compiler. by means of the pragma CPP_Class, that some tagged types have been defined in the C++ side; this is required because the dispatch table associated with these tagged types will be built on the C++ side and therefore it will not have the Ada predefined primitives. (The GNAT compiler then generates the elaboration code for the portion of the table that holds the predefined primitives: Size, Alignment, stream operations, etc). Next, for each user-defined primitive operation we must indicate by means of pragma CPP_Virtual that their body is on the C++ side, and by means of pragma CPP_Import their corresponding C++ external name. The complete code for the previous example is as follows:

```
package My_Cpp_Interface is
   type I1 is interface;
   procedure P (X : I1) is abstract;

   type I2 is interface;
   procedure Q (X : I1) is abstract;
   function R (X : I2) return Integer is abstract;

   type Root is tagged record with
      R_Value : Integer;
   end record;
   pragma CPP_Class (Root);

   procedure Root_Op (Obj : Root);
   pragma CPP_Virtual (Root_Op);
   pragma Import (CPP, Root_Op, "_ZN4Root7Root_OpEv");

   type A is new Root and I1 and I2 with record
      A_Value : Float;
   end record;
   pragma CPP_Class (A);

   procedure P (Obj : A);
   pragma CPP_Virtual (P);
   pragma Import (CPP, P, "_ZN1A4PEv");

   procedure Q (Obj : A);
   pragma CPP_Virtual (Q);
   pragma Import (CPP, Q, "_ZN1A4QEv");

   function R (Obj : A) return Integer;
   pragma CPP_Virtual (R);
   pragma Import (CPP, R, "_ZN1A4REv");

   function S (Obj : A) return Float;
   pragma CPP_Virtual (S);
   pragma Import (CPP, S, "_ZN1A7SEi");

   function Constructor return A'Class;
   pragma CPP_Constructor (Constructor);
   pragma Import (CPP, Constructor, "_ZN1AC2Ev");
end My_Cpp_Interface;
```

With the above package we can now declare objects of type A and dispatch calls to the corresponding subprograms in the C++ side. We can also extend A with further fields and primitives, and override on the Ada side some of the C++ primitives of A.

It is important to note that we do not need to add any further information to indicate either the object layout, or the dispatch table entry associated with each dispatching operation. For completeness we have also indicated to the compiler that the default constructor of the object is also defined in the C++ side.

In order to further simplify interfacing with C++ we are currently working on a utility for GNAT that automatically generates the proper mangled name for the operations, as generated by the G++ compiler. This would make the pragma Import redundant.

7 Conclusion

We have described part of the work done by the GNAT Development Team to implement Ada 2005 interface types in a way that is fully compatible with the C++ Application Binary Interface (ABI). We have explained our implementation of abstract interface type conversions, including the special support required for variable sized tagged objects. We have also given an example that shows the power of the combined use of the GNAT and G++ compilers for mixed-language object-oriented programming.

The implementation described above is available to users of GNAT PRO, under a switch that controls the acceptability of language extensions (note that these extensions are not part of the current definition of the language, and can not be used by programs that intend to be strictly Ada95-conformant). This implementation is also available in the GNAT compiler that is distributed under the *GNAT Academic Program* (GAP) [15].

We hope that the early availability of the Ada 2005 features to the academic community will stimulate experimentation with the new language, and spread the use of Ada as a teaching and research vehicle. We encourage users to report their experiences with this early implementation of the new language, in advance of its much-anticipated official standard.

Acknowledgments

We wish to thank Robert Dewar, Cyrille Comar, Gary Dismukes, and Matthew Gingell for the discussions that helped us to clarify the main concepts described in this paper. We also wish to thank the dedicated and enthusiastic members of AdaCore, and the myriad supportive users of GNAT whose ideas, reports, and suggestions keep improving the system.

References

1. J. Gosling, B. Joy, G. Steele, and G. Bracha. *The Java Language Specification (3rd edition)*. Addison-Wesley, 2005. ISBN: 0-321-24678-0.
2. E. International. *C# Language Specification (2nd edition)*. Standard ECMA-334. Standardizing Information and Communication Systems, December, 2002.

3. ISO/IEC. *Programming Languages: C++ (1st edition).* ISO/IEC 14882:1998(E). 1998.
4. Ada Rapporteur Group. *Annotated Ada Reference Manual with Technical Corrigendum 1 and Amendment 1 (Draft 15): Language Standard and Libraries.* (Working Document on Ada 2005).
5. S. Taft, R. A. Duff, and R. L. Brukardt and E. Ploedereder (Eds). *Consolidated Ada Reference Manual with Technical Corrigendum 1. Language Standard and Libraries.* ISO/IEC 8652:1995(E). Springer Verlag, 2000. ISBN: 3-540-43038-5.
6. CodeSourcery, Compaq, EDG, HP, IBM, Intel, Red Hat, and SGI. *Itanium C++ Application Binary Interface (ABI)*, Revision 1.83, 2005. http://www.codesourcery.com/cxx-abi
7. Ada Rapporteur Group. *Abstract Interfaces to Provide Multiple Inheritance.* Ada Issue 251. http://www.ada-auth.org/cgi-bin/ cvsweb.cgi/AIs/AI-00251.TXT.
8. Ada Rapporteur Group. *Object.Operation Notation.* Ada Issue 252, Available at http://www.ada-auth.org/ cgi-bin/cvsweb.cgi/AIs/AI-00252.TXT.
9. Ada Rapporteur Group. *Protected and Task Interfaces.* Ada Issue 345, Available at http://www.ada-auth.org/cgi-bin/cvsweb.cgi/ AIs/AI-00345.TXT.
10. Ada Rapporteur Group. *Null Procedures.* Ada Issue 348, Available at http://www.ada-auth.org/cgi-bin/ cvsweb.cgi/AIs/AI-00348.TXT.
11. Ada Rapporteur Group. *Single Task and Protected Objects Implementing Interfaces.* Ada Issue 399. Available at http://www.ada-auth.org/cgi-bin/cvsweb.cgi/ AIs/AI-00399.TXT.
12. J. Miranda, E. Schonberg. *GNAT: On the Road to Ada 2005.* SigAda'2004, November 14-18, Pages 51-60. Atlanta, Georgia, U.S.A.
13. J. Miranda, E. Schonberg, G. Dismukes. *The Implementation of Ada 2005 Interface Types in the GNAT Compiler.* 10th International Conference on Reliable Software Technologies, Ada-Europe'2005, 20-24 June, York, UK.
14. J. Miranda, E. Schonberg, K. Kirtchov. *The Implementation of Ada 2005 Synchronized Interfaces in the GNAT Compiler.* SigAda'2005, November 13-17. Atlanta, Georgia, U.S.A.
15. AdaCore. *GNAT Academic Program.* http://www.adacore.com/academic_overview.php

Using Mathematics to Improve Ada Compiled Code

Ward Douglas Maurer

Computer Science Department,
George Washington University,
Washington, DC 20052, USA
maurer@gwu.edu

Abstract. We have developed two mathematical techniques which, used together, can increase the speed of Ada compiled code, in two ways. We can eliminate most subprogram call overhead, involving stack pointer adjustment when a subprogram is called and when it returns. We can also eliminate most static scoping overhead, requiring the use of multiple base registers when procedures are nested. In particular, all this overhead can be eliminated in the absence of recursion. One of our techniques is based on an analogy with a variant of the well-known critical path method. The other is based on a new result in directed graph theory, which has many potential applications in addition to the one presented here.

1 Introduction

The problem being addressed here is that of how to reduce, as much as possible, two kinds of overhead in Ada compiled code. One of these is associated with pushing an allocation record on the public stack when a subprogram is called, and popping it when the subprogram returns. The other is associated with finding local variables of a procedure in which the current procedure is nested, at one or more levels. All this overhead can be eliminated in the non-recursive case, as indicated in section 3 below. However, an improved Ada compiler would be unacceptable if it eliminated overhead only in this case, despite the fact that Ada is used in practice mostly for safety-critical systems using coding rules that normally forbid recursion.

We have developed two mathematical techniques which, used together, can eliminate most of this overhead. One of our techniques is based on an analogy with a variant of the well-known critical path method. The other is based on a new result in directed graph theory, which has many potential applications in addition to the one presented here.

We shall assume familiarity with offsets of variables in allocation records and with the usual rules for pushing and popping these records on the public stack; and also with the static chain method and the display method for gaining access to variables when procedures are nested. These are described in several programming language texts, such as [1].

L.M. Pinho and M. González Harbour (Eds.): Ada-Europe 2006, LNCS 4006, pp. 191–202, 2006.

2   The Critical Path Method

In section 3 below, we will show how to eliminate all subprogram call overhead, and all base register swapping, in the absence of recursion. This will be done by an analogy with the AOV (activity on vertex) version of the critical path method (CPM), which was originally developed for managing large industrial projects.

An industrial project is made up of tasks, sometimes known as activities. Each task takes a certain amount of time, represented by an integer. Several tasks may take place simultaneously. Certain tasks must be finished before other tasks can be started. CPM is used in determining when each task can start; how long the entire project will take; and what to do in case some tasks take more time than they were supposed to.

In using CPM, we form a directed graph; in the AOV version, each task is a node of the graph. (In the other version, AOE or Activity On Edge, tasks correspond to edges, rather than nodes, of the graph.) An edge $P_1 \to P_2$ in the graph denotes the fact that task P_1 must be complete before P_2 can start. For every path in the graph, $P_1 \to P_2 \to \ldots \to P_n$, it therefore follows that P_1 must be complete before P_n can start.

It should be clear that such a graph must be acyclic; it would make no sense for P_1 to be required to finish before P_1 itself can start. It is well known that the graph therefore has a topological sort (see, for example, [2], pages 549-551), meaning that its nodes can be ordered as $P_1, P_2, \ldots, P_n$, in such a way that, for every edge $P_i \to P_j$, we have $i < j$. In what follows, we assume that such an order has been imposed.

We associate a length, $length(P)$, with each task P, which is the amount of time P will take, considered in discrete increments. (In CPM this is an estimated length, to be revised later; but we ignore this detail, since it will not be needed in our analogy.) It is then necessary to find $start(P)$ and $finish(P)$ for each P, where $start(P) + 1$ is the time at which P should start, and $finish(P)$ is the time at which P will then finish. These calculations are made by considering all nodes in the order $P_1, P_2, \ldots, P_n$ of the topological sort. For every initial node P_j of the graph (including P_1), we have $start(P_j) = 0$; for every other node P_j, $start(P_j)$ is the maximum value of all $finish(P_i)$ over all nodes P_i for which there are edges from P_i to P_j, since P_j cannot start until all these P_i have finished. In either case, we have $finish(P_j) = length(P_j) + start(P_j)$.

It is customary to add an artificial node T at the end of the project, with an edge to it from every terminal node. This allows us to calculate $start(T)$, which is the total time taken by the project. CPM now continues by determining a critical path in the project, in order to guide managers if certain tasks actually take longer than their estimated times. As before, we ignore this detail here, since it will not affect our analogy.

An example of all this is given in Figure 1. Here $length(P_i)$ is given initially for each P_i, and we now proceed to calculate $start(P_i)$ and $finish(P_i)$, as follows:

$start(P_1) = 0$ (since P_1 is an initial node)
$finish(P_1) = length(P_1) = 10$

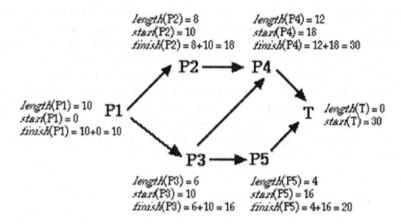

Fig. 1. A sample CPM project graph, showing *length*, *start*, and *finish* values

$start(P_2) = finish(P_1) = 10$
$finish(P_2) = length(P_2) + start(P_2) = 8 + 10 = 18$
$start(P_3) = finish(P_1) = 10$
$finish(P_3) = length(P_3) + start(P_3) = 6 + 10 = 16$
$start(P_4)$ is the maximum of $finish(P_2)$ and $finish(P_3)$, i. e., $max(18, 16) = 18$

$finish(P_4) = length(P_4) + start(P_4) = 12 + 18 = 30$
$start(P_5) = finish(P_3) = 16$
$finish(P_5) = length(P_5) + start(P_5) = 4 + 16 = 20$
$start(T)$ is the maximum of $finish(P_4)$ and $finish(P_5)$, i. e., $max(30, 20) = 30$

3   The Call Graph

We proceed now with our analogy. This time the P_i are subprograms in a computing project, and there is an edge from P_i to P_j in the graph if P_i calls P_j. Such a graph is known as a *call graph*, and these have been studied by Ryder [3]. Unlike a project graph, a call graph G may contain cycles, and such a cycle always represents recursion. Ordinary recursion is represented by a self-loop in G, from some P_i to itself, where P_i calls P_i; mutual recursion is represented by a more general cycle, $Q_1 \rightarrow Q_2 \rightarrow \ldots \rightarrow Q_k = Q_1$, where Q_1 calls Q_2, which calls Q_3, and so on back to Q_1 again.

We start by assuming no recursion, so that the call graph is acyclic; therefore, we may apply the method of the preceding section. This time, $length(P_i)$ is the number of bytes in the allocation record of P_i, while $start(P_i)$ is the offset of the first of these bytes. The offsets of the other bytes range from $start(P_i)$ through $start(P_i) + length(P_i) - 1$. The total allocation size needed for the entire project is $start(T)$; and this number of bytes is reserved when execution starts.

Our overall aim, here, is to associate with every temporary variable V in every subprogram a single offset. Since this offset never changes, it may be used for every reference to V, throughout the lifetime of the project. There is one and only one base register, whose value never changes during execution.

Some of the allocation records share space, since they will never be needed at the same time. However, as we show at the end of section 4 below, this will never be true of the bytes that can be referenced by a nested subprogram. Specifically, suppose that Q_2 is nested in Q_1; Q_3 is nested in Q_2; and so on up to Q_k. Then the local variables of Q_1, Q_2, and so on up through Q_k can always be referenced simultaneously; none of them will ever overlap.

4   A Call Graph Example

Call graphs are illustrated in Figure 2, which describes the following project (omitting most of the statements):

```
procedure P1 is
    S: Short_Integer;  —— 2 bytes
    F: Float;  —— 4 bytes
begin
    . . . P2;
    . . . P3; . . .
end P1;
procedure P2 is
    I: Integer;  —— 4 bytes
begin
    . . . P4; . . .
end P2;
procedure P3 is
    C1: Character;  —— 1 byte
    C2: Character;  —— 1 byte
begin
    . . . P4;
    . . . P5; . . .
end P3;
procedure P4 is
    D: Long_Float;  —— 8 bytes
begin
    . . .
end P4;
procedure P5 is
    . . .
begin
    . . .
end P5;
```

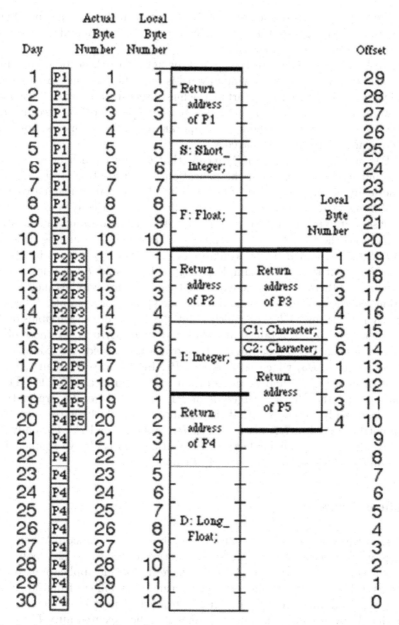

Fig. 2. Actual byte numbers for this project, with local byte numbers and offsets

The call graph of this project is the same as Figure 1. Thus $P1$ calls $P2$ and $P3$, and therefore there are edges from $P1$ to $P2$ and $P3$; both $P2$ and $P3$ call $P4$, so there are edges from both of these to $P4$; and so on. The length of $P1$ is 10, as in Figure 1, since there are 10 bytes needed in the allocation record of $P1$ — four, as always, for the return address; two for S: Short_Integer;

which takes up two bytes; and four for F: Float; which takes up four bytes. The length of $P2$ is 8, since there is, again, a four-byte return address, and also a four-byte I: Integer; and so on.

Note that the given offsets (at the right of the figure) are those for a grow-down stack; each offset for a stack growing upward is one less than the corresponding actual byte number (since these start at 1, while offsets start at zero). Also, in our figure, we omit, without loss of generality, parts of the allocation records other than the return address and the local temporary variables, such as subprogram parameters and registers to be saved.

In CPM, an edge from Q_1 to Q_2 means that Q_1 must finish before Q_2 can start. In our compiling method, the allocation record of $Q1$ (call it $A1$) must metaphorically finish before that of $Q2$ (call it $A2$) can start; meaning that the offsets of bytes in $A1$ are all less than (and thus metaphorically "earlier" than) all the offsets of bytes in $A2$, so that $A1$ and $A2$ become disjoint, on the stack. This is because the values of the temporary variables of Q_1 must be preserved when Q_1 calls Q_2, and must be available for use when Q_2 returns to Q_1. On the other hand, in the CPM example of Figure 1, $P2$ and $P3$ are done at the same time, since there is no edge connecting them. In our compiling method, the allocation records of $P2$ and $P3$ share the same space. For example, $P3$ cannot start until $P2$ returns to $P1$, at which point the values of the variables of $P2$, being temporary, are not retained and thus may be overwritten by those of $P3$.

Suppose now that some of these subprograms are nested; for example, $P5$ could be nested in $P3$, which is nested in $P1$. In that case $P5$ can reference the local variables of $P3$ and $P1$ in addition to its own local variables. This is possible because the allocation records of $P1$, of $P3$, and of $P5$ are mutually disjoint. Informally we can see that, for example, $P3$, which shares space with $P2$, cannot be nested in $P2$, because then $P1$ could not call $P3$. Formally, this kind of condition always holds because the static chain is always a subchain of the dynamic chain (see, for example, [4], Lemma 3.7).

5   Loop Trees

All this, as we have said, works only in the absence of recursion. When there is recursion, it is necessary, as we see in section 6 below, to use loop trees, as introduced by this author in [4]. These have important applications to flow graphs, as well as to call graphs; and their terminology follows from flow graph applications. Here an edge in a flow graph, from statement U to statement V, means that V is, or can be, the next statement to be executed after U (see, for example, [5]). We summarize the general theory in this section, and then go on to its specific application to Ada.

Semantically, outer loops in a flow graph correspond to nontrivial strongly connected components of it (this is not always true syntactically). Here such a component is trivial if it has no edges, and therefore exactly one node. An outer loop L contains at least one entry point, that is, a vertex with an edge to it from outside L, if and only if it does not contain the start vertex of the graph. By choosing a head H for L, either one of its entry points or the start vertex, and then eliminating from L all edges (called *loopbacks*) which lead to H, we obtain the *body* B of L. A first-level inner loop is then a nontrivial strongly connected component of B.

This process may be iterated as many times as necessary, to obtain loops at all levels. The process works for any directed graph, including call graphs. The loops (in this sense) of such a graph G may be arranged in a *loop tree*, with G as the root and the loops as nodes, where descendants of L in the loop tree correspond to loops contained in L. A graph may have more than one loop tree, since a loop may have more than one entry point. A *structured graph* is one which has a unique loop tree; and it may be proved (see the end of [4]) that the structured graphs are exactly the reducible graphs in the sense of Allen and Cocke (see [5]).

The *skeleton* of a graph G is G after removing all loopbacks, as defined above, at all levels. The skeleton of G is acyclic, and therefore, as we have seen, has a topological sort. By putting the loopbacks in again, we arrive at the fundamental theorem of loop trees: any directed graph can always be ordered in such a way that the only reverse edges, relative to the ordering, are the loopbacks.

Loop trees can, without too much difficulty, be found automatically; the only slight difficulty is in the determination of strongly connected components. The easiest way to do this is by doing two depth-first searches, one on the original graph and one on its transpose. The order of starting points in the second search is the reverse of the order of finish times in the first search (see [2], pages 552-557). Another method of finding these components, which avoids the necessity of precomputing the transpose, has been found by Gabow [6].

There is a stronger version of the fundamental theorem in which every loop, at every level, is required to be a contiguous subsequence of the given ordering (see [4], Theorem 1.2). If a graph G has n vertices, represented by the integers 0 through $n-1$, this allows an entire loop tree of G to be represented by two arrays, each indexed from 0 through $n-1$. The first of these, called *order*, is such that $order(k)$ is the kth vertex in the ordering. The second, called *loops*, is such that $loops(k) = j + 1$ where $order(j)$ is the last vertex in the loop with head equal to $order(k)$. If $order(k)$ is not the head of a loop, then $loops(k) = k$.

6   Insert and Remove Operations

The use of loop trees to treat recursion is an extension of a method that is more easily understood in the case of a simple cycle $Q_1 \to Q_2 \to \ldots \to Q_k = Q_1$ in the call graph G. Suppose that the removal of the single edge $Q_{k-1} \to Q_k$ from G leaves an acyclic graph. We now topologically sort that graph, and apply to it the method of the preceding section. This will work so long as Q_{k-1} does not actually call $Q_k = Q_1$.

Suppose now that $start(Q_1) = U$ and $finish(Q_{k-1}) = V$. In other words, the first byte of the allocation record for Q_1 is at $SP + U$, and the last byte of the allocation record for Q_{k-1} is at $SP + V - 1$. When Q_{k-1} calls $Q_k = Q_1$, then, we want the first byte of the allocation record for Q_1, at recursion level 2, to be at $SP + V$. Any reference to this byte with base-displacement addressing, however, will have U in its displacement field. It will work, then, only if $V - U$ is added to SP, producing a new value SP' such that $SP' + U = SP + (V - U) + U = SP + V$.

The treatment of this single cycle proceeds from three observations about adding $V - U$ to SP. First, this also works for any other byte in the allocation record of Q_1. Supposing that there are K bytes in this record, they will be at $SP + U$ through $SP + U + K - 1$ at recursion level 1. At recursion level 2, there is room for them at $SP + V$ through $SP + V + K - 1$. Therefore, byte J of this record will be at $SP + U + J - 1$, and the displacement for it is $U + J - 1$. After adding $V - U$ to SP, and using this same displacement, the effective address is $SP' + U + J - 1 = SP + (V - U) + U + J - 1 = SP + V + J - 1$. This is exactly where we expect it to be, at recursion level 2.

Second, and more important, this also works for any byte in the allocation record of any Q_i, for $2 \le i \le k - 1$. If $start(Q_i) = X_i$, then, at recursion level 1, byte J in the allocation record for Q_i will be at $SP + X_i + J$, and its displacement in base-displacement addressing will be $X_i + J$. Rewriting $SP + X_i + J$ as $SP + U + (X_i - U + J)$, we see that it is byte $X_i - U + J$ among the $V - U$ bytes making up the allocation records of all Q_i for $2 \le i \le k - 1$. At recursion level 2, we lay out space for all these allocation records (we do not necessarily use them all, of course), starting at $SP + V$. Byte $X_i - U + J$ among these will therefore be at $SP + V + (X_i - U + J) = SP' + X_i + J$, where $SP' = SP + V - U$ as before. Thus the displacement $X_i + J$ still works properly.

Finally, all of this also works at recursion levels 3 and higher. At recursion level 2, the last byte of the allocation record for Q_{k-1} is at $SP' + V - 1$. When Q_{k-1} calls $Q_k = Q_1$, then we want the first byte of the allocation record for Q_1, at recursion level 3, to be at $SP' + V$. A reference to this byte, with base-displacement addressing, will work if $V - U$ is added once more to SP', producing SP'', and $SP'' + U = SP' + (V - U) + U = SP' + V$. The same arguments as above may then be used iteratively.

We refer to the adding of $V - U$ to SP as an *insert* operation. It must be undone when $Q_k = Q_1$ returns to Q_{k-1}; this is a *remove* operation. These operations are stack pointer adjustments, like those which we are making unnecessary. This is why we say that we can eliminate *most* (not all) subprogram call overhead, as mentioned in section 1 above.

Whenever there is an operation that must take place when F calls G, there is a question as to whether F should do the operation just before calling G, or whether G should start by doing the operation itself. In this case, there is a definite answer. An insert must be done when Q_{k-1} calls Q_1, but not when Q_1 is called from outside the cycle; therefore Q_1 cannot do the insert, which must be done by Q_{k-1}. In general, when a subprogram P makes a call which is a loopback in the call graph, then P performs the insert operation; then makes the call; and then performs the corresponding remove operation.

7 Structured Graphs

We now show how insert and remove operations may be used in a call graph which is more general than just a simple cycle. We restrict ourselves first to graphs in which each loop has one and only one entry point, or structured graphs (see section 5 above). Let P be called by P', and suppose that this call represents a loopback in the call graph. Suppose that, as above, an insert operation takes place within P' just before it calls P, and a remove operation takes place within P' just after P returns. Then it is not hard to see that this call to P must introduce a new recursion level for P.

We can see this as follows. Suppose that, as above, an insert operation takes place when P' calls P and when this call is a loopback. By the definition of a loopback (in section 5 above), P must be an entry point of some loop L in the loop tree, where P' is also contained in L. If P is the start vertex of G, then it is already on the dynamic chain. Otherwise, P is an entry point of L, and therefore the only entry point of L, since G is structured. In that case L must have been entered at P, and P is again already on the dynamic chain. In either case, P is now at the next higher recursion level.

Consider now the cycle consisting of the path on the dynamic chain from P to P', followed by the edge from P' to P. Since L is a loop, it is strongly connected; since P is in L, this cycle C is completely contained in L. All the subprograms on C are on the dynamic chain when P' calls P, and so space has already been set up on the stack for their allocation records. When P' calls P, and the insert operation is done, space is effectively again set up for all these subprograms. Any such subprogram which is actually called will have its allocation record in the proper place.

8 General Graphs and Pseudo-recursive Calls

We now consider general graphs which are not structured; that is to say, a loop might have more than one entry point. Here we have a new problem, because a loopback $N \to N'$ is defined with respect to a particular choice of head N' for the loop. All we can do is to choose one head H for each loop; perform insert and remove operations in loopbacks relative to H; and then handle alternate entry points in a different way. We shall now see how this can be done.

As a simple example, let us look again at the cycle of section 6 above. We assumed there that Q_1 was the only entry point to this cycle. Suppose, however, that Q_3 is also an entry point; and suppose that we continue to use the method described in that section. That is, just before Q_{k-1} calls $Q_k = Q_1$, an insert operation is done; and, just after Q_1 returns, a remove operation is done. Does this still work? The answer is that it does, although not for an obvious reason.

When the cycle is entered at Q_1, the call from Q_{k-1} to Q_1 is a recursive call; it starts what it calls (in this case Q_1) at a new recursion level. Whenever that happens, adjusting the stack pointer is clearly necessary, since only in that way are proper references made to local temporary variables at the new recursion level. When the cycle is entered at Q_3, however, the call from Q_{k-1} to Q_1 is not recursive; Q_1 is at recursion level 1 when it is called.

It is, therefore, unnecessary to adjust the stack pointer when Q_1 is called, in this case. However, it does no harm, other than using some unnecessary space which was reserved on the stack for the allocation records of Q_1 and Q_2. That space was never used, and the new space reserved for these records, at recursion level 2, is actually being used at level 1; but the speed, and the correctness, of the code are unaffected.

We refer to the call from Q_{k-1} to Q_1, in this case, as a *pseudo-recursive call*. It is not a real recursive call, but it is compiled as if it were. It can, as here, be followed by a real recursive call; in this case, the call from Q_2 to Q_3. No insert operation takes place here, and none is needed, because the insert was already done when Q_{k-1} called Q_1. Further details of this are given in [4].

9   Base Registers

It remains to be seen how many base registers are needed in the general case. In the worst case, a simple example, involving k subprograms, for any $k > 1$, shows that k base registers are required. Let the subprograms be Q_1, Q_2, and so on up to Q_k, where Q_i is nested in Q_{i-1} for $2 \leq i \leq k$; and let each Q_{i-1} possibly (but not always) call itself before it calls Q_i. If Q_k uses the temporary variables of all the Q_i, for $1 \leq i \leq k$, then k base registers are required, one for each Q_i. This is because Q_k has no way of knowing, for each Q_i, whether it called itself or not; all these decisions (did Q_i call itself? yes or no?) are independent of each other; and each decision determines where the temporary variables of Q_i are.

For this reason, we cannot, as mentioned in section 1 above, eliminate all static scoping overhead. We can, however, eliminate most of it, because the example above is contrived. Indeed, there are many cases in which only one base register is needed, even in the presence of arbitrary nesting depth. Suppose that, in the example above, none of the Q_i makes a call to itself; and that the call to Q_1 from Q_{k-1} is the only loopback in the project. Then it is not hard to see that, as before, we can get by with one base register. At recursion level 1, allocation records are on the public stack for Q_1 through Q_{k-1}. When Q_{k-1} calls Q_1, an insert operation takes place, providing space on the public stack for allocation records at level 2 for all these subprograms. The result is that, when Q_j is called, for any j, $2 \leq j \leq k$, the allocation records for all Q_i, for $1 \leq i \leq j$, are available for the use of Q_j at recursion level 2. The same techniques then work at higher levels.

We now solve the problem posed at the start of this section.

Theorem 1. *Let G have the loop tree Z, and let U and V be nodes in G, such that V is nested in U. Suppose that every loop in Z which contains V also contains U. Then U and V can share a base register.*

The proof of this theorem is given in [4] (Theorem 3.1).

In the second example of this section, there is only one loop L in the loop tree, and L consists of the subprograms Q_1 through Q_{k-1}. Here Q_i is nested in

Q_{i-1}, for $2 \leq i \leq k - 1$. All these subprograms are in L, and so the hypotheses of the theorem are satisfied; hence all of these can share a base register, and only one base register is needed for the project. In the first example of this section, however, each Q_i calls itself, for $1 \leq i \leq k - 1$, and therefore there is an edge in the call graph from each Q_i to itself. Each Q_i, therefore, together with this edge, is a separate loop in the loop tree. As we saw, Q_i is nested in Q_{i-1}, for $2 \leq i \leq k - 1$; but, this time, each Q_i is in a loop which does not contain Q_{i-1}, and the hypotheses of the theorem are not satisfied. Indeed, as we saw, none of the Q_i, in general, can share a base register with any other.

10   Conclusions and Suggestions for Further Work

Using mathematics, we have developed methods for saving time in the execution of Ada code. The reason that these methods work is easy to understand as long as the compiled code contains no recursion. It is considerably harder to understand, but relatively easy to apply, when recursion is present.

Our methods result in greater savings when the target processor has a small number of registers. On a machine with 32 general-purpose registers, several of these can be dedicated to use as base registers. On a register-sparse machine, on the other hand, if there are several base registers, their values may well have to be kept in memory and loaded into actual registers when necessary. Reducing the number of base registers results in greater savings in this case.

Further work needs to be done on the actual implementation of the methods presented here, and an empirical determination of efficiency improvement for real examples including both small and large Ada programs. Comparison should then be made between the efficiency problems suggested here and other such problems, including those concerned with complex floating point operations, internal bus limitations, and limitations of graphic hardware. It should be understood that the author of this paper is a mathematician, who is not, at the time of writing, associated with any actual Ada compilation project. This is the only reason for the fact that we have no data on how much savings actually accrue in practice with our methods.

Acknowledgments

The author is grateful to Prof. Michael B. Feldman, and to four anonymous reviewers, for checking this paper for errors and inconsistencies; and to colleagues and students for help with LaTeX.

References

1. Sebesta, R.W.: Concepts of Programming Languages. 7th edn. Addison-Wesley, Boston (2005)
2. Cormen, T.H., Leiserson, C.E., Rivest, R.L., Stein, C.: Introduction to Algorithms. 2nd edn. McGraw-Hill, New York (2001)

3. Ryder, B.G.: Constructing the Call Graph of a Program. IEEE Trans. on Software Eng. 1 (1979) 216-226
4. Maurer, W.D.: Loop Trees for Directed Graphs and Their Applications. Technical Report TR-GWU-CS-05-004. Computer Science Dept., George Washington Univ., Washington (2005)
5. Hecht, M.S., Ullman, J.D.: Flow Graph Reducibility. SIAM J. on Computing 1 (1972) 188-202
6. Gabow, H.N.: Path-Based Depth-First Search for Strong and Biconnected Components. Inf. Processing Letters 74 (2000) 107-114

Replication-Aware Transactions: How to Roll a Transaction over Failures

Mohsen Sharifi and Hadi Salimi

Computer Engineering Department
Iran University of Science and Technology
msharifi@iust.ac.ir, h_salimi@mail.iust.ac.ir

Abstract. The CORBA standard adopted by OMG supports reliability using two orthogonal mechanisms: *Replication* (by means of FT-CORBA standard) and *Transaction* (with the aid of OTS standard). Replication represents a *roll-forward* approach in which a failed request is re-directed into another replica that is alive. On the other hand, transaction represents a *roll-back* approach in which a system reverts into its last committed state upon any failure. Current researches show that integrating these two approaches is essential in 3-tier systems, wherein the replication protects system processes from failures in the middle tier, and the transaction concept ensures the data consistency in the data tier. All proposed methods for reconciling these two concepts are unanimous that the transaction approach suffers from poor performance due to the use of two-phase commit protocol. In this paper we introduce a new *replication-aware* transaction model based on replicated objects. This kind of transaction can jump over the failures that the replicas come across without rolling the whole transaction back (we call it *roll-over*). Instead, the failed objects would be removed from the replica list and re-created somewhere else if needed. Implementation results of our model show better transaction throughput in comparison with known approaches.

1 Introduction

There are two different attributes of fault tolerance for enterprise systems: protection of data against corruption and protection of processes against failures. Data protection means using techniques that guarantee no loss or inconsistencies exist in data. On the other hand, process protection represents methods that ensure that at least one processing unit will be available every time to reply client requests.

To protect data against loss or inconsistency, systems are usually equipped with transaction processing capability. This feature ensures that no partial execution of an operation is allowed. This means that transactions execute completely or not at all [5]. To protect the processes of a system against failures, these processes are usually replicated [6], so that a failed process is replaced with a fresh one.

Object Management Group (OMG) has released two specifications related to fault tolerance, namely, Fault Tolerant CORBA (FT-CORBA) [1] and Object Transaction Service (OTS) [2]. FT-CORBA provides reliability for enterprise applications by replicating CORBA objects so that, if one of the replicas fails, another one can

L.M. Pinho and M. González Harbour (Eds.): Ada-Europe 2006, LNCS 4006, pp. 203–214, 2006.

provide continuous service to the clients. On the other hand, the OTS provides reliability by introducing commit and abort concepts to provide consistency even in the presence of faults. In other words, FT-CORBA yields *liveness* by replicating the CORBA objects, but OTS fulfills the *consistency* or *safety* attribute of a system.

In this paper, we present a *replication-aware* flat transaction model with a new termination style, called *roll-over*. This termination means that although there had been errors during the execution of a flat transaction on a group of replicated objects, the transaction can be committed safely. By means of this method, the replica objects that had failed will be removed from the list of object replicas.

The remainder of this paper is organized as follows. Sect. 2 provides a summarized background on FT-CORBA and OTS required in our discussions. Sect. 3 describes some notable related works. Sect. 4 presents an important limitation of the existing methods. Sect. 5 presents our proposed approach. Sect. 6 illustrates some experimental results of our approach, and finally Sect. 7 concludes the paper.

2 Background

In the rest of this section, we describe the current CORBA standards that provide reliability for the constructed systems. These services include: FT-CORBA and OTS.

2.1 FT-CORBA

Support for availability is provided by the standard that has recently been adopted by OMG, namely, FT-CORBA [1]. This standard implements system availability by replicating objects. In the case of a replica failure, a new replica can take over the failed one, generally without the client's awareness.

In this standard, the concept of IOGR (Interoperable Object Group Reference) is introduced. An IOGR specifies an object reference that contains multiple IORs, each of which represents a replica object reference. The client ORB can easily iterate through the replica references and try to make calls to other replicas in the case of failures.

In FT-CORBA a unit called Replication Manager (RM) manipulates the creation, replication and deletion of replicated objects. RM replicates objects and distributes the replicas across the system. It is also responsible for constructing IOGRs that clients use to contact the replicated objects.

Replica faults are detected by a unit inside each host, namely, Fault Detector (FD). Detected faults are reported to Fault Notifier (FN), which filters them and distributes fault event notifications to RM. Based on these notifications, RM initiates appropriate actions to enable the system to recover from faults.

FT-CORBA defines three different replication styles: (1) *active*, (2) *warm-passive* and (3) *cold-passive*. In active replication, all members of an object group receive and simultaneously process the same sequence of client requests in an independent way. Consistency is guaranteed by assuming that, when provided with the same input in the same order, replicas will produce the same output. In warm-passive replication, the basic principle is that clients send their requests to a primary, which executes the requests and sends update messages to the backups. The backups do not execute the invocation, but apply the changes produced by the invocation execution at the primary. In a cold-passive replication strategy, clients send their requests to a unique primary member of the group which is the only one who executes the requests. After the operation has completed, the state of this primary gets recorded in a message log. When faults occur, the recovery is done using the state information and messages recorded in the message log. In this case, the state gets transferred to a new primary member object.

2.2 OTS

CORBA provides support for safety using the Object Transaction Service (OTS) standard [2]. OTS supports interfaces for synchronizing a transaction across the objects of a distributed and object-based application. A transaction is initiated by a client, and can involve multiple objects. The scope of a transaction is defined by a transaction context, which is shared by all the objects that take part in that transaction. The context is associated with the client thread that initiated the transaction. This context is implicitly bound to subsequent invocations that the client makes, until the client decides to terminate the transaction. If no fault occurs during the execution of a transaction, the changes produced as a consequence of the client's requests are committed. In the case that a fault occurs, any changes to object states that had occurred within the scope of the current transaction are rolled back and discarded.

Each object that intends to take part in a transaction is required to register a special kind of object in the transaction called *resource* object. At the end of a transaction, OTS performs the two-phase commit protocol by issuing requests to the resources registered for the transaction.

3 Related Works

Researches that have so far focused on integrating replication and transaction can be categorized into two different groups. The first group includes those methods in which the integration of legacy concepts of transaction and replication are considered. Old transaction concepts have focused on concurrency and locking methods in database management systems. Legacy concepts of replication are also known as *process groups* in which more than one process is responsible for performing the same task. On the other hand, the second group includes those techniques that try to integrate the new concepts of transaction and replication. These approaches have mainly focused on integrating transaction and replication on distributed systems, especially the ones that have been constructed by means of CORBA. So, the previous attempts at reconciling replication and transaction are discussed under two headings with the focus on: (1) traditional concepts and (2) new concepts.

3.1 Traditional Concepts

In this section we will highlight research efforts that have attempted to solve specific aspects of integrating transactional and group communication protocols.

Some old researches believe that these two models are also rivals. Some of them [7] claim that transactional processing systems are better suited to group communication-enabled ones. Those researches that are group communication supporters [8] have the opposite idea.

A more complete approach is presented in [9]. In this work, the role of group communication in building transaction processing systems is explored. The viewpoint of this paper is that group communication primitives are mechanisms that provide transactional semantics.

The idea of *Group Transactions* was first defined in [10]. This approach tries to integrate the two concepts using a new transactional model. This work also proposes that the transactional servers can also be a group of processes which either work individually or cover each other when a failure occurs.

[11] presents another transaction model, namely, *e-Transaction*. This model is proposed on behalf of enterprise systems in which the middle tier only contains replicated stateless application servers. This model also guarantees to be executed exactly once when errors occur.

3.2 New Concepts

Integrating OTS and FT-CORBA capabilities in order to bring end-to-end reliability to CORBA applications is still an open issue [4]. Some researches [13] believe that integration of these two services requires more facilities to make them interoperable. On the other hand, other works [3] claim that unification of these two standards is possible by applying some changes to the protocols that these services are based on.

A comparison between transactional systems and the ones that use group communication is presented in [12]. This work assumes that future distributed applications will increasingly rely on middleware services. This research shows that transactions can be used to support replication without the need for process groups. It is shown that if the underlying infrastructure supports process groups, these groups can be exploited effectively for binding service replication, for providing faster switching to backups and for supporting active replication.

A CORBA-based infrastructure for unification of OTS and FT-CORBA in 3-tier systems is introduced in [14]. This infrastructure tries to bring reliability to systems by means of replicating application servers and transaction coordinators. This makes it possible to use OTS and FT-CORBA together to achieve higher availability and reliability.

Felber and Narasimhan [3] have proposed a protocol to use transactional mechanisms in the implementation of replicated objects. This protocol can also address the problem of determinism in nested interactions between replicated objects. Using this technique, 3-tier systems would be able to use replication-based availability in their middle tier and at the same time use transaction-based safety in their back-end systems, which are typically database management systems.

4   Limitation of Current Researches

Almost all available implementations of FT-CORBA standard (like Eternal [16], Electra [17] and FRIENDS [18]) rely on *total-order multicast protocols* [15] to keep object replicas consistent. These protocols ensure that all messages sent to a set of objects (processes) are delivered to all of these objects (processes) in the same total order. The underlying totally ordered multicast mechanisms guarantee that all of the replicas of an object receive the same messages in the same order; therefore, they perform the operations in the same order. This ensures that the states of the replicas are consistent at the end of each operation.

Failure of replica objects during the execution of an update operation is still another concern. FT-CORBA standard assumes that no source of non-determinism exists in the system, so all the replicas will reach the same final state after an update execution. Some other FT-CORBA implementations consider non-deterministic behavior for replica consistency. For example, Eternal supposes that if a replica object fails, while performing an operation, the remaining replicas in its object group continue to perform the operation and return the result. In this case, the failed replica is simply removed from the group by object group membership mechanisms while the operation continues to be performed. The failure is thus transparent to other object groups involved in the operation. This replica consistency scheme substantially quickens recovery from faults.

Although the so-called multicast protocols that are frequently used in constructing fault tolerant systems are beneficial, there are cases in which using only these techniques cannot guarantee system safety. Fig. 1 depicts a case in which the object O1 intends to do an atomic operation on a set of replicated objects (G) and a non-replicated object (O2). First, O1 makes a successful call to the group of replicated objects. Next, O1 performs another call to a non-replicated object, O2. The problem is that if O2 fails because of encountering an error, the state changes on replicated objects cannot be discarded.

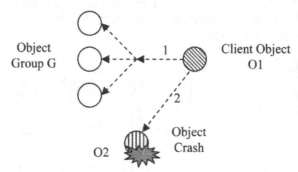

Fig. 1. A case in which the total-order multicast protocol cannot guarantee system safety

According to the above scenario, it can be concluded that the total-order multicast protocols are especially beneficial to guarantee the message delivery to the members of some object groups. They also guarantee to deliver the messages in the same total order. Although the use of these protocols can prevent the objects from going to unsafe states, other sources of inconsistency exist that cannot be resolved using these protocols. As an example, we showed how an object crashing during an atomic operation can lead to an unwanted state.

It seems that the use of transaction technique can solve the mentioned problem. But the transaction model that OTS supports is based on two-phase commit protocol and is flawed with rolling the whole transaction back when encountering any error. In the next section, we propose a new transaction model which works on behalf of replicated objects. As Sect. 6 shows, this model is preferable for dealing with replicated objects, compared to the traditional model that OTS supports.

5 The Proposed Approach

As discussed in Sect. 4, there are cases in which using only multicast protocols cannot guarantee the safety of a system. As an example, we showed how the crash of an object in an atomic operation can lead to system inconsistency. On the other hand, equipping the system with transaction processing capabilities may lead to roll many changes back due to any replica failure.

From another point of view, any failure in the scope of a transaction that is executing on a group of replicated objects can be easily discarded. If the replicated objects are stateless, any failure on a replica can be recovered just by selecting another replica to provide the expected service. Due to this mechanism (called *roll-forward*), the failure can easily be compensated. In the case of statefull objects, forwarding the request to another replica cannot be helpful when a failure occurs, because the states of other replica objects need to remain consistent. In this case, removing the failed object from the group inhibits the roll back of the whole transaction. We call this action *roll-over*, which means that the transaction can be rolled over a failure.

Fig. 2 depicts three different transaction models. In Fig. 2.a, an object crash in the scope of a transaction that is executing on a set of unreplicated objects has lead to roll the whole transaction back. In this case, in step 0, the transaction is issued and in steps 1 and 2, the first object is updated. In step 3 the request for updating the second object is failed because of the crash of this object. So, the transaction will be rolled back, without any state change.

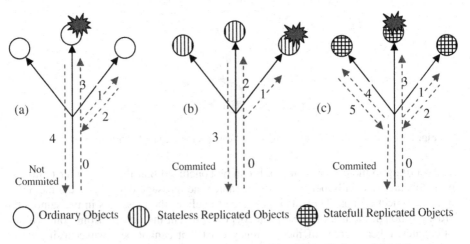

Fig. 2. Three different transaction models: (a) roll-back (b) roll-forward (c) roll-over

Fig. 2.b presents a transaction on a group of stateless replicated objects. The transaction has committed successfully by redirecting the failed request to a live replica. As depicted, although the request in step 1 has failed, but this failure has recovered just by redirecting it to another replica (step 2). Finally, Fig. 2.c shows a case that a transaction is executed across a group of statefull and replicated objects. In this case, although there is a failure during the transaction in step 3, the transaction has committed successfully by removing the failed replica from the relevant object group.

5.1 Implementation of Roll-Over Mechanism

To implement the proposed roll-over approach, we have extended the OTS service in such a way that it can ignore the failures that statefull replica objects come across. In this case, all recoverable objects, including statefull replica objects, register their resource objects in OTS. The difference in registering the resource by replica objects is that they register their resources with a name that can be easily identified by OTS. Using this technique, the OTS Resource Manger is able to distinguish ordinary resource objects from the ones that are registered by replica objects.

When the OTS Resource Manager performs the two-phase commit protocol on registered resources, those resources that belong to replicated objects can be easily detected by their registered name. The Resource Manger can easily ignore the failure occurred in a replica. To clarify the approach, parts of the code for the registerResource and prepare methods in the OTS Resource Manager is given below:

```
void
ResourceManager::registerResource(CosTransactions::Resource_ptr r,
const char* name)
{
    ResourceRecord  record;

    Record.name = name;   // and other initializations for record

    if (strstr(name , "~$Replicated$~"))
            record.setReplicated(true)
    else    record.setReplicated(false);

    resources_.push_back(record);
}

CosTransactions::Vote ResourceManager::prepare(Heuristic& h)
{
    ResourceList::iterator iter = resources_.begin();

    while (iter != resources_.end())
    {
        CosTransactions::Resource res = apply(*iter).resource;
        CosTransactions::Vote v = res -> prepare();

        switch(v)            {
        case CosTransactions::VoteRollback:
            if (res -> isReplicated())
                resources_.Remove(res);
            else return v;

        //other cases come here
        }
    }
}
```

In the code related to *prepare* method, when the Resource Manager receives a *VoteRollback* vote from a resource, if the registered resource belongs to a replicated object, the resource is easily said to forget about the transaction and is removed from the resource list. So this resource will not take part in the next step of the two-phase commit protocol.

5.2 Removing the Failed Replica from Its Group

The elimination of a replica that has failed during a transaction is performed by its registered resource. Using this mechanism, each resource object issues a crash message to its owner object whenever a failure occurs. The replica object (resource owner) then marks its state as *NotAlive*. This state causes the replica object to be detected as a failed object by the local fault detector. The local fault detector informs the Replication Manager of the failure. Now, the Replication Manager is responsible for recreating the failed replica somewhere else. It is also possible for the resource object to encounter a fault. In this case, the fault will be explicitly detected by its local fault detector the next time it pings the local servant.

5.3 Support for Group Failure Detection

Failure of all the objects belonging to an object group is still another concern. This case may occur when all the replica objects are running on the same host. The crash of this host will cause all the replicas to shut down. Disconnection of hosts, the ones that a group of replica objects are running on, from the network may be another reason for group failure. Group failure can also occur if at a given time there exists only one replica in the system and that replica comes across a failure.

The approach that we have proposed up to here is not able to tolerate this kind of fault; in the case of a group failure, the transaction server will commit the transaction even if the entire replica objects fail. In other words, our extended transaction service will roll over all the failures regardless of considering a group failure.

To tolerate this special kind of failure, the information about whether all the members of an object group have failed or not should be specified in the revised OTS. To achieve this, the names in which resource objects have registered themselves in the transaction service must be changed in such a way that replicas' group can be determined. As depicted in Fig. 3, this name is composed of two parts. The first part is a constant string as used in the program code above. The second part is the identifier of the group that the replica object belongs to. This identifier can easily be retrieved from the replica's IOGR. By means of this name, OTS is able to roll the transaction back if all group members fail during the transaction.

Fig. 3. The structure of a resource name registered by a replica object

6 Performance Measurement

We have developed a prototype environment (adopted from [14]) to evaluate our proposed approach. It is based on an open source ORB, namely, ORBacus [20] and our extended version of ORBacus OTS implementation [19] from Object-Oriented Concepts, Inc. We have also implemented a light-weight Replication Manager Service to manage replica manipulation. Our experiments were carried out on a number of Pentium III PCs over a 100 Mbit/Sec LAN. Each PC was equipped with 256 Mbytes of RAM and ran Microsoft Windows XP© with SP1.

The experimental application architecture is shown in Fig. 4. A client invokes the replicated server objects to do a simple bank balance transfer operation. An interceptor is registered at the client side and dispatches the client requests to all target replica objects, which are distributed across the network, using *active* replication style. The account objects then update their states which are stored in the MS SQL Server DBMS.

Each balance transfer request is carried out in the scope of a transaction which is initiated by the client. All replica objects are updated during the execution of this transaction. If any account object fails during this period, the transaction server will not roll the transaction back; instead, it commits the transaction with the remaining objects. In the prepare and commit phase, OTS ignores any partial failures caused by a replicated object. The failed replica objects are detected by means of local fault detectors. The recovery from fault is performed by reporting the fault to Replication Manager and creating the failed replica again.

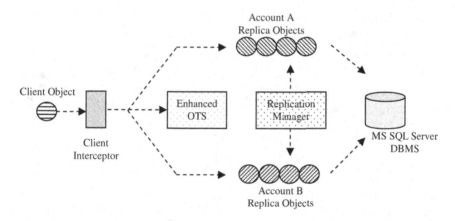

Fig. 4. An architectural view of the implemented environment

We ran the described application on the chosen hardware platform with different configurations. The following parameters were changed in each run: the number of each account replica objects (N), the probability of a replica failure (P) and the preferred transaction model supported by OTS. In each configuration, we measured the overall transaction throughput (T) in terms of the number of committed transactions per second. The results are summarized in Fig. 5.

As depicted in Fig. 5, the transaction throughput (T) increases when the roll-over approach is used, especially in faulty environments. When there is no fault in the system (P=0), both approaches lead to the same value of T. In a fully faulty environment (P=1), the two approaches lead to the same value of T (T=0) again. As the number of replica objects increases, the roll-over approach shows better performance compared to roll-back approach. The reason is that when a transaction is issued on a crowded object group, the probability of roll-back increases and hence more transactions fail to commit.

An interesting point about the roll-over approach, in contrast to roll-back approach, is that when P varies between 0 to 0.5 (or 0.7 for more crowded groups) the value of T increases. The rate of this increase also deteriorates as N decreases. The reason is that as the failure probability increases, more replica objects are prone to crash. So, fewer objects are able to do a successful commit operation. In this case, the roll-over approach commits the transaction with a fewer number of objects and hence the whole transaction duration decreases and more transactions can commit in a defined interval. The failed objects need to be recreated in the system again, but because the cost of recreation of an object is much less than writing the value of the object into a database table, the roll-over approach shows better performance. We expect decrease in performance in case of heavy objects.

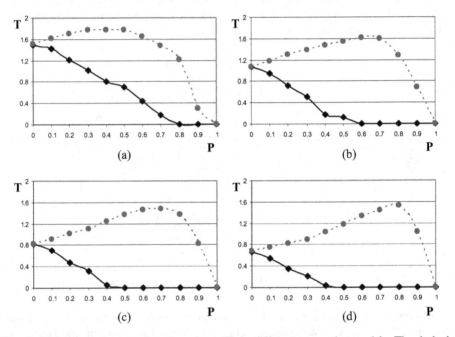

Fig. 5. The measured transaction throughput (T) in different transaction models. The dashed curves show T for roll-over approach, and the solid curves show T for roll-back approach. (a) N=2, (b) N=3, (c) N=4 and (d) N=5.

Although our experimental results show better performance for roll-over approach, there are cases in which this mechanism may not be helpful. As an example, consider the organization of objects shown in Fig. 1. In this case, the transactions that use the roll-over model will pass the replicated objects by rolling over the failures that may occur in this group, but may crash due to O2 failure. So, roll-over approach brings some extra object commits that will be rolled back finally. This extra commits will be the cause of poor performance in this scenario.

Table 1. A feature-wise transaction model comparison

Object Type	Object State	Recovery Mechanism	OTS Change	Transaction Type	Replication Style
Ordinary Objects	Stateless or Statefull	Roll-Back	No	Flat or Nested	N/A
Replicated Objects	Stateless	Roll-Forward	No	Nested	Active
	Statefull	Roll-Over	Yes	Flat	Warm-Passive or Active

A feature-wised comparison for different transaction models with respect to replicated objects is presented in Table 1.

7 Conclusion and Further Work

In this paper we showed that current replica consistency techniques that are based on total order multicast protocols cannot guarantee system safety. To solve this problem, we presented a new transaction model that can be applied to object replicas. This model is based on the fact that a failure in the scope of a transaction that is running on a group of replicated objects can be easily ignored. To achieve a good performance, we extended the OTS in support of our model. We also implemented a prototype to evaluate this extension. The experimental results showed that this model is particularly beneficial to crowded object groups within faulty environments. In the case of replica groups that contain fewer objects, this approach is not recommended due to high probability of a group failure.

The current research will be complemented in future by modeling the proposed approach with Stochastic Petri Nets, and also by extending the model to support the *active with voting* replication style.

References

1. Object Management Group: Fault Tolerant CORBA (Final Adopted Specification). OMG Technical Committee Document, formal/01-12-29, December 2001.
2. Object Management Group: Object Transaction Service Specification. Version 1.4, OMG Technical Committee Document, formal/03-09-02, September 2003.
3. Felber, P., Narasimhan, P.: Reconciling Replication and Transactions for the End-to-End Reliability of CORBA Applications. In the Proceedings of International Symposium on Distributed Objects and Applications (DOA'02), pp. 737-754, October 2002.
4. Felber, P., Narasimhan, P.: Experiences, Strategies and Challenges in Building Fault-Tolerant CORBA Systems. IEEE Transactions on Computers, Vol. 53, No. 5, May 2004.
5. Gray, J., Reuter, A.: Transaction Processing: Concepts and Techniques. Morgan Kaufmann Publishers, San Mateo, CA, 1993.
6. Pullum, L.: Software Fault Tolerance Techniques and Implementations. Artech House Publishers, Norwood, MA, 2001.

7. Cheriton, D.R., Skeen, D.: Understanding the Limitations of Causally and Totally Ordered Communication. In the Proceedings of 14th ACM Symposium on Operating Systems Principles. Operating Systems Review, 27 (5), pp. 44-57, December 1993.

8. Rebuttals from Cornell, Operating Systems Review, 28 (1), January 1994.

9. Schiper, A., Raynal, M.: From Group Communication to Transactions in Distributed Systems. CACM, 39(4), April 1996.

10. Martinez, M.P., Peris, R.J., Arevalo, S.: Group Transactions: An Integrated Approach to Transaction and Group Communication. Workshop on Concurrency in Dependable Computing, June 2001.

11. Frolund, S., and Guerraoui, R.: Implementing e-Transactions with Asynchronous Replication. IEEE Transactions on Parallel and Distributed Systems, vol. 12, No. 2, pp. 133-146 (2001).

12. Little, M.C., Shrivastava, S.K.: Integrating Group Communication with Transactions for Implementing Persistent Replicated Objects. Lecture Notes in Computer Science, Vol. 1752, Springer-Verlag, 2000.

13. Frolund, S., Guerraoui, R., CORBA Fault-Tolerance: why it does not add up. In the Proceedings of the IEEE Workshop on Future Trends in Distributed Systems, Cape Town, December 1999.

14. Zhao, W., Moser, L.E., Melliar-Smith, P.M.: Unification of Replication and Transaction Processing in Three-Tier Architectures. In the Proceedings of the International Conference on Distributed Systems, 2002.

15. Tanenbaum, A.S., Steen, M.V.: Distributed Systems: Principles and Paradigms. Prentice Hall, 2002, ISBN: 0-13-088893-1

16. Moser, L.E., Melliar-Smith, P.M, Narasimhan, P.: Consistent Object Replication in the Eternal System. Theory and Practice of Object Systems, 4(2):81-92, 1998.

17. Maffeis, S.: Run-Time Support for Object-Oriented Distributed Programming. PhD thesis, University of Zurich, Feb. 1995.

18. Fabre, J.C., Perennou, T.: FRIENDS: A Flexible Architecture for Implementing Fault Tolerant and Secure Distributed Applications. In the Proceedings of the 2nd European Conference on Dependable Computing (EDCC), LNCS 1150, pp.3-20, Springer Verlag, 1996.

19. Object Oriented Concepts, Inc. ORBacus OTS, Version 1.2, 2000. http://ooc.com

20. Object Oriented Concepts Inc. ORBacus 4.1.1, http://ooc.com

The Arbitrated Real-Time Protocol (AR-TP): A Ravenscar Compliant Communication Protocol for High-Integrity Distributed Systems*

Santiago Urueña[1], Juan Zamorano[1], Daniel Berjón[2],
José A. Pulido[2], and Juan A. de la Puente[2]

[1] Technical University of Madrid (UPM)
Department of Computer Architecture and Technology (DATSI)
E28660 Boadilla del Monte, Spain
{suruena, jzamora}@datsi.fi.upm.es
[2] Technical University of Madrid (UPM)
Department of Telematic Systems Engineering (DIT)
E28040 Madrid, Spain
{berjon, pulido, jpuente}@dit.upm.es

Abstract. A new token-passing algorithm called AR-TP for avoiding the non-determinism of some networking technologies is presented. This protocol—based on RT-EP, a research protocol also based on transmission control techniques—allows the schedulability analysis of the network, enabling the use of standard Ethernet hardware for Hard Real-Time behavior while adding congestion management. It is specially designed for High-Integrity Distributed Hard Real-Time Systems, being fully written in Ada and taking advantage of some of the new Ada 2005 features, like the Ravenscar Profile.

1 Introduction

A Distributed Hard Real-Time System must not respond later than expected to its inputs. Therefore the timing behavior of all of its actions shall be bounded, including the access to the network. However, some network technologies do not have a deterministic media access control —usually due to collisions in the shared medium—, being thus not directly usable by applications with real-time constraints. A possible solution is to add a transmission control layer [1] to the communication stack to avoid this unpredictable behavior, and thus making the access to the network predictable.

This paper describes the *Arbitrated Real-Time Protocol* (AR-TP), a communication protocol designed for safety-critical embedded hard-real time systems that employs token passing for avoiding collisions. These high-integrity systems exhibit a set of strict requirements not found in other application fields, heavily derived from the entailed certification process. The certification of an application can be difficult or even impossible if no constraints are imposed to the development process.

Ada has always provided a good foundation for the development of real-time embedded applications, as well as for those with the more demanding safety-critical requirements. Because the unrestricted usage of some high level constructions of some

---

* Work supported by MEC, project TRECOM (TIC2002-04123).

L.M. Pinho and M. González Harbour (Eds.): Ada-Europe 2006, LNCS 4006, pp. 215–226, 2006.

programming languages can lead to unpredictable code behavior, the protocol has been designed to be compliant with the Ada Ravenscar Profile [2], a subset that restricts the Ada tasking features in such a way that defines a computational model that allows current response time analysis techniques [3] [4]. The current implementation of AR-TP as well as the network interface card driver are fully programmed in the Ada Ravenscar profile, also taking advantage of some other features added by Ada 2005 [5] like execution time clocks, task termination procedures or the partition elaboration policy.

Although most communication protocols could be coded using the Ravenscar Profile, its timing analysis can be difficult to obtain or too pessimistic (and thus useless). AR-TP has been specifically designed to be easily implemented under those restrictions, as well as predictable enough for modeling its temporal behavior. Now that the Ravenscar profile has been standardized by ISO as part of the Ada 2005 language revision, it is time to look forward and, together with deterministic protocols like AR-TP, to develop a Distributed Ravenscar Profile that paves the way for certifying High-Integrity Distributed Hard Real-Time systems.

This paper is organized as follows. Section 2 discusses some networking technologies used in embedded and real-time systems. Section 3 gives a detailed description of the protocol, whereas section 4 explains the implementation. Section 5 evaluates the properties of the Arbitrated Real-Time Protocol. Finally, section 6 presents the conclusions of this work.

2   Networking Technologies for Real-Time Systems

Fieldbuses like CAN Bus [6] were the communication networks traditionally used in automation systems because they fulfilled the requirements of distributed hard real-time systems, including predictability (deterministic behavior), low cost and reliability [7]. But nowadays these networks cannot provide the required bandwidth for the more demanding distributed real-time systems [8]. For example, CAN Bus cannot improve its bandwidth because it is limited by the propagation time. Therefore developers are looking for cost-effective alternatives, including network technologies that were not designed for systems with real-time requirements.

Two widely-used Local Area Network (LAN) technologies that do not have a deterministic behavior are IEEE 802.3 [9] (commonly known as *Ethernet*), and the IEEE 802.11 family of standards [10] (also known as *Wi-Fi*). These technologies are by far the most used communication networks in office environments, and through the years they have increased their bandwidth and decreased their cost, becoming *de facto* networking standards. This ensures that they will continue to be maintained and improved in the future.

These advantages over other communication networks make both technologies appealing options for the development of distributed systems. Industrial versions of Ethernet and Wi-Fi have been developed to support more aggressive conditions, like those faced in automation and other industrial environments, hardening network interfaces and wires. But their non-deterministic arbitration mechanism, designed for a shared physical medium, prevents their direct use as a communication network with real time constraints.

The arbitration mechanism of Ethernet (CSMA/CD) monitors the physical medium until no signal is detected, sending the message when the Interframe Gap (IFG) time has expired (96-bit times, i.e. 9.6 μs at 10 Mbit/s). If a collision is detected during the transmission of the frame, the node stops transmitting the message, sends a jam signal to ensure that other stations detect the collision too, and waits for a random time before trying to send the message again. This random wait in the arbitration mechanism is the main cause of the non predictability of Ethernet (Wi-Fi has an analogous behavior).

The use of transmission control techniques to avoid non-determinism is an effective method that can be implemented by a portable software layer above full-conforming standard hardware, and without modifying the device drivers. This method can work with any network topology, including Wi-Fi, half-duplex Ethernet, full-duplex Ethernet, or a heterogeneous network made of any combination of hubs, switches, bridges, repeaters or other network devices. However, some of them do not support the use of switches or bridges for full performance.

3   Description of the Protocol

3.1   Overview

The Arbitrated Real-Time Protocol (AR-TP) is a research real-time communication protocol for local area networks with a non-deterministic shared media like half-duplex Ethernet, Wi-Fi, or other wireless networks. It is based on RT-EP (Real-Time Ethernet Protocol) [11], a research multipoint local area network protocol designed to achieve full predictability over half-duplex Ethernet thanks to the addition of a transmission control layer for avoiding collisions. In RT-EP a station is not allowed to put any frame on the network until it receives a special frame, called *token*, which gives it the right to transmit. Stations are organized into a logical ring where, as the network is a shared medium, every station receives all the frames.

In RT-EP the token is first circulated through all stations to write onto this special frame the priority of their messages. When the token arrives to the last node, the right to transmit is finally granted to the station with the highest priority message. When the data message has been transferred, the token is circulated again to start another negotiation cycle. The protocol is fully distributed, and is prepared to detect and solve some types of faults, like the loss of a token or a failing station.

Under RT-EP the maximum blocking time for a message can be computed because the random wait introduced by the Media Access Control of Ethernet is completely eliminated. Moreover, as fixed priorities are assigned to messages, there are mature schedulability techniques for analyzing the timing behavior of the network, thus being adequate for distributed systems with hard-real time requirements. Other advantages of the protocol are its fault-tolerance mechanisms (e.g. there is no single point of failure) and especially that it works with unmodified Ethernet hardware.

However, the performance of RT-EP is lower than other protocols because a high number of arbitration packages are needed for every transferred message. This means that the network bandwidth is decreased, and that the nodes must circulate the token even when there are no messages to transmit (a delay is introduced before sending every token in order to reduce the CPU overhead). Other issues of RT-EP are that it is

Ethernet specific, and that it reduces the Maximum Transfer Unit (MTU) of the network due to the addition of a new header to data messages. AR-TP was developed in order to eliminate some drawbacks of RT-EP —specially the performance and CPU overhead— while maintaining its advantages —predictability and fault-tolerance— as well as adding other features derived from the requirements. The main differences of AR-TP with respect to RT-EP are that more than one message could be sent in the transmission phase, and the addition of a framework for handling network overloads.

The bandwidth is increased in AR-TP because up to n messages could be sent in each transmission phase, as well as other improvements like decreasing the number of packets needed in the arbitration. Therefore the ratio between info data and control data is higher, the overhead of the protocol is lower and thus the throughput is increased. Moreover, less control messages are used in AR-TP than in RT-EP. However, the higher the cycle time, the worse the maximum blocking time —a vital concern of hard-real time systems—, so the optimum value of n is constrained by the characteristics of the system. It depends on the number of stations, the maximum size of data messages, and the worst admissible blocking time. In addition, AR-TP exploits the control messages for including an additional service: the token contains the global number of messages currently waiting to be sent. By monitoring this new parameter the stations are capable to prevent and handle network congestions.

3.2   Detailed Description

Consider a distributed system composed by M stations interconnected by a communications network, where each station can be a producer or/and a consumer, i.e. sends data messages or receives data messages (or both). All the producer nodes of the network are organized into a logical ring where each station has been assigned a unique network identifier (ID). Each node must be informed about the configuration of the ring to know the ID of its successor and predecessor.

In AR-TP the access to the (shared) medium is controlled by the use of a token. The possession of this special message gives the station the right to transmit. It also contains information about the number of messages waiting to be transmitted, and the ID of the stations with the highest priority messages. After the initialization of the system, when the logical ring has been established, the first communication cycle starts when the node with the lowest ID creates a new token. This token is initialized by setting to zero the number of enqueued frames (messages waiting to be sent) and the sequence number. Each communication cycle has two phases: the *arbitration phase* and the *transmission phase*.

At the arbitration phase the token circulates through all the stations to determine the nodes with the n highest priority messages. While holding the arbitration token, each station checks the n priority slots of the token, where empty slots have priority 0. If one or more slots have recorded a lesser priority than any of the messages of the current station, it overwrites those slots with the priority of its messages and its ID. But if the station has no messages or the preceding nodes have filled all the slots with higher priorities, it does not modify these fields of the token. If the number of enqueued messages of this station has changed with respect to the previous cycle, it modifies the token field with the global number of enqueued messages, and then transmits the token to its successor.

When the arbitration token arrives to the last node, it will have recorded the ID of the stations with the highest priority messages. Then this last station, just after determining whether any of its messages has higher priority than the other nodes, modifies the message type to the "transmission token" value, starting the transmission phase. At this phase the token is circulated among the "winning" stations to allow them to send their messages. The token is updated with the new global number of enqueued messages. When all the messages have been sent, the transmission phase ends, starting a new communication cycle.

The last node that has transmitted a data message puts the new token in the next arbitration phase. This new token is circulated immediately unless no frames were sent at the transmission phase of the previous cycle. In that case, if the priority of zero messages were recorded in the token at the end of the arbitration phase, a delay W is introduced before starting the next cycle to reduce the transmission of control packets when there are no messages to send. It should be noted that the new initiator of the arbitration phase is probably different in every cycle.

Due to the fault-tolerance mechanisms, the behavior of the protocol requires some time-outs to detect the token loss, as well as a failing station. Refer to the paper about RT-EP [11] for more information.

3.3 Temporal Behavior

As stated above, temporal predictability is of paramount importance when certifying a hard real-time system. The *response time* of the protocol is defined as the time elapsed since the message is passed to the AR-TP layer at the sender node, until its arrival at the destination node. All operations are bounded, and schedulability analysis can be done. The *cycle time* of AR-TP can be modeled as shown below. The k-th cycle time $Cycle_k$, of a system with M producer nodes can be obtained from the following equation:

$$
Cycle_k = \overbrace{(t_{delay} + t_{token}) \cdot M}^{arbitration\ phase} + \begin{cases} W & n_k = 0 \\ \overbrace{\sum_{i=1}^{n_k} (t_{delay} + Msg_{i,k})}^{transmission\ phase} & n_k > 0 \end{cases} \tag{1}
$$

where t_{token} is the token transmission time, t_{delay} is the delay between messages, n_k is the number of messages sent in the k-th arbitration phase, $Msg_{i,k}$ is the transmission time of the i-th message of the cycle k, and W is the wait time.

The delay between messages (t_{delay}) is imposed by the hardware, e.g. in Ethernet is equal to the IFG (0.96 μs at 100 Mbit/s). This delay could also be "incremented" by software for other purposes like to leave enough execution time to process the token for some slow nodes (e.g. microcontrollers). Note that in RT-EP this delay between messages is used to reduce the CPU overhead of the stations (mainly when there are no messages to send), whereas in AR-TP the wait time W is used for this purpose, and only this wait is introduced when there are no enqueued messages. Of course $W \geq t_{delay}$.

Under AR-TP, the response time of any message is bounded. The best response time of the protocol is when the last node of the arbitration phase wants to send a minimum-size message with a higher priority than any of the other stations just before writing the final token, i.e. the minimum-size message is produced just before the start of the transmission phase, being the first to be sent, i.e.

$$R_{best} = t_{token} + t_{delay} + Msg_{min}, \tag{2}$$

where Msg_{min}, is the transmission time of a minimum size message. However, the best case is not used to analyze the schedulability of a hard real-time system, but the worst case. The response time in the worst case has to take into account the blocking time caused by the non-preemptability of the network, potentially causing a priority inversion. The maximum blocking time B occurs when the initial node produces a message just after the arbitration token has been transmitted, having to wait the whole arbitration phase as well as the longest transmission phase. Please, refer to other papers about this protocol [12] for a more complete timing analysis.

This blocking time depends heavily on the number of messages sent by cycle (n), the delay time (t_{delay}) and the size of the maximum message (Msg_{max}). The system designer can adjust any of these parameters to obtain an adequate blocking time, while maximizing the throughput of the network and minimizing the CPU overhead. The value of n can be as high as the allowed by the maximum admissible blocking time. If the application needs a very tight response time, n can be reduced to 1, giving the same blocking time as RT-EP (in fact the response time is slightly better because there are less arbitration frames in AR-TP than in RT-EP).

The priority of a message is proportional to the temporal constraints of its data, i.e. the closer the relative deadline the higher its assigned priority. This fixed priority assigned to a message is obtained by using timing analysis techniques, deduced from the maximum blocking time. However, although the current implementation uses Fixed Priority Scheduling, the message priorities do not need to be fixed, and they could be scheduled using dynamic techniques like Earliest Deadline First, for example.

3.4   Congestion Management

The system is said to be overloaded when it has to process more jobs than it can cope with, due to the lack of resources. Overloads can happen by an unforeseen event not taken into account at development time, or during operation due to an implementation bug. Therefore, although temporal analysis is conducted during system design to obtain a correct behavior, dependable systems must be prepared to handle overloads at runtime. The protocol has been designed to cope with network overloads (congestions), i.e. when there are too many messages to be sent by the nodes without violating their time constraints. Usually, under the nominal mode of operation, the priority of a message is proportional to the temporal constraints of its data, as stated above. However, when the system is overloaded not all messages will be sent before the violation of their deadlines, therefore the priority of the message should be proportional to the criticality of the data, and not the urgency.

To achieve this behavior, in AR-TP each message has associated two priorities, one used when the system is in the nominal operating mode, and the other when the network is under an overload. A network congestion is detected when the number of enqueued messages at the end of the previous cycle exceeds a determined threshold O_1. Each station checks this value reading the last token sent in the previous cycle. In the next arbitration phase the overload priority will be considered instead of the regular one. The network congestion is considered to be finished when the number of enqueued messages decreases to a given constant O_2, where $O_1 \geq O_2$. Two thresholds are used for the mode change instead of one to avoid overload mode bouncing. The value of both constants depends on the network bandwidth, the number of nodes of the ring, as well as the maximum size of messages, being thus system specific.

The whole algorithm has been designed to have a constant computational complexity, i.e. $O(1)$ in the big O notation: in the average case, only a constant number of frames has to be examined before updating the arbitration token (the upper bound is the maximum number of messages allowed in a transmission phase), even when a mode change have just occurred. To this end, the current implementation uses two output queues in every node —one ordered by the regular priority whereas the other is ordered by the congestion priority— and thus there is no need after a mode change to reorder the messages.

During a congestion it is highly probable that some messages violate their time constraints while being enqueued, so, to avoid sending obsolete data, each message has also assigned an absolute deadline that must be checked before recording its priority in an arbitration token. Of course, the sender task of that message is informed when this happens. However, in the worst case, all the messages of a node can have violated their deadlines before being sent. Therefore, the entire queue would be examined dropping all messages while searching for the highest priorities, having thus a linear complexity. A background task is introduced for dropping all enqueued messages that have violated their deadlines, trying to avoid this situation.

4 Implementation

A preliminary version of the AR-TP protocol has been developed with the GNAT/ORK [13] cross-compilation system for PC-compatible computers. The target computers are Advantech PCM-3350 single board computers, which are PC/104 compatible and include an AMD Geode processor at 300 MHz as well as an Intel i82559 LANCE (Local Area Network Controller for Ethernet). The i82559 can operate the network at 10 or 100 Mbit/s and it was designed for the PCI bus. It must be noted that the stations are interconnected by a 100 Mbit/s Ethernet hub and not by a switch, which would introduce a noticeable transmission delay as well as extra traffic.

The intended middleware layers for high integrity distributed applications are shown in figure 1. The whole system —the low level driver and the AR-TP protocol layer— has been implemented from the scratch following the Ravenscar profile, which is supported by the Open Ravenscar Kernel. It is planned to add new low-level drivers for other network technologies, e.g. wireless local area networks.

The Ravenscar profile provides a foundation adequate indeed for the development of the low level Ethernet driver, as it retains nearly every element from the Ada language needed for low-level development, such as representation clauses, which greatly

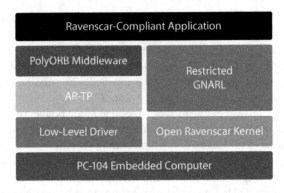

Fig. 1. General architecture

improve code readability. In fact, the Ravenscar profile definition provides much more than is really needed for this particular piece of software, which was finally written using full sequential code except for the use of a single protected object to handle the interrupts generated by the network adapter in the way described in Annex C of the Ada Reference Manual [5]. There are also no explicit dependencies on ORK, so the code should be readily usable under any other operating system that provides an Ada runtime library with the minimum tasking capabilities needed to support the interrupt handling.

The driver provides two sending procedures, one enables the programmer to send Ethernet frames from a single memory buffer, with type checking, while the other sends whatever data is stored in several raw data buffers in sequence, which is useful to avoid data copying when using a layered network architecture in which each network layer attaches a header to the packet coming from the upper level. Using this procedure each header may be contained in a different buffer and there is no need to copy anything. Both sending procedures are blocking, as the time needed to execute the call is fairly small and constant for a given package size and it simplifies memory management, making it unnecessary to keep track of whether a memory buffer has already been read. Neither of the sending procedures returns any feedback about the success of the sending operation because the adapter does not provide reliable information on this subject so all error detection logic is left for the upper software layers.

Two receiving methods are provided in a blocking variant, which returns data if there was any frame waiting to be read or waits until there is. Since blocking calls cannot be cancelled under the restrictions of the Ravenscar profile, a non-blocking variant is also provided, which returns immediately either with valid data or signaling the absence of such data. Both variants can be used interchangeably during the same program with no ill effects. No operation requires dynamic memory allocation, whose use can be freely decided by the implementor of the upper level.

The Ravenscar profile has also been expressive enough for supporting the required behavior of the AR-TP layer. It has two tasks: the main task and a background task. The latter continuously traverses through the two output queues discarding the messages that have violated their deadlines. The main task implements the logic of AR-TP, and is in charge of checking incoming messages, processing the token, and transmitting the adequate frames. This task must be assigned a higher priority than any other task using the network disrupting the communication. Both tasks make use of CPU time clocks for measuring their worst-case execution time.

Finally, it must be said that the guide of usage of the Ravenscar profile [14] has been a great reference for the implementation of the whole system. A preliminary middleware prototype has been built by using the Ravenscar compliant version of PolyORB [15], which provides a Distributed System Annex (DSA) implementation. However, this preliminary prototype was built by using the raw Ethernet driver and therefore the AR-TP layer has still to be integrated. Furthermore, in the future it is planned to design a new Partition Communication Subsystem interface —taking advantage of the new Ada 2005 permission to provide an implementation dependent one— to fully exploit the features of AR-TP within the DSA.

5   Evaluation

Metrics of the best-, average- and worst-case response times have been obtained for a set of operations of the protocol, using an AR-TP prototype on a cluster of three PC/104 nodes, as described in section 4. The test application was designed to stress the network at the same instant in every node. Some hooks were added to the protocol source code for obtaining precise execution time measures of operations. Also, all the frames put in the network were captured by the host with the help of a packet sniffer, traffic later analyzed for exact time measurements.

The metrics were taken for different configurations of the protocol. The maximum size of the data was varied between 75–1500 bytes, while the number of messages per transmission phase (n) was given the values 1, 3, and 5. (When the value of n equals to 1, the performance of the protocol is equivalent to RT-EP.) The delay used between messages at the arbitration phase was 100 μs.

The processing of the token is a relevant metric of AR-TP. The execution time needed to check and modify the slots of the token at the arbitration phase depends on the number of slots of the token (n), but not on the maximum size of the messages. As can be seen in table 1, the token processing time does not increase significantly with the number of messages per cycle.

Table 1. Measures of the prototype implementation

Frame size (octets)	n	Token check time (μs)			Arbitration time (μs)		
		Best	Average	Worst	Best	Average	Worst
	1	6.08	6.11	8.78	733	810	1062
75	3	6.97	7.00	10.48	709	973	1065
	5	7.01	7.13	11.06	741	836	1169
	1	4.79	5.82	9.50	733	821	1162
500	3	6.91	7.00	11.08	737	831	1414
	5	5.00	5.07	9.78	741	838	1179
	1	6.08	6.12	9.52	733	812	1355
1500	3	5.00	6.08	10.65	734	835	1357
	5	5.00	6.92	10.73	717	827	1365

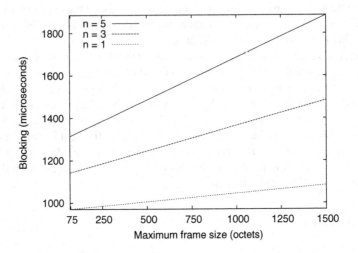

Fig. 2. Blocking time for 3 stations

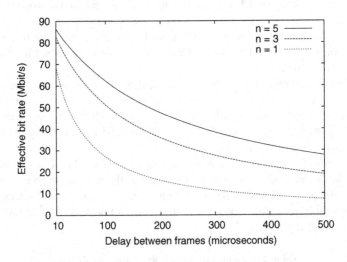

Fig. 3. Effective bit rate for 3 stations sending messages of 1500 octets

Another interesting metric of the protocol is the duration of an arbitration phase. It can be seen in the table that the arbitration phase barely grows with the number of messages per cycle. This is derived from the previous result, i.e. if the time needed to check the token grows slowly with the number of slots the arbitration phase will exhibit the same behavior. This result demonstrates that the increase in the number of messages sent at the transmission phase does not introduce a penalty in the arbitration phase. Therefore the lower the number of arbitration frames per data messages the higher the network throughput with respect to RT-EP. However, as said in section 3.1, the blocking time increases with the maximum size of data messages and the number of packets sent each transmission phase as can be seen in figure 2. At 100 Mbit/s, the blocking time for a 3-node system with 5 messages per cycle can have a blocking time as high as 2 ms (with the maximum MTU).

Finally, the overhead introduced by the protocol must be considered. The effective bit rate achieved with AR-TP depends on many factors, and is directly proportional to the average size of data messages and the number of packets sent each transmission phase, and inversely proportional to the number of stations and the token processing time. The last one (t_{delay}) is the main bottleneck of the protocol, being highly sensitive to the delay between messages, as shown in figure 3. It should be noted that neither the CPUs are very fast nor the current prototype is optimized, so better token processing execution times could be achieved. However, it also should be noted that in practice pure shared Ethernet cannot achieve its 100% capacity due to collisions. Depending on the traffic pattern, the network can be saturated with a much lower load.

In summary, AR-TP has a better performance than RT-EP, but still its full predictability has a price. The system designer must make a trade-off between the network throughput and the blocking time when configuring the protocol parameters.

6   Conclusions

As the complexity of distributed real-time systems grows, their hardware resources must be increased. The networks traditionally used in this type of systems are becoming not capable of transmitting the required amount of information, therefore faster network technologies are being used, and even those without a real-time behavior like Ethernet or Wi-Fi. This paper has presented AR-TP, a protocol that employs transmission control techniques to avoid the non-determinism of Ethernet or Wi-Fi, making them usable for hard real-time systems.

This token-passing protocol can be implemented by a portable software layer above full-conforming standard hardware, working with any network technology and topology, including Wi-Fi, half-duplex Ethernet, full-duplex Ethernet, or a heterogeneous network made of any combination of hubs, switches, bridges, repeaters or other network devices. It offers advanced network scheduling policies (including congestion management), static temporal analysis techniques, and its distributed architecture guarantees a fault-tolerant protocol well suited for wireless networks. However, although it has better performance than other protocols, a trade-off must be done between the network throughput and the maximum blocking time.

The protocol has been fully implemented in the Ada programming language, taking advantage of some Ada 2005 features like the Ravenscar Profile, execution time clocks and task termination procedures. Ada is well suited for the development of hard-real time applications and high-integrity systems, specially the Ada 2005 revision which includes several facilities not found in other programming languages —like the Ravenscar profile—, or not in a portable manner —like execution time clocks, or the scheduling policies.

Future work is directed towards the integration of the protocol with communication middlewares like PolyORB, as well as designing a Partition Communication Subsystem —taking advantage of the new Ada 2005 permission to modify it— to fully exploit all the features of AR-TP within the DSA. Also, it is planned to explore the behavior of AR-TP in implementation for Wireless Local Area Networks.

References

1. Pedreiras, P., Almeida, L., Gai, P.: The FTT-Ethernet protocol: Mergin flexibility, timeliness and efficiency. In: 14th Euromicro Conference on Real-Time Systems, IEEE Computer Society Press (2002) 1–10
2. Burns, A., Dobbing, B., Romanski, G.: The Ravenscar tasking profile for high integrity real-time programs. In Asplund, L., ed.: Reliable Software Technologies — Ada-Europe'98. Number 1411 in LNCS, Springer-Verlag (1998) 263–275
3. Audsley, N., Burns, A., Richardson, M., Tindell, K., Wellings, A.: Applying new scheduling theory to static priority preemptive scheduling. Software Engineering Journal 8(5) (1993)
4. Sha, L., Abdelzaher, T., Årzén, K.E., Cervin, A., Baker, T., Burns, A., Buttazzo, G., Caccamo, M., Lehoczky, J., Mok, A.K.: Real time scheduling theory: A historical perspective. Real-Time Systems 28 (2004) 101–155
5. Taft, S.T., Duff, R.A., Brukardt, R.L., Plöedereder, E., eds.: Consolidated Ada Reference Manual. Language and Standard Libraries. International Standard ANSI/ISO/IEC-8652:1995(E) with Technical Corrigendum 1. Volume 2219 of Lecture Notes in Computer Science. Springer-Verlag (2001)
6. R. Bosch Gmbh Germany: CAN Specification-Version 2.0 Part A. (1991)
7. Thomesse, J.: Fieldbuses and interoperability. Control Engineering Practice 7(1) (1999) 81–94
8. Song, Y.: Time constrained communication over switched ethernet. In: 4th IFAC International Conference on Fieldbus Systems and their Applications, Nancy, France (2001)
9. The Institute of Electrical and Electronics Engineers New York, USA: IEEE Std. 802.3-2002. (2002)
10. The Institute of Electrical and Electronics Engineers New York, USA: IEEE Std. 802.11-2003. (2003)
11. Martínez, J.M., González Harbour, M.: RT-EP: A fixed-priority real time communication protocol over standard ethernet. In Vardanega, T., Wellings, A., eds.: Reliable Software Technologies - Ada-Europe 2005. Volume 3555 of LNCS., Springer-Verlag (2005)
12. Urueña, S., Zamorano, J., Berjón, D., Pulido, J.A., de la Puente, J.A.: Schedulability analysis of AR-TP, a Ravenscar compliant communication protocol for high-integrity distributed systems. In: 14th International Workshop on Parallel and Distributed Real-Time Systems, Island of Rhodes, Greece (2006)
13. de la Puente, J., Ruiz, J., Zamorano, J.: An open Ravenscar real-time kernel for GNAT. In Keller, H.B., Plöedereder, E., eds.: Reliable Software Technologies — Ada-Europe 2000. Number 1845 in LNCS, Springer-Verlag (2000) 5–15
14. Burns, A., Dobbing, B., Vardanega, T.: Guide for the use of the Ada Ravenscar profile in high integrity systems. Ada Letters XXIV(2) (2004) 1–74
15. Vergnaud, T., Hugues, J., Pautet, L., Kordon, F.: PolyORB: a schizophrenic middleware to build versatile reliable distributed applications. In: Proceedings of the 9th International Conference on Reliable Software Techologies Ada-Europe 2004 (RST'04). Number 3063 in LNCS, Palma de Mallorca, Spain, Springer Verlag (2004) 106–119

Interchangeable Scheduling Policies in Real-Time Middleware for Distribution*

Juan López Campos, J. Javier Gutiérrez, and Michael González Harbour

Departamento de Electrónica y Computadores
Universidad de Cantabria, 39005 - Santander, Spain
{lopezju, gutierjj, mgh}@unican.es

Abstract. When a middleware layer is designed for providing semi-transparent distribution facilities to real-time applications, a trade-off must be made between the expressiveness and control capabilities of the real-time parameters used, and the simplicity of usage. Middleware specifications such as RT-CORBA or Ada's Distributed Systems Annex (DSA) rely on the use of priorities to map the timing requirements of the application, thus restricting the possible scheduling policies. This paper presents a generic technique to express complex scheduling and timing parameters of distributed transactions, allowing real-time middleware implementations to change their scheduling policies for both the processing nodes and the networks. The technique has been tested in an implementation of Ada's DSA, providing two interchangeable policies: a fixed-priority scheduler, and a complex contract-based flexible scheduler.

1   Introduction

As real-time embedded systems grow in complexity and cover an increasing number of application areas, the need for real-time distribution grows accordingly. Developing software that can be migrated in a semi-transparent way from a single node platform to different distributed platforms with different interconnection architectures requires the use of a distribution middleware that takes care of all the communication implied, without explicit intervention of the application. There are different distribution middleware technologies, such as CORBA [8], which supports the distributed object paradigm, or the Distributed Systems Annex (DSA) in Ada 95 [12], which is mainly based on remote procedure calls (RPCs) and also supports distributed objects.

The advantages of these distribution middleware technologies are that they provide a level of abstraction that allows the application developer to concentrate on the problem being solved, independently of the platform used to execute it, and without having to program explicit message passing. Later, at configuration time, the particular mapping of software elements to processing nodes and communication networks is established, allowing the flexibility of migrating to different platforms,

---

* This work has been funded in part by the Spanish *Ministry of Science and Technology* under grant number TIC2002-04123-C03-02 (TRECOM), and by the IST Programme of the European Commission under project IST-2001-34140 (FIRST).

L.M. Pinho and M. González Harbour (Eds.): Ada-Europe 2006, LNCS 4006, pp. 227–240, 2006.
© Springer-Verlag Berlin Heidelberg 2006

and the ability to explore different configurations. Explicit message passing makes the application not well structured and difficult to analyse.

If distribution middleware is to be used in real-time applications, it is necessary that the application developer has some way of mapping the timing requirements of the application into system parameters that can be used by the system to guarantee the required timing properties. In addition, the services provided and used by the middleware, such as dynamic task creation, the scheduling policies, or the networks and communication protocols must be designed so that the system is capable of guaranteeing predictable response times. For these reasons distribution middleware specially adapted to real-time systems has been specified and implemented. One of these specifications is real-time CORBA [19]. Another one is the DSA in the Ada language [12]; although it is not specifically designed to support real-time applications, it is possible to develop implementations that provide hard real-time guarantees [10] [11] [5].

Both of these middleware technologies, RT-CORBA and Ada's DSA, are based on fixed priority scheduling. The timing requirements of the application must be mapped on to priorities assigned to the user tasks and also to the tasks implementing the remote procedure handlers or the servers. In addition, if a fixed priority communication network is used, the application must also specify the priorities of all the messages involved [5]. This requirement somehow limits the "transparency" of distribution, but it is well known that in real-time applications a model of all the activities being performed must be known, and there must be ways to influence their timing behaviour. This applies to both hard and soft real-time applications, despite the fact that the timing models are required to be more precise for hard real-time.

The fixed priority approach is simple in the sense that the application just has to specify a number that can be dynamically assigned to tasks and messages, and fixed priority scheduling is widely available and simple to implement. However, many realtime applications being built today have a mixture of complex timing requirements that require the use of advanced scheduling policies capable of flexibly managing the available resources [2]. Moving towards more complex scheduling policies means that a single number such as a priority or a deadline is not enough to express the application requirements. Distribution middleware must be adapted to support these complex scheduling parameters that cannot be changed or transmitted dynamically. It must also be adapted to support changeable scheduling policies that can fit specific application requirements.

In this paper we present some ideas that allow a distribution middleware to manage complex scheduling parameters specified by an application in a way that minimizes overhead. We also show how these ideas can be used to adapt an implementation of Ada's DSA. For this particular implementation we show the API that the application has to use to set the scheduling parameters, and the way in which a new scheduling policy can be added to the system.

The paper is organized as follows. First, in Section 2 we present the model used to describe the event flow of a distributed real-time system, and its influence on the new approach for distribution middleware. In Section 3 we discuss the particular aspects of the communication layer in an implementation of Ada's DSA, and in Section 4 we show the corresponding API. In Section 5 we show how to introduce a new scheduling policy under the new approach. Section 6 contains a simple example that illustrates the usage of the API, while Section 7 provides a case study and evaluates the ease of usage. Finally, Section 8 contains our conclusions.

2 The Transactional Model Applied to Distribution Middleware

Traditional distributed architectures built with RT-CORBA or Ada's DSA are based on the client-server architecture or the distributed objects model [10]. However, for analysing the response time of a real-time distributed application it is common to use the event-driven transactional model [7] (not to be confused with the transactional model used in database applications), in which events arriving at the system trigger the execution of activities, which can be either task jobs in the processors or messages in the networks. These activities, in turn, may generate additional events that trigger other activities, and this gives way to a chain of events and activities, possibly with end-to-end timing requirements, called the transaction (see Fig 1). It is easy to show how an application designed with distributed objects or under the client-server architecture can be modelled and analysed using the transactional model.

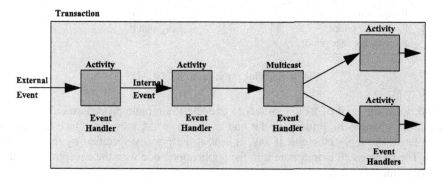

Fig. 1. Model of a transaction

To allow the highest degree of flexibility and the best timing results, it is useful to allow the application developer to assign the scheduling parameters of each activity involved in a transaction in an independent way [4]. This contradicts the traditional way of assigning scheduling parameters used in common distributed middleware specifications and implementations. For instance, in RT-CORBA we can assign a priority to a server, or it can inherit the priority of the calling client. None of these alternatives is completely satisfactory, because scheduling analysis might show that in a particular system configuration the optimum solution is to execute the server at a low priority when called from a high priority server, and use a high priority when called from particular a low priority client [4].. It is the transaction in which the server is being executed that should be used to determine the priority, but not with the rigidity that inheriting the client's priority imposes.

To allow a flexible use of the transactional model we proposed in [5] a modification of the GLADE [11] implementation of Ada's DSA, called RT-GLADE, in which the application developer was able to assign all the priorities involved in an RPC: the priority of the client task, the priorities of the query and reply messages, and the priority of the RPC handler in the server side. As it can be seen in Fig 2, the underlying implementation automatically sets the priority of the query message, and encodes into it the priorities of the RPC handler and of the reply message. The system then chooses

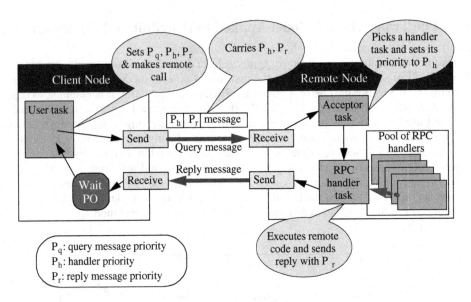

Fig. 2. Handling priorities in RT-GLADE

a task from the pool of RPC handlers to execute the remote procedure call, and dynamically changes its priority to the one specified in the message. Once the call is completed, the reply message, if any, is sent at the priority specified by the application. The remote call is transparent to the application code with the exception that the priorities must be set.

However this solution is tied to the use of fixed priorities, and does not work if more complex scheduling policies are used. Sending the scheduling parameters of the RPC handler and the reply message through the network is inefficient if these parameters are large in size. Dynamically changing the scheduling parameters of the RPC handler may also be inefficient. Both problems appear in the contract-based scheduling framework described later in Section 5, where the scheduling parameters represent a contract with tens of parameters, and for which dynamically changing a contract requires an expensive renegotiation process.

The solution proposed in this paper consists of explicitly creating the network and processor schedulable entities required to establish the communication and execute the remote calls, and identifying the created schedulable entities with a short identifier that can be easily encoded in the messages transmitted (see Fig. 3):

- For the processing nodes, the schedulable entities in the server side are the RPC handlers. Instead of having a pool of RPC handler tasks, we will create these tasks explicitly, each with their own appropriate scheduling parameters.
- For the network, the schedulable entities are communications ports that are used to establish the scheduling parameters that will be used for messages sent through that particular port. We will identify each of these ports through the two endpoints used to send and receive messages at either node. We will assume that the scheduling parameters are assigned to the port through its send endpoint. The endpoints are created and assigned their scheduling parameters explicitly.

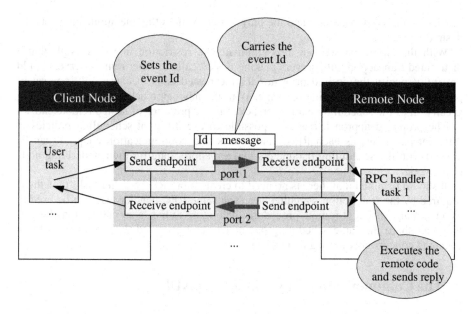

Fig. 3. Explicitly created schedulable entities

For identifying these schedulable entities we will relate to the transactional model and use an identifier that represents the event that triggers the activity executed by the schedulable entity. We call it an Event_Id.

To achieve distributed communication in an application developed with the proposed approach it is necessary to create the following elements, as shown in Fig. 3:

- A send endpoint must be created in the client's node to send the message with the RPC query, containing information about the destination node and port.
- A receive endpoint must be created in the remote node for an RPC handler task to wait for the RPC reply message; it must specify the same port used in the caller's send endpoint.
- An RPC handler task must be created in the remote node to execute the remote call; it will directly wait for messages arriving at the corresponding receive endpoint in the remote node.
- A send endpoint must be created at the remote node to send back the RPC reply to the client; it must contain information on the destination node (where the client's partition is) and a port.
- A receive endpoint must be created in the client's node for the calling task to await the reply message; it must use the same port specified in the remote node's send endpoint.

It is also necessary to establish the corresponding scheduling parameters for each of the above elements, both in the processors and in the networks. This is usually done in the configuration or initialization part of each of the software components used. This configuration could be automatically generated by a tool that would obtain the information from the model of the transaction. Once configured, the usage of the new scheme is almost transparent, and the only requirement is that the application sets the desired Event_Id.

With this approach we can also eliminate the restriction in RT-GLADE that a distributed transaction with servers making nested calls to other remote servers could not fully specify the desired priorities for the nested calls, because only one set of priorities is sent in the calling message. With the new approach it is possible to fully specify all of the scheduling parameters, even in the presence of nested remote calls.

The proposed approach makes it possible to use different scheduling policies in different partitions, as each RPC handler task and communication endpoint can be created with the scheduling parameters that are appropriate for their underlying node or network.

It should be noted that there is no need to create more RPC handler tasks than those required by the transaction's architecture. The same RPC handler task can be used to execute many different remote procedures belonging to the same partition, as long as they can share the same scheduling parameters and provided they don't need to be executed concurrently among themselves.

3   The Communication Layer in RT-GLADE

In this section we will explain the modifications made to the original RT-GLADE communication layer in order to implement the proposed approach for inter-changeable scheduling policies. The main architectural changes are:

- Removal of the Acceptor_Task: the purpose of these tasks was to receive messages directly from the network and process part of their information to then dynamically set the priority of the selected RPC handler tasks and awaken them. This is not necessary any more, so these tasks are removed in the new implementation, making it more efficient.
- Removal of the pool of RPC handlers: they were in charge of executing the calls in the remote node. In the new implementation the RPC handler tasks are created explicitly, and they wait for messages from the network directly, using the communication endpoints also created explicitly.
- Removal of the wait mechanism for a remote call reply: now the same user task that made the RPC waits directly for the reply because the communication endpoint is already created and known.

In order to identify the schedulable entities we create a special identifier called Event_Id. This identifier is specified by the application and used when creating the schedulable entities, which are the communication endpoints and the RPC handlers. Before an RPC is invoked, the application task must set the Event_Id associated with the current transaction, thus identifying the send and receive endpoints at its partition. This Event_Id is added to the RPC query message, so that the RPC handler task can read it and determine the send endpoint to which the reply should be sent in the remote node.

Internally, there is a mapping established between this Event_Id and the corresponding information relative to the communication layer; in particular, the identifiers of the required communication endpoints. It is possible to reduce the number of RPC handler tasks by grouping the execution of remote code placed in the same remote node through the same RPC handler.

4 The Application Interface for Ada's DSA

The application program interface appears in three packages: Rt_Glade_Types, containing basic data types; Rt_Glade_Event_Id_Handling, containing the only operations that are required to be invoked from the user code, to set or get the Event_Id for a remote call; and Rt_Glade_Scheduling, which contains the abstract types used to explicitly create and set the scheduling parameters of the communication endpoints and RPC handlers.

For representing the network elements, we will assume that there could be several networks, each identified with a value of the type Network_Id. A node is identified with a value of the type Node_Id. Reception queues at the destination node and network are identified by a port Id of the type Port_Id. These three types appear in package Rt_Glade_Types.

The Event_Id is stored as a task attribute in order to be easily used inside the RT-GLADE communication layer, as we did in the original RT-GLADE with the priorities involved in each RPC. The call used to set the Event_Id for a remote call is:

```
procedure Set_Event_Id (Id : Rt_Glade_Types.Event_Id);
```

There is also a function that may be called by an RPC handler task to get the Event_Id carried inside the query message that activated the current execution.

Package Rt_Glade_Scheduling contains two abstract tagged types and their corresponding classwide access types. The first of these types, Task_ Scheduling_ Parameters, represents the scheduling parameters of an RPC handler task. The second type, Message_Scheduling_Parameters, represents the scheduling parameters used for the messages sent through a specific endpoint. Both types must be extended to represent actual parameters required by the underlying scheduling policies.

```
type Task_Scheduling_Parameters is abstract tagged private;
type Task_Scheduling_Parameters_Ref is
   access all Task_Scheduling_Parameters'Class;
type Message_Scheduling_Parameters is abstract tagged pri-
vate;
type Message_Scheduling_Parameters_Ref is
   access all Message_Scheduling_Parameters'Class;
```

The primitives used to customize the communication layer by creating the RPC handler tasks and the communication endpoints are:

- Procedure Create_Query_Send_Endpoint creates a send endpoint for query messages. The arguments are the Event_Id that will be associated with this endpoint, the network that will be used to send the messages, the destination node and port in that network, and the scheduling parameters used for sending the messages.

- Procedure `Create_RPC_Handler` creates a receive endpoint for the query message and an RPC handler that waits at that receive endpoint. The arguments passed are the network and port from where the receive endpoint must receive the messages, the associated `Event_Id`, and the scheduling parameters used for the RPC handler.
- Procedure `Create_Reply_Send_Endpoint` creates a send endpoint for sending the reply messages to the originating partition. The necessary arguments are the `Event_Id` that will be associated with this endpoint, the network that will be used to send the messages, the destination node and port in that network, and the scheduling parameters for sending the messages.
- Procedure `Create_Reply_Receive_Endpoint` creates a receive endpoint from where the application task can read the reply message. Its arguments are the associated `Event_Id` and the network and port from where the receive endpoint must receive the messages.

Corresponding operations are provided to destroy the created endpoints or handlers, but their specification is omitted here for saving space.

For creating all the elements shown in Fig 3 the application has to take the following actions when initializing software components involved in a remote call:

- Choose an unused `Event_Id` (`My_Event_Id`), an unused port in the remote node (`Remote_Port`), and an unused port in the client's partition node (`Calling_Port`).
- In the client's node, create the send endpoint by invoking `Create_Query_Send_Endpoint` using the desired scheduling parameters and network, specifying the node where the remote partition is located, and using `Remote_Port` and `My_Event_Id`. And create the receive endpoint by invoking `Create_Reply_Receive_Endpoint` using the desired network, and using `Calling_Port` and `My_Event_Id`.
- In the remote node, create the RPC handler and the receive endpoint by invoking `Create_RPC_Handler` using the desired scheduling parameters and network, and using `Remote_Port` and `My_Event_Id`. And also create the send endpoint by invoking `Create_Reply_Send_Endpoint` using the desired scheduling parameters and network, specifying the node where the calling node is located, and using `Calling_Port` and `My_Event_Id`.

After this initialization, RPCs can be made and they will be automatically directed through the appropriate endpoints and RPC handler by just specifying `My_Event_Id`, with procedure `Set_Event_Id` described above.

5   Implementation of Specific Scheduling Policies

Once a system supports a new scheduling policy, adapting the RT-GLADE implementation to use it requires extending the abstract types declared in `Rt_Glade_Scheduling`. The same applies to a new real-time communication protocol using a new scheduling policy for the messages.

The extension for the task and message scheduling parameters types requires that at least the scheduling parameters for the new policy are included among the new attributes of both types. In addition, the `Rt_Glade_Scheduling` specifies in its private part two abstract primitive operations of these types that must be defined. Their specification is:

```
procedure Create_Task
   (Params     : in Task_Scheduling_Parameters;
    Endpoint : in Rt_Glade_Types.Receive_Endpoint_Id;
    Tid        : out Ada.Task_Identification.Task_Id);
procedure Create_Send_Endpoint
   (Params     : in Message_Scheduling_Parameters'Class;
    Node       : in Rt_Glade_Types.Node_Id;
    Net        : in Rt_Glade_Types.Network_Id;
    Port       : in Rt_Glade_Types.Port_Id;
    Endpoint : out Rt_Glade_Types.Send_Endpoint_Id);
```

Procedure `Create_Task` creates an RPC handler task and associates the parameters to it in a manner appropriate to the scheduling policy being used. The handler waits for messages (from any source) arriving at the specified endpoint. Each message carries the `Event_Id` of the sender. If the call requires a reply, the handler sends the reply message through the send endpoint associated with the `Event_Id` carried in the message, unless the `Event_Id` is changed by the handler code.

Procedure `Create_Send_Endpoint` creates a send endpoint for the specified node, net and port and associates the parameters to it in a manner appropriate to the scheduling policy being used.

For the purpose of demonstrating the ability to change the scheduling policy, we have implemented two extensions of the `Rt_Glade_Scheduling` package, one for the traditional fixed priority scheduling, but under the new approach, and the other one for a complex contract-based flexible scheduling policy [3].

For the fixed priorities, we have implemented the extension in a child package called `Rt_Glade_Scheduling.Priorites`. The particularization of the two tagged types for this case are:

```
type Task_Priority is new Task_Scheduling_Parameters with record
   RPC_Handler_Priority:System.Garlic.Priorities.Global_Priority;
end record;
```

```
type Message_Priority is new Message_Scheduling_Parameters with record
   Endpoint_Priority : System.Garlic.Priorities.Global_Priority;
end record;
```

The `Create_Task` operation creates an RPC handler task and sets its priority to the value specified in the `Task_Scheduling_Parameters` object. We do the same in `Create_Send_Endpoint` for the communication endpoints.

The First Scheduling Framework (FSF) [3] is a framework for a scheduling architecture that provides the ability to compose several applications or components to build a real-time system, and to flexibly schedule the available resources while guaranteeing hard real-time requirements. It is is based on establishing service contracts that represent the complex and flexible requirements of the application, and which are managed by the underlying system to provide the required level of service. FSF is applied both to processor and networks. From the application's perspective, the requirements of an application component are written as a set of contracts, which are negotiated with the underlying implementation. To accept a set of contracts, the system has to check if it has enough resources to guarantee all the minimum requirements specified, while keeping guarantees on all the previously accepted contracts negotiated by other application components. If as a result of this negotiation the set of contracts is accepted, the system will reserve enough capacity to guarantee the minimum requested resources, i.e., processor capacity and network bandwidth, and will adapt any spare capacity available to share it among the different contracts that have specified their desire or ability for using additional capacity.

In summary, the FSF contracts are the scheduling parameters of the tasks and messages under this framework, and they are very different in nature from the plain fixed priorities.

To use this scheduling framework, we have created a child package called `Rt_Glade_Scheduling.Fsf` in which we have extended the types to hold an FSF contract as a scheduling parameters. In addition, the operations `Create_Task` and `Create_Send_Endpoint` perform the contract negotiation. It is important to set in the contract, at least, the minimum budget, and the maximum period to ensure a minimum amount of system resources.

6   Example Using the Proposed Approach

In this subsection we will show how to build a simple application using the approach presented in this paper. For simplicity, we will use the fixed priorities scheduling scheme. In this application, shown in Fig 4, we are going to perform a remote add operation. The application is composed of two partitions, each placed in a different node. Partition `p1` contains the code of the main program, `menu`, and the initialization code for that partition, `P1_Init`, while partition `p2` contains the code implementing the calculator, `Calculator`, and the initialitation code, `P2_Init`. The Event Ids and the network ports are chosen arbitrarily from those still available.

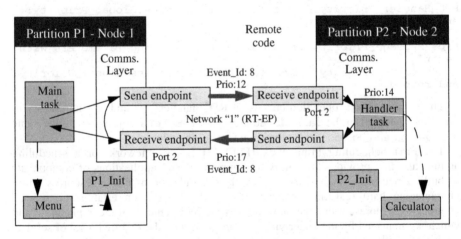

Fig. 4. Example using fixed priorities in the new version of RT-GLADE

The menu procedure code is as follows:

```
with Calculator, RT_Glade_Event_Id_Handling, P1_Init;
procedure Menu is
   A,B,Sum:Integer;
Begin

   -- Initialize the communications endpoints
   P1_Init;
   -- Set the event id for subsequent RPCs
   Rt_Glade_Event_Id_Handling.Set_Event_Id(8);
   loop
      ...
      Sum := Calculator.Add (A, B); -- remote call
      ...
   end loop;
end Menu;
```

The P1_Init procedure is used to initialize all the neccesary elements to establish the communications in partition p1:

```
with Ada.Real_Time, Rt_Glade_Scheduling;
with Rt_Glade_Scheduling.Priorities;
procedure P1_Init is
   R_Message_Params :
      Rt_Glade_Scheduling.Message_Scheduling_Parameters_Ref;
begin
   -- Create the send endpoint for the query messages
   R_Message_Params:= new Rt_Glade_Scheduling.Priorities.
      Message_Priority'
         (Rt_Glade_Scheduling.Message_Scheduling_Parameters
          with Endpoint_Priority=>12);
   Rt_Glade_Scheduling.Create_Query_Send_Endpoint
      (Params=>R_Message_Params.all, Node=>2,
       Net=>1, Port=>2, Event=>8);

   -- Create the receive endpoint for the reply messages
   Rt_Glade_Scheduling.Create_Reply_Receive_Endpoint
      (Net=>1, Port=>2, Event=>8);
end P1_Init;
```

The Calculator package is a normal ada implementation with the only difference that the package has to be categorized with the pragma Remote_Call_Interface which makes all the procedures callable remotely.

```
package Calculator is
   pragma Remote_Call_Interface;

   function Add (A : in Integer; B : in Integer) return Integer;
end Calculator;
```

The P2_Init procedure is a main partition program to initialize all the neccesary elements to establish the communications in p2:

```
with Rt_Glade_Scheduling, Rt_Glade_Scheduling.Priorities;
with Ada.Real_Time;
procedure P2_Init is
   R_Task_Params :
```

```
      Rt_Glade_Scheduling.Task_Scheduling_Parameters_Ref;
   R_Message_Params :
      Rt_Glade_Scheduling.Message_Scheduling_Parameters_Ref;
begin
   -- Create the RPC handler
   R_Task_Params:=new Rt_Glade_Scheduling.Priorities.

      Task_Priority'
         (Rt_Glade_Scheduling.Task_Scheduling_Parameters
            with RPC_Handler_Priority=>14);
   Rt_Glade_Scheduling.Create_RPC_Handler
      (Params=>R_Task_Params.all, Net=>1, Port=>2, Event=>8);

   -- Create the send endpoint for the reply message
   R_Message_Params:= new Rt_Glade_Scheduling.Priorities.
      Message_Priority'
         (Rt_Glade_Scheduling.Message_Scheduling_Parameters
            with Endpoint_Priority=>17);
   Rt_Glade_Scheduling.Create_Reply_Send_Endpoint
      (Params=>R_Message_Params.all, Node=>1,
        Net=>1, Port=>2, Event=>8);
end P2_Init;
```

As we can see, once the initialization code for creating the communication endpoints and the RPC handler is written, the only change to the application code is the setting of the Event Ids.

7   Case Study and Evaluation of Application Complexity

We have evaluated the impact of migrating a real application that had been built using the fixed-priority version of RT-GLADE to the new proposed approach for scheduling, in particular using the FSF contracts mentioned in Section 5. The application is a simulated tile inspection plant that uses a real industrial robot arm and a video acquisition system, running on a MaRTE OS operating system [1] and using the RT-EP real-time communication protocol [6]. To minimize the number of RPC handler tasks, we have grouped all the calls for a particular transaction and to a given partition into a single RPC handler, calculating its budget as the sum of the worst case execution times of all the RPCs involved. With this approach, every transaction in the application code has been assigned a single Event_Id that identifies its communication endpoints and the associated RPC handler task.

The number of source code lines that were necessary to make the networks contracts for seven distributed transactions was 14*7 = 98 lines to create 14 send endpoints, 7*8 = 56 lines to create 7 RPC handlers and associated receive endpoints in the remote nodes, and 7 lines to create the 7 receive endpoints in the calling tasks. Besides we added 13 "with" lines, and 7 lines to specify the Event_Ids of each distributed transaction. So in total we have added just 181 lines of code, to a program of more than 13.000 lines.

In summary, we did not require any changes to the architecture when migrating from the original version of RT-GLADE to the new version. Changes were only required for the creation of the network contracts, the communication endpoints, and the RPC handlers, and for the specification of Event_Ids. The amount of new lines of code is very small, compared to the size of the application. We can conclude that having a well-documented architecture and real-time model of the application makes it very easy for a designer to use the FSF contracts, or any other special-purpose scheduling policy, for a distributed application under the new RT-GLADE implementation.

8 Conclusions

We have proposed an approach to support generic scheduling parameters and policies in real-time distributed middleware. This approach follows the transactional model in which the scheduling parameters are determined by the sequence of events that are activated inside a real-time transaction, allowing the highest degree of flexibility and resource usage. Complex scheduling policies, such as those used to achieve flexible scheduling using contracts or reservations can be handled with the proposed approach, even if the size of the scheduling parameters is large, or if dynamic changes of these parameters are expensive. With the new approach we can define the scheduling parameters of whole distributed transactions with complete freedom, even in the presence of nested remote procedure calls.

The approach has been tested in an implementation of Ada's DSA, by providing two interchangeable policies: a fixed-priority scheduler, and a complex contract-based flexible scheduler. The new implementation continues to conform to Ada's DSA and is independent of the kind of scheduling parameters used. The architecture of this implementation is simpler than before, although it may require more space as the pool of RPC handlers is replaced by a possibly larger set of explicitly created handlers. In summary the new implementation is more flexible, and has more control on the scheduling of the different elements involved in the distributed transactions, at the price of requiring more intervention from the application and using more tasks and network access points.

References

1. M. Aldea and M. González. "MaRTE OS: An Ada Kernel for Real-Time EmbeddedAp-plications". Proceedings of the International Conference on Reliable Software Technolo-gies, Ada-Europe 2001, Leuven, Belgium, Springer LNCS 2043, May 2001.
2. Bruno Bouyssounouse and Joseph Sifakis (Eds.) "Embedded Systems Design. TheAR-TIST Roadmap for Research and Development", Springer LNCS Vol. 3436, 2005.
3. M. Aldea, et al. "FSF: A Real-Time Scheduling Architecture Framework". Proceedings of the 12th IEEE Real-Time and Embedded Technology and Applications Symposium,San Jose, CA, USA, April 2006.
4. J.J. Gutiérrez García, and M. González Harbour. "Prioritizing Remote Procedure Calls in Ada Distributed Systems". Proceedings of the 9th International Real-Time Ada Work-shop, ACM Ada Letters, XIX, 2, pp. 67-72, June 1999.
5. Juan López Campos, J. Javier Gutiérrez, Michael González Harbour, "The Chance for Adato Support Distribution and Real-Time in Embedded Systems". Proceedings of the 8thInternational Conference on Reliable Software Technologies, Ada-Europe, Springer LNCS 3063, June, 2004, ISBN:3-540-22011-9, pp. 91,105.

6. José María Martínez and Michael González Harbour, "RT-EP: A Fixed-Priority Real Time Communication Protocol over Standard Ethernet". Proceedings of the 9th International-Conference on Reliable Software Technologies, Ada-Europe, York, Springer, LNCS-3555, June, 2005.
7. J.L. Medina Pasaje, M. González Harbour, J.M. Drake Moyano, "MAST Real-Time View: Graphic UML Tool for Modeling Object-Oriented Real-Time Systems". Proceedings ofthe 22th IEEE Real-Time Systems Symposium, London, UK, December, 2001, ISBN:0-7695-1420-0, pp. 245,256.
8. Object Management Group. CORBA Core Specification. OMG Document, v3.0 formal/02-06-01, Julio 2003.
9. Object Management Group. Realtime CORBA Specification. OMG Document, v2.0 formal/03-11-01, November 2003.
10. L. Pautet, T. Quinot, and S. Tardieu. "CORBA & DSA: Divorce or Marriage". Proc. Of the International Conference on Reliable Software Technologies, Ada-Europe'99, Santander, Spain, in Lecture Notes in Computer Science No. 1622, pp.211-225, June 1999.
11. L. Pautet and S. Tardieu. "GLADE: a Framework for Building Large Object-Oriented Real-Time Distributed Systems". Proc. of the 3rd IEEE Intl. Symposium on Object-Oriented Real-Time Distributed Computing, (ISORC'00), Newport Beach, USA, March 2000.
12. S. Tucker Taft, and R.A. Duff (Eds.). "Ada 95 Reference Manual. Language and Standard Libraries". International Standard ISO/IEC 8652:1995(E), in LNCS 1246, Springer, 1997.

Author Index

Lecture Notes in Computer Science

For information about Vols. 1–3908

please contact your bookseller or Springer

Vol. 3962: W. IJsselsteijn, Y. de Kort, C. Midden, B. Eggen, E. van den Hoven (Eds.), Persuasive Technology. XII, 216 pages. 2006.

Vol. 3960: R. Vieira, P. Quaresma, M.d.G.V. Nunes, N.J. Mamede, C. Oliveira, M.C. Dias (Eds.), Computational Processing of the Portuguese Language. XII, 274 pages. 2006. (Sublibrary LNAI).

Vol. 3959: J.-Y. Cai, S. B. Cooper, A. Li (Eds.), Theory and Applications of Models of Computation. XV, 794 pages. 2006.

Vol. 3958: M. Yung, Y. Dodis, A. Kiayias, T. Malkin (Eds.), Public Key Cryptography - PKC 2006. XIV, 543 pages. 2006.

Vol. 3956: G. Barthe, B. Gregoire, M. Huisman, J.-L. Lanet (Eds.), Construction and Analysis of Safe, Secure, and Interoperable Smart Devices. IX, 175 pages. 2006.

Vol. 3955: G. Antoniou, G. Potamias, C. Spyropoulos, D. Plexousakis (Eds.), Advances in Artificial Intelligence. XVII, 611 pages. 2006. (Sublibrary LNAI).

Vol. 3954: A. Leonardis, H. Bischof, A. Pinz (Eds.), Computer Vision – ECCV 2006, Part IV. XVII, 613 pages. 2006.

Vol. 3953: A. Leonardis, H. Bischof, A. Pinz (Eds.), Computer Vision – ECCV 2006, Part III. XVII, 649 pages. 2006.

Vol. 3952: A. Leonardis, H. Bischof, A. Pinz (Eds.), Computer Vision – ECCV 2006, Part II. XVII, 661 pages. 2006.

Vol. 3951: A. Leonardis, H. Bischof, A. Pinz (Eds.), Computer Vision – ECCV 2006, Part I. XXXV, 639 pages. 2006.

Vol. 3950: J.P. Müller, F. Zambonelli (Eds.), Agent-Oriented Software Engineering VI. XVI, 249 pages. 2006.

Vol. 3947: Y.-C. Chung, J.E. Moreira (Eds.), Advances in Grid and Pervasive Computing. XXI, 667 pages. 2006.

Vol. 3946: T.R. Roth-Berghofer, S. Schulz, D.B. Leake (Eds.), Modeling and Retrieval of Context. XI, 149 pages. 2006. (Sublibrary LNAI).

Vol. 3945: M. Hagiya, P. Wadler (Eds.), Functional and Logic Programming. X, 295 pages. 2006.

Vol. 3944: J. Quiñonero-Candela, I. Dagan, B. Magnini, F. d'Alché-Buc (Eds.), Machine Learning Challenges. XIII, 462 pages. 2006. (Sublibrary LNAI).

Vol. 3943: N. Guelfi, A. Savidis (Eds.), Rapid Integration of Software Engineering Techniques. X, 289 pages. 2006.

Vol. 3942: Z. Pan, R. Aylett, H. Diener, X. Jin, S. Göbel, L. Li (Eds.), Technologies for E-Learning and Digital Entertainment. XXV, 1396 pages. 2006.

Vol. 3941: S.W. Gilroy, M.D. Harrison (Eds.), Interactive Systems. XI, 267 pages. 2006.

Vol. 3940: C. Saunders, M. Grobelnik, S. Gunn, J. Shawe-Taylor (Eds.), Subspace, Latent Structure and Feature Selection. X, 209 pages. 2006.

Vol. 3939: C. Priami, L. Cardelli, S. Emmott (Eds.), Transactions on Computational Systems Biology IV. VII, 141 pages. 2006. (Sublibrary LNBI).

Vol. 3936: M. Lalmas, A. MacFarlane, S. Rüger, A. Tombros, T. Tsikrika, A. Yavlinsky (Eds.), Advances in Information Retrieval. XIX, 584 pages. 2006.

Vol. 3935: D. Won, S. Kim (Eds.), Information Security and Cryptology - ICISC 2005. XIV, 458 pages. 2006.

Vol. 3934: J.A. Clark, R.F. Paige, F.A. C. Polack, P.J. Brooke (Eds.), Security in Pervasive Computing. X, 243 pages. 2006.

Vol. 3933: F. Bonchi, J.-F. Boulicaut (Eds.), Knowledge Discovery in Inductive Databases. VIII, 251 pages. 2006.

Vol. 3931: B. Apolloni, M. Marinaro, G. Nicosia, R. Tagliaferri (Eds.), Neural Nets. XIII, 370 pages. 2006.

Vol. 3930: D.S. Yeung, Z.-Q. Liu, X.-Z. Wang, H. Yan (Eds.), Advances in Machine Learning and Cybernetics. XXI, 1110 pages. 2006. (Sublibrary LNAI).

Vol. 3929: W. MacCaull, M. Winter, I. Düntsch (Eds.), Relational Methods in Computer Science. VIII, 263 pages. 2006.

Vol. 3928: J. Domingo-Ferrer, J. Posegga, D. Schreckling (Eds.), Smart Card Research and Advanced Applications. XI, 359 pages. 2006.

Vol. 3927: J. Hespanha, A. Tiwari (Eds.), Hybrid Systems: Computation and Control. XII, 584 pages. 2006.

Vol. 3925: A. Valmari (Ed.), Model Checking Software. X, 307 pages. 2006.

Vol. 3924: P. Sestoft (Ed.), Programming Languages and Systems. XII, 343 pages. 2006.

Vol. 3923: A. Mycroft, A. Zeller (Eds.), Compiler Construction. XIII, 277 pages. 2006.

Vol. 3922: L. Baresi, R. Heckel (Eds.), Fundamental Approaches to Software Engineering. XIII, 427 pages. 2006.

Vol. 3921: L. Aceto, A. Ingólfsdóttir (Eds.), Foundations of Software Science and Computation Structures. XV, 447 pages. 2006.

Vol. 3920: H. Hermanns, J. Palsberg (Eds.), Tools and Algorithms for the Construction and Analysis of Systems. XIV, 506 pages. 2006.

Vol. 3918: W.K. Ng, M. Kitsuregawa, J. Li, K. Chang (Eds.), Advances in Knowledge Discovery and Data Mining. XXIV, 879 pages. 2006. (Sublibrary LNAI).

Vol. 3917: H. Chen, F.-Y. Wang, C.C. Yang, D. Zeng, M. Chau, K. Chang (Eds.), Intelligence and Security Informatics. XII, 186 pages. 2006.

Vol. 3916: J. Li, Q. Yang, A.-H. Tan (Eds.), Data Mining for Biomedical Applications. VIII, 155 pages. 2006. (Sublibrary LNBI).

Vol. 3915: R. Nayak, M.J. Zaki (Eds.), Knowledge Discovery from XML Documents. VIII, 105 pages. 2006.

Vol. 3914: A. Garcia, R. Choren, C. Lucena, P. Giorgini, T. Holvoet, A. Romanovsky (Eds.), Software Engineering for Multi-Agent Systems IV. XIV, 255 pages. 2006.

Vol. 3911: R. Wyrzykowski, J. Dongarra, N. Meyer, J. Waśniewski (Eds.), Parallel Processing and Applied Mathematics. XXIII, 1126 pages. 2006.

Vol. 3910: S.A. Brueckner, G.D.M. Serugendo, D. Hales, F. Zambonelli (Eds.), Engineering Self-Organising Systems. XII, 245 pages. 2006. (Sublibrary LNAI).

Vol. 3909: A. Apostolico, C. Guerra, S. Istrail, P. Pevzner, M. Waterman (Eds.), Research in Computational Molecular Biology. XVII, 612 pages. 2006. (Sublibrary LNBI).